KASHMIR ART, ARCHITECTURE AND TOURISM

ENCYCLOPAEDIA OF KASHMIR SERIES - 2

Kashmir Art, Architecture and Tourism

Edited by

Suresh K. Sharma & S.R. Bakshi

ANMOL PUBLICATIONS PVT LTD

New Delhi

ANMOL PUBLICATIONS PVT LTD
4374/4B, Ansari Road, Daryaganj
New Delhi-110 002

Kashmir Art, Architecture & Tourism

First Edition 1995
ISBN 81-7488-055-0

PRINTED IN INDIA

Published by J L. Kumar for Anmol Publications Pvt Ltd, New Delhi, and Printed at Mehra Offset Press.

Preface

The picturesque valley of Kashmir situated on the northern extremity of India, occupies a position of unique and strategic importance in the sub-continent of India. It excels in beauty, art, architecture, culture and tradition, rivers, mountains, flora and fauna than several regions of the world. So far so, some eminent writers have compared this Himalayan range with that of Switzerland. Whereas, Kashmir bore the pangs of various onslaughts from North-West, Switzerland enjoyed peaceful postures for centuries.

This volume displays authentic representations of the art, architecture and sculpture of ancient and modern Kashmir alongwith an illustrative account on tourism, impact on the economy, environmental society and culture of this beautiful area.

We have collected the material from several libraries and some of them are—Nehru Memorial Museum and Library, Indian Council of World Affairs Library, Gandhi National Museum and Library, Indian Council of Historical Research Library, University of Delhi Library, etc.

We feel much beholden to the authorities of these institutions for their academic support during our researches.

Finally, we owe a deep sense of admiration for Usha Sharma, Jyotsna Tewari, Gagan, Shilpa and Naresh with regard to their constant help provided in many ways.

Editors
Suresh K. Sharma
S.R. Bakshi

Preface

Contents

CHAPTER 1

ANCIENT MONUMENTS OF KASHMIR

By

R. C. Kak

Kashmir proper is an irregularly oval valley 84 miles long from north-east to south-west by 20 to 25 miles broad. Its height above the sea level is everywhere over 5,000 feet. It is enclosed on all sides by ranges of snow-capped mountains, which vary at different points from 12,000 to 18,000 feet in height. The correctness of the local tradition regarding its lacustrine origin in remote prehistoric times has been demonstrated by the disovery of marine fossils and other characteristic features in the surrounding mountains and uplands. Politically it was, ordinarily, limited to its geographical frontiers, the mountain ramparts; but the neighbouring hill principalities of Prunts (Poonch) and Rajauri were often within its sphere of influence. The extent of that influence usually depended upon the personality of the ruler for the time being. Some of its more energetic kings extended their sway to the north and north-west of the Panjab, and one king, Lalitaditya (in the middle of the eighth century), is credited with having effected the conquest of Kanauj.

The valley itself was divided into two great territorial divisions, Maḍavarajya, the southern half, and Kramarajya, the northern half; Srinagar, the capital, was included in the former. Maḍavarajya, modern Maraz, is represented by the present-day wazarat or district of Anantnag, and Kramarajya by the wazarat of Baramula. The large lateral valleys drained by the Sindh and the Lidar formed integral parts of their respective districts. The two rural divisions were in their turn subdivided into smaller areas—known in later times as parganas—which consisted of groups of villages ranging in number from a dozen to perhaps a hundred or more. The capital, though forming part of Maraz, practically constituted an independent unit; and owing to its situation at the point of contact of the two main divisions, its compactness, the presence of the court, its large population, its organised public opinion, and the superior culture of its inhabitants, it was the most important of all. Its alliance or opposition almost always proved a decisive factor in determining the fortunes of war. Its position in the centre of a large, fertile, and populous valley, interested by navigable rivers, canals and lakes, not only made it a point of vantage commercially, but also sufficiently accounts for the failure of all the attempts made from time to time to remove it from its present position to some other place.

The most striking features of the Kashmir landscape are its mighty mountain ramparts, its beautiful lakes and rivers and its dry brown karewas. The former have largely determined the political fortunes of the little country they encircle. It is the inaccessibility and practical impregnability of these natural defences rather than the valour of Kashmiri troops that has so often turned the tide of invasion from the valley, when far more powerful kingdoms succumbed to it. This inaccessibility, again, enabled Kashmir to preserve and consolidate its peculiar social and economic conditions up to very recent times. While, thus, the mountains long served as effectual barriers against foreign invasion, and as a sure means of conservation of indigenous culture, they do not appear to have proved equally effectual in preventing natives of the valley from seeing something of the world which lay beyond their circumscribed horizon. Kashmir played a notable part in the propagation of Buddhism in foreign lands, especially in China and Tibet. We may mention a single instance. Kumarajiva's distinguished scholarly labours in China during the regime of the later Chin dynasty (A.D. 384-417) gained for him the title of Tungsheo, which interpreted means that "although young in years he was ripe in the wisdom and virtues of old age." He is referred to as "one of the four suns of Buddhism," and is credited with the introduction of a new alphabet. In mediaeval times when, according to the great Muslim scholar Alberuni, Kashmir had closed her gates to intercourse with foreign lands, her pandits lived as honoured guests at the courts of Indian princes; for instance, Bilhana, the well-known author of the Vikramankadevacharita, was the court poet of Vikramaditya VI (A.D. 1075-1126) of Kalyana in Southern India (modern Kalyani in the Nizam's Dominions). The numerous rivers and lakes, besides being invaluable as commercial waterways and producers of a variety of much prized foodstuffs, have from time immemorial been the means of innocent and inexpensive pleasure to the people. The former, specially the Vitasta, the largest of them all, have also been important in the physical history of the valley. Indeed, with the exception of the uplands commonly called wudars or karewas, which date back to the lacustrine epoch, the whole of the valley owes its formation to deposits of river alluvium. This deposition of silt is still in progress, and consequently the level of the low-lying parts of the valley, particularly those where the Vitasta, carrying the drainage of the whole valley, debouches into the Wular lake, is year by year being slowly but steadily raised. According to Brahman tradition, every lake and river and spring of the valley has a divine origin and a scared mission to fulfil—viz., washing away the sins of the faithful. The Vitasta is, above all, the sacred river, and is said to contain within its waters all that is holy in the world. Indeed Kashmir itself is considered to be the holiest of all the holy lands; it is called the Rishibhumi, "the land of sages," Saradapitha,"the eternally pure seat of the goddess Sarada." It has not only its own Prayaga (the Vitasta corresponding to the Jumna and the Sindh to the Ganges) and its own Kurukshetra, but it has also the replica of almost every other important river or spring that is held in reverence in India.

The uplands or wudars, officially known as karewas, range in height from 100 to 300 feet and in area from 5 to 6 square miles to over 50 square miles each. With one or two exceptions they are dependent for their productivity upon rainfall. In ancient times, when the population of the country was probably much larger than at present, not only these wudars, which are still for the most part under cultivation, but also the comparatively high mountain slopes, were cultivated, as it evidenced by the existence to this day of innumerable terraces surrounded and supported by cyclopean walls at Pandrethan, Avantipur, and almost everywhere. The chief crop and, therefore, the staple food of Kashmir is rice; though maize, barley, and wheat are sown in unirrigated uplands.

With the exception of a few Sikhs and Rajputs who have settled here during the last century, the whole of the valley is occupied by Kashmiri-speaking people, who are linguistically, and perhaps ethnologically also, distinct not only from the Indians of the plains, but also from Gujars, Khakhas, and Bombas, was inhabit the neighbouring hills. The substratum of their language, after its Sanskrit super-structure has been removed, appears to be akin to Dardic, which under various names and forms is spoken by the Kanjutis of Hunza and Nagar, Kafirs of the Karakoram, and other tribes inhabiting the great mountain barrier which separates North-western India from Central Asia.

The comparative immunity from fear of foreign domination, due to the strength of the country's natural defences and to the practical impregnability of the routes leading to it, the abundance and variety of wholesome and nutritious food, the mild and salubrious climate, the narrowness of the geographical horizon—the Kashmiri could see his whole world from the roof of his house—are largely responsible for molnding the character of the inhabitants of the Happy Valley, a character which has remained unaltered for many centuries.

SOURCES OF KASHMIR HISTORY

Our knowledge of the political, social, and economic conditions which prevailed in early Kashmir is exceptionally ample, and is derived from a variety of sources. References to the country and its people are found in the literature of the Greeks, the Chinese, and the Arabs, as well as in Indian literature. Incomparably the most authoritative and informative are, naturally, the indigenous writers of Kashmir.

GREEK NOTICES.—Speaking of the geographical position of the country, which he calls by the name of Kaspeiria, Ptolemy remarks that it is situated "below the sources of the Bidaspes (Vitasta) and of the Sandabal (Chandrabhaga) and of the Adris (Iravati)." He further states that it lies between the Daradrai or Darads on the Indus and Kylindrine or the land of the Kulindas on the Hyphasis (Bias) and eastwards. His definition of its territorial limits is considerably exaggerated.

The passage in the Bassarika of Dionysios of Samos, preserved by Stephanos of Byzantium, which makes mention of the Kaspeiroi as a tribe famous among the Indians for their fleetness of food, probably refers to the Kashmiris, whose marching powers, owing to the mountainous nature of their country, are greater than those of the Indians of the plains.

CHINESE NOTICES.—The information which the Chinese records have left us is much more ample. The earliest reference which can with certainty be attributed to Kashmir is dated A.D. 541. It describes the northern part of India as a country "enveloped on all sides like a precious jewel by the snowy mountains, with a valley in the south which leads up to it and serves as the gate of the kingdom." But by far the greatest Chinese authority on Kashmir is the pilgrim Hsüan-tsang, who visited

Kashmir in A.D. 631 and spent two years there studying "the Sutras and Sastras."

A fairly detailed description of the country is contained in the itinerary and life of Hsüan-tsang, who was accorded a princely welcome by the ruler of Kashmir. He entered Kashmir by way of Baramula. He found Buddhism flourishing though not predominant. On his nearing the capital the king came out to receive him, and invited him to a sumptuous feast at the palace. He gave him twenty scribes to copy the sacred books and Sastras, and also deputed five men to wait on him and to furnish him, free of expenses, with whatever he required.

Speaking of the state of learning in Kashmir, he says that "this country from remote times was distinguished for learning, and their priests were all of high religious merit and conspicuous virtue as well as marked talent and power of clear exposition of doctrine; and though the other priests (i.e., of other nations) were in their own way distinguished, yet they could not be compared with these, so different were they from the ordinary class."

Regarding the extent of the country, its products, and its people, he says that "it (Kashmir) was above 7,000 li (1,400 miles) in circuit, surrounded by high steep mountains over which were narrow, difficult passes, and the country had been always impregnable. The capital, which had a large river on its west side, was 12 or 13 li (about 2 1/2 miles) from north to south and 4 to 5 li (nearly a mile) from east to west. The district was a good agricultural one and produced abundant fruits and flowers; it yielded also horses of the dragon stock, saffron, and medicinal plants. The climate was very cold in season with much snow and little wind. The people wear serge and cotton (pai- tieh). They were volatile and timid; being protected by a dragon they crowed over their neighbours; they were good-looking, but deceitful; they were fond of learning and had a faith which embraced orthodoxy and heterodoxy (i.e., Buddhism and other religious). Buddhist monasteries were above 100 in number, and there were 5,000 Buddhist brethren; and there were four Asoka topes each containing above a pint (shêng) of the bodily relics of the Buddha."

The territories of Prunts and Rajauri were at the time of Hsüan- tsang's visit subject to the king of Kashmir.

The next Chinese pilgrim who has left us an account of Kashmir is Ou-k'ong, who reached Kashmir in 759 A.D. Here he tool his full vows as a regular monk. He resided in the country for four years, spending his time mainly in visiting holy places and in studying Sanskrit. He states that the number of Buddhist convents was more than three hundred; which shows that Buddhism was in a much more flourishing condition than in the preceding century when Hsüan- tsang visited Kashmir.

A somewhat earlier and more interesting reference is furnished by the annals of the T'ang dynasty of China. "These mention the arrival at the imperial court of the first embassy from Kashmir sent by king Tchen-t'o-lo-pi-li (in or shortly after A.D. 713), and that of another embassy sent by his brother and successor, Mu-to-pi." These kings are to be identified with Chandrapida and Muktapida-Lalitaditya mentioned in the Rajatarangini. Besides the information that Hsüan-tsang gives, the only item of interest that this account furnishes is a reference to the Mo-ho-to-mo- loung or Mahapadma lake (present Wular lake), Po-lo-ou-lo-po-lo, Pravarapura, the old and official name of Srinagar, and Mi-na-si- to, the Vitasta river, which flowed on the west of the capital.

From this last statement, as well as from the testimony of Hsüan- tsang, it may be inferred that in the seventh and eighth centuries the city of Srinagar lay only on the right bank of the river and had not yet extended to the left bank. This expansion must have taken place some time before the end of the tenth century A.D., as Alberuni (see below) speaks of the city being situated on both banks of the river.

ARAB NOTICES.—The above is practically all that the Chinese have to tell us about Kashmir. The next foreigner from whom we get information of real value is Alberuni, the great Muhammadan scholar who flourished at the court of Mahmud of Ghazni (A.D. 996-1031). He tell us that, owing to the victories of Mahmud over the Hindus, the Hindu sciences have retired far away from those parts of the country conquered by us and have fled to places where our hand cannot yet reach—Kashmir, Benares, and other places.

Notwithstanding the numerous difficulties which the contemporary political conditions of India placed in the way of his collecting accurate statistics of the remote valley, Alberuni seems to have succeeded in the attempt better than might have been expected; for his account of Kashmir is much fuller than that of other parts of India and appears to show that among his informants, if not among his actual teachers, there were Kashmiri scholars. Regarding the people and the country he remarks as follows :

The inhabitants of Kashmir are pedestrians, and they have no riding animals. The nobles among them ride in palankins called kati carried on the shoulders of men. They are especially anxious about the natural strength of the country, and therefore take always great care to keep a strong hold upon the entrances and routes leading into it. In consequence it is very difficult to trade with them. In former times they used to allow one or two foreigners, particularly Jews, to enter their country; but at present they do not allow any Hindu, whom they do not know personally, to enter, much less other people.

The best known entrance to Kashmir is from the town Babrahan (in the district of Hazara).... The city of Kashmir covers a space of four farsakh, being built along both banks of the river Jailam, which are connected with each other by bridges and ferry-boats.

He adds that four farsakh below Addisthan, the capital, is a swamp of one square farsakh; that the people have plantations on its borders, and that Kashmir has no Varshakala (rainy season), but a snow-fall beginning with Magh up to the middle of Chaitra, when continual rains set in.

Kashmir holds the same rank among holy places as Benares, Kurukshetra, etc.

"The second of the month of Chaitra is a festival to the people of Kashmir called Agdus, and celebrated on account of a victory gained by their king Muttai over the Turks."

Alberuni counts five days' march "to be beginning of the ravine whence the river Jailam comes"—that is, to the entrance of the gorge through which the river flows immediately below Baramula. This estimate agrees closely with the actual road distance between Muzafferabad and Baramula, which is given by Mr. Drew as 84 miles. At the other or Kashmir end of the ravine, Alberuni places quite correctly the watch station Dvar (Skr. Dvara), the position of which, as we shall see below, is marked to this day by the site of the old gate known as Drang.

"Thence leaving the ravine you enter the plain, and reach in two more days Addishtan, the capital of Kashmir, passing on the road the village Ushkara." All this is perfectly accurate. Adhisthana, the capital, is, of course, meant for Srinagara, and Ushkara for Ushkur opposite Baramula, the ancient Hushkapura already mentioned by Hsüan-tsang. Alberuni's mention of Ushkur, which is on the left river bank, shows that then as now the ordinary road from the "Gate of Varahamula" to Srinagar passed on the left or southern side of the valley. Two marches are still counted for this part of the journey.

"Marching on the right side (of the river), you pass through villages, one close to the other, south of the capital, and thence you reach the mountain Kularjak, which is like a cupola, similar to the mountain Dunbawand (Damawand). The snow there never melts. It is always visible from the region of Takeshar and Lauhawar (Lahore)."

Besides describing the valley with great accuracy, Alberuni makes mention of the adjacent hill territories of Bolor (Baltistan) and the Dard tracts of "Gilgit, Aswira, and Shiltas" (modern Gilgit, Hasor, and Chilas). He also speaks of the fortresses of Lauhur (Skr. Lohara), in the Loharin valley on the way to Poonch, and Rajagiri as the strongest places he had ever seen.

He closes his account with a reference to the town of Rajavari (Skr. Rajapuri), the modern Rajauri. In Hindu times it was the capital of a small hill state, situated immediately to the south of the Pir Pantsal range and often tributary to Kashmir. Alberuni distinctly names it as the farthest place to which the Muhammadan merchants of his time traded, and beyond which they never passed.

INDIAN NOTICES.—The information that we can glean regarding Kashmir from the works of ancient Indian writers other than those of Kashmiri origin is extremely meagre. The great grammarian Panini and his commentator Patanjali make a bare mention of the name Kasmīra and its derivative Kāsmīra. The Mahabharata and the Puranas refer to the Kāsmīras and their ruler, but in a fashion so general and vague that nothing but the situation of the country in the hill region to the north can be concluded therefrom.

Varahamihira, the will-known Indian astronomer, who probably lived about A.D. 500, had even more hazy notions regarding the location of Kashmir, inasmuch as he mentions it along with a number of purely mythical countries and people such as "the kingdom of the dead" (Nastarajya), "the gold region," "the one-footed people," etc. His mention of Abhisaras, Daradas, etc., who were undoubtedly living on the borders of Kashmir, does not help much in gaining knowledge of the valley as it existed at that time.

"Perhaps the most specific piece of information regarding Kashmir that Sanskrit literature outside the valley can furnish is conveyed in the term kāsmīra or kāsmīraja, which designates the saffron, and also, according to the lexicographers, the root of the kustha, or Costus speciosus. As both saffron and kustha have been from early times famous products of Kashmir, the origin of the term is clear enough.

KASHMIRI AUTHORS.—In strong contrast to the lack of definite geographical knowledge displayed by Indian authors is the refreshing abundance of historical and topographical detail in the works of Kashmiri authors. This splendid array of authoritative guides begins with the Nilamatapurana and continues practically without break to the present time. The age of the Nilamata is uncertain; but there is evidence to show that in one form or the other it was extant in the early middle ages. Beginning with the legend regarding the lacustrine origin of the valley and its drainage after the death of Jalodbhava, the water demon, who infested the lake and made human habitation on its shores impossible, the Purana gives us a detailed list of the holy places of Kashmir. To each name it appends a more or less comprehensive topographical description, which is of great value in identification of the numerous places mentioned.

Analogous in nature, but far later in date, are the Mahatmyas of the different tirthas or places of pilgrimage. These works give lengthy accounts of the legendary origin of the holy places of Kashmir, and the religious merit accruing to the fortunate pilgrim who pays a visit to each sacred spot. They also furnish a complete survey of the sacred places places of Kashmir.

By far the greatest amount of our information regarding ancient and mediaeval Kashmir is supplied by indigenous historians, of whom Kalhana is the oldest and most informative. He composed his Rajatarangini, the river of kings, in A.D. 1148-49. Born in a Brahman official family, and learned in the traditions of his country both from oral and written sources, Kalhana was specially fitted for his self-imposed task, which he has executed with conspicuous ability. His father, Champaka, was the minister of king Harsha (A.D. 1089-1101), but after the murder of his master in A.D. 1101 neither father nor son appears to have taken office under the succeeding rulers. With the characteristic reticence of ancient Indian authors he has left no information regarding his own life and pursuits. The indirect evidence of his chronicle, however, compensates to some extent for his silence by revealing the character and intellectual equipment of the man. He had a keen, observant eye, considerable sense of humour, vivid poetic imagination, and extensive knowledge of human nature. His impartiality in according praise or blame to his royal contemporaries, no less than to the kings of the past, shows that he was no sycophant. Though by birth he was a worshipper of Siva, he respected other sects and religious almost as much as he did his own form of faith. His appreciation of the material conditions of his country, his topographical detail, his use of archaeological and numismatic evidence in the compilation of his history, give his work not only an absorbing interest in itself, but also an honourable place among histories of the mediaeval world.

It has, however, shortcomings which cannot be ignored. His chief defect is his want of critical acumen. He seldom quotes an opinion or a statement with a view to refute it. He is not able to distinguish between the legendary and genuine elements of tradition. Owing partly to this defect and partly, probably, to want of authentic sources, the first four books of his chronicles are little more than dynastic lists, interspersed here and there with anecdotes. It is from the seventh century A.D. that history in the modern sense begins. This does not mean that the earlier part of the chronicle is on that account without interest. On the contrary, it has very great value, not only because it mentions the great historic names of Asoka, Kanishka, etc., but also because it presents us with a fairly detailed account of the general condition of the kingdom before we reach the centuries which immediately precede the time of Kalhana, and for which he had genuine oral and written information. The latter consisted of a number of ancient histories written before Kalhana's time, of which he appears to have made extensive use. Unfortunately all of them are now lost. This makes it impossible to distinguish what is original from what is borrowed in Kalhana's Rajatarangini. Perhaps this work, which probably served as a convenient and comprehensive manual of Kashmir history for subsequent generations, was not a little responsible for the gradual disuse and final disappearance of the literary records which were available in his time. The period which he knew personally or the knowledge of which he owed to living witnesses is treated by him with an exhaustiveness which leaves little to be desired, especially when we bear in mind that Kalhana regarded himself primarily as a poet, and composed the Rajatarangini as a didactic poem for the edification of his countrymen. Kalhana's chronicle has been published, with an excellent translation, exhaustive introduction, numerous explanatory notes, and a valuable monograph on the ancient geography and coinage, etc., of Kashmir, by Sir Aurel Stein. This monumental work is indispensable for the proper understanding of the social and political conditions of pre-Muslim Kashmir.

Exactly three centuries passed before a successor was found to continue Kalhana's work. He was another Kashmiri Brahman, Jonaraja, who was the contemporary and court historian of Zain- ul-abidin (A.D. 1421-1472). His treatment of the centuries between him and his great predecessor is very superficial. The greater part of his work as well as of the history of Srivara, his pupil, who continued his master's task, is devoted to the reign of their patron Zain-ul-abidin. Prajyabhatta and Suka, two other historians who followed Srivara, bridge another century and terminate their labours with the conquest of the valley by Akbar in A.D. 1587.

Thenceforward, Sanskrit chronicles ceased to be written; for, though Akbar tolerated and even encouraged Sanskrit learning, in such an out-of-the-way place as Kashmir it was no doubt at a discount, at any rate in an official sense. But with the decay of Sanskrit learning the Kashmiris characteristic love of history and tradition did not wane and wither away.

Before bidding farewell to our Kashmiri Sanskrit writers, we must make mention of the poets from whose works can be gleaned some useful information. The most important among them is Kshemendra, the well-known historian, whose books, composed in the second and third quarter of the eleventh century, form important landmarks in several fields of Indian literature. In the Samayamatrika, one of his most original poems, which is intended to describe the snares of courtesans, he gives us, among other stories, an amusing account of the wandering of his chief heroine, Kankali, through the length and breath of Kashmir. The numerous places which form the scene of her exploits can all easily enough he traced on the map. More than once curious touches of true local colour impart additional interest to these references. To Kshemendra's poem we owe, for example, the earliest mention of the Pir Pantsal pass (Panchaladhara) and its hospice (maṭha). There too we get a glimpse of the ancient salt trade which until lately continued to follow that route.

Bilhana, the poet, who has been alluded to above, has also left in his Vikramankadevacharita a glowing picture of the beauties of Kashmir in general, besides giving a description of his rural home at Khunamusha, which is known today as the rakh (game preserve) of Khunamoh.

Mankha, the contemporary of Kalhana, has left a similar description of Kashmir and Srinagar.

These accounts serve the additional purpose of enabling us to corroborate the statements of Kalhana from independent evidence.

The book known as the Lokaprakasa is a curious mixture of the ordinary dictionary and a practical handbook dealing with various topics of administration and private life in Kashmir. Though much of the information given in it is decidedly old and probably from the hand of our well-known Kshemendra, there are unmistakable proofs in the form and contents of the book that it has undergone considerable alterations and additions down even to the seventeenth century. It supplies the earliest list of Kashmir parganas; and there are also the names of numerous localities inserted in the forms for bonds, hundis, contracts, official reports, and the like, which form the bulk of Prakasas ii and iv.

In Mughal times and later, a host of Muslim and Hindu historians writing in the official Persian language recorded the events that occurred in their own lifetime, as well as the traditions which they heard from living witnesses. None of them, however, reached the standard of Kalhana. What little they tell of the Hindu period they borrowed from him, and borrowed in a most perfunctory manner. The most important among these later historians are Haidar Malik of Tsodur, a contemporary of the emperor Jahangir; Narayan Kaul, who complied his history in A.D. 1721; Hasan, who wrote in the last quarter of the eighteenth century; and Birbal Katsur, who is still more recent.

Besides the indigenous Sanskrit and Persian chronicles, we have notices of foreigners who collected information or visited Kashmir from time to time and recorded what they heard, or saw with their own eyes. Of these Mirza Haidar Doghlat of Kashgar, who conquered the valley in A.D. 1540 and ruled it in the name of Humayun till A.D. 1551, the historian Firishta, and Abul Fazl, the minister of Akbar, are the most instructive. Abul Fazl's account is specially interesting. Besides supplying detailed information regarding the administration of the country, its products and industries, it furnishes an account of its chief places and objects of note, a list of thirty-eight parganas or administrative divisions with their respective land revenue figures in kind and in cash, and of the tribes residing in each. It also furnishes a short resume of the history of Kashmir, which Abul Fazl had got summarised from indigenous sources.

Among the European travellers who visited Kashmir before the valley became the fashionable summer resort of India, the earliest to contribute to our knowledge of it is the French physician Bernier, who accompanied Aurangzeb in his journey to Srinagar in A.D. 1664. He has left many interesting descriptions of the "merveilles," as he calls them, of Kashmir, as well as of the general condition of the country in Aurangzeb's time. The travels of Foster afford a peep into the state of tyranny that prevailed in the valley during the Pathan regime. Moorcroft, Vigne, Hügel, Honigberger, and Jacquemont are valuable for the Sikh times.

In addition to the numerous sources of Kashmir history above mentioned, we have to take into account the extraordinarily tenacious oral traditions, which have been handed down from generation to generation. They remove uncertainty in the identification of many ancient names given in the chronicles, and in certain cases they supplement the information furnished.

CHAPTER 2

THE ARCHITECTURAL MONUMENTS OF KASHMIR

BY

Sachchidananda Sinha

"Ancient India has nothing more worthy of its early civilisation than the grand remains in Kashmir; the massive, the grotesque, the elegant, in architecture, may be admired in many parts of India, but nowhere there is to be seen the counterpart of the classically graceful, yet symmetrically massive, edifices of Kashmir which, though inferior to Palmyra or Persepolis in stateliness, are in beauty of position so immensely superior to either"—wrote a qualified European critic. There are in Kashmir splendid and wonderful ruins, of cut lime-stone, dating from the third to the eighth century, to demonstrate that the ancient Kashmiris were great architects, and produced a beautiful and impressive style distinct from the Buddhist

and Hindu architecture of other parts of India. It betrays, to some extent, Greek influence in its pediments, and its fluted columns with base-shaft, and capital. But the pillars were spaced further apart than in Greek architecture, and pediments pitched higher, and the temples crowned with pyramidal roofs tapering to a single lotus blossom, with the interior walls enriched with deep reliefs. In recent years much excavation and restoration have been carried out, and the results had been carefully recorded and surveyed, in 1933, by Mr. Ram Chandra Kak, in his excellent work, Ancient Monuments of Kashmir.

This comprehensive and useful book should be kept handy by all visitors to Kashmir, interested in its many archaeological monuments.

The best preserved of these stone temples are at Awantipura and Martand, both within easy distance of Srinagar. For a general sketch of the chief temples, one cannot do better than quote from the luminous article on the Architecture of Kashmir, by the late Mr. T. S. Growse, which brings into prominent relief their striking features. As he put it :—"Owing to the great thickness of the walls, and the massiveness of the plinth upon which the temples are raised, the exterior proportions are much more imposing than would be expected from the insignificant interior. Though less suggestive of Greek influence than the detached pillars of the colonnades, the pilasters, with their definitely proportioned base-shaft and capital, the square architraves of the doorways, and the triangular pediments that surmount them, but still more the chastened simplicity of outline and the just subordination of merely decorative details, are at a glance seen to be classic rather than oriental. Beyond the points above enumerated, the resemblance ceases; the porches are curved into a bold trefoiled arch of similar character with English Gothic of the first pointed period, and the roof, instead of being flat and out-of-slight, is a high pitched pyramid, broken, however, into two compartments by a horizontal band carved with dentils and triglyphs. In short, the adaptation of classic forms was complete just so far as the differences of climate and the conventionalities of religion allowed; hence the roof became a prominent feature in the design."

Harwan has perhaps the oldest monument in Kashmir, containing the only remains of its kind in India. A temple and some tablets—built in the first or second century—have been unearthed here, which date the monument as belonging to the Kushan period, when Kashmir was closely connected with Central Asia, The remains are situated only a few furlongs below the water reservoir at Harwan, which is close to

Srinagar, and well deserve a visit for their great historic interest.

The temple crowning the Takht-i-Suleiman, or Shankaracharya—which rises to the height of 1,000 feet above the plain, and overlooks Srinagar, and spreads away to the foot of the opposite but somewhat lower eminence called the Hari Parbat—is one of the earliest in Kashmir. The first religious edifice on this commanding site was built by the son of the great Buddhist Emperor, Asoka, about 200 B.C. which was subsequently rebuilt, and dedicated to Mahadeva by Raja Gopadittya, who reigned in the sixth century of the Christian era. Restored, from time to time, it stands today at the top of the hill, and its platform commands a superb view of the valley of Kashmir, and the city of Srinagar.

Of more interest and in much more perfect preservation is the small cave temple at Bhaumajo, which is about half a mile from the village of Bawan, near Khanabal. The entrance to the cavern, which is more than sixty feet above the level of the river, is carved into an architectural doorway, and a passage fifty feet in length leads from it to the door of the temple, which is a simple cella ten feet square, raised on a boldly-moulded plinth and approached by a short flight of steps. The square doorway is flanked by two round-headed niches and is surmounted by a high triangular pediment reaching to the apex of the roof with a trefoiled tympanum. This is perhaps the earliest perfect specimen of Kashmir temple, and dated from the fifth or the sixth century of the Christian era.

The little shrine at Payech—on the Srinagar-Khanabal motor road—comes next in point of antiquity, and in intrinsic beauty and elegance of outline is far superior to all the existing remains of similar dimensions. The cella, which is only eight feet square, and has an open doorway on each of the four sides, is composed of only ten stones, the four corners being each a single stone, the sculptured tympanums over the doorways of four others, while two more compose the pyramidal roof, the lower of these being an enormous mass eight feet square by four feet in height. It has been ascribed by General Cunningham to King Narendraditya.

Of somewhat later date are the temples at Wangat, in two groups, up the Liddar valley, at the distance of a few hundred yards from each other, and consisting respectively of six and eleven distinct buildings. In close proximity is a sacred spring called Nagbal, and by it the footpath leads up the heights of Haramuck to the mountain lake of Gangabal, a celebrated place of pilgrimage,. The luxuriant forest growth had over-thrown and buried almost completely several of the smaller temples, while on summit of the largest a tall pine had taken root. The architecture is of a slightly more advanced type than at Payech, the most striking feature being the bold projection and lofty trefoiled arches of the lateral.

Of very similar character, but in more perfect preservation, is the temple at Bhaniyar, which stands on the very edge of the high road leading from Rawalpindi to Srinagar. The actual shrine is a cella of larger dimensions than usual, being 131/2 feet square in the interior, with walls 61/2 feet thick, supported on a basement, a 4 feet square, of singularly noble proportions. It is the earliest example that still retains its original enclosure, a cloistered quadrangle measuring 145 by 120 feet. Though the final touches of the chisel have been effaced by time, the colonnade is in other respects almost perfect. The wall is pierced by a series of pedimented and trefoiled arches forming shallow recesses for the accommodation of priests and pilgrims.

The celebrated temple of Martand is of far more imposing dimensions than any other existing example. It alone possesses in addition to the cella, sanctuary, choir and nave. The nave is 18 feet square, and the total length of the building is 63 feet. The sanctuary alone is left entirely bare, the two other compartments are lined with rich panelling and sculptured niches. The roof has been completely removed, and lies in vast masses round the wall of the buildings; it is calculated that the height cannot have been less than 76 feet. The western entrance, approached by a wide flight of steps, now encumbered with ruins, is surmounted by a magnificent trefoiled arch, and flanked by two side chapels, one connected with the nave by the extension of their roof over the narrow intervening passage. On the other sides of the temple are similar arches with closed doorways below. The pillared quadrangle, which is 200 by 142 feet in dimension, varies in no essential point from that at Bhaniyar, but the carving is rather more elaborate. There are in all eighty-four colonnade as distinctly recorded in the Rajatarangini as the work of the famous King Lalitaditya, who reigned from 699 to 735. From the same authority we gather that the temple itself was built by Ramaditya, who probably died in the first half of the fifth century after Christ. Standing on a fine bluff, two to three hundred feet above the valley, it commands an extensive and beautiful view of the Kashmir valley :—

On slope of vast and undulating plain
In solemn solitude, of noble art,
The ancient ruins of Martand remain
Built for Sun-worship once. Has the true part
Of thy prone columns faded like a dream ?
Engirdled by the everlasting hills,
O Temple of the Sun! His radiant beam
Illumes this broken altar, and still fills
These shattered halls at dawn with his clear light,
Though human hands may no more loving tend.
The Sun's pure glory is God's symbol bright,
Thus thy great destiny can never end :
Still eloquent of prayers, though stones decay
And forms of ancient creeds have passed away.

From "The Ruined Temple of Martand" in Mrs. Percy Brown's Chenar Leaves.

On the right bank of the Jhelum, about half-way between the towns of the Srinagar and Anantnag (Islamabad) stood the capital of the famous King Avanti Verma, called after his name as Avantipur. His reign extended from the year 858 to 883. The gateways of both are standing and the colonnade of the smaller temple. The style corresponds with that of the Martand quadrangle; but the semi- attached pillars of the arched recesses are enriched with elaborate carving of very varied character, while the large detached columns are somewhat less elegantly proportioned. They possess a wealth of carving unparalleled in Kashmir.

Shankara Varma, who succeeded Avanti varma and reigned from 883 to 901, dedicated to Mahadeva two temples at his capital, now identified with the modern Pattan, where two stately temples are still standing. Each is a simple cella; but in the larger one the side porches are so deep as to constitute separate chambers. In both the architecture is of the same character as at Martand, and of equal excellence. Here and there the carving is sharp and fresh, but the larger one was much injured by the earthquake of 1885.

The temple of Pandrethan is, next to Martand, the best known of all, in consequence of its close proximity to the capital. The domed roof is well worth inspection, being covered with sculpture of such purely classic design that an uninitiated person, who saw a copy of it on paper, would at once take it for a sketch from a Greek or Roman original. The temple is 18 feet square, with a projecting portico on each side, and displays a confused exuberance of decoration, more especially the repetition of pediment and trefoil, clear indications of a later date. It was erected by a Minister of king Partha, who governed Kashmir from 913 to 921.

Pandrethan's shrine farewell : Thy stones are falling
And totter to a final, sad decay :
What echoes of heart's worship here are calling!
What visions of thy early mystic sway!

From "Pandrethan" in Mrs. Percy Brown's Chenar Leaves

Pari-Mahal ("the place of fairies") is a massive building, now in ruins, standing on the side of the mountain on the southern side of the Dal lake, which was erected in the Moghal time for astronomical observations. It has a garden attached to it, with six terraces. The retaining wall is ornamented with a series of arches, and it has a domed ceiling.

"Peri Mahal!" strange and romantic name
Bestowed by folk-lore on this ancient pile
Above the Dal lake's shore :
The ruin hoar remains, its sad stern brow
O'erhangs the shining lake in frowning gloom,
Deserted— brooding lone—it's mystic doom!
I'll flee! lest spell malign befall me now

From "Peri Mahal" (The Fairies' Palace) in Mrs. Percy Brown's Chenar Leaves.

Taper (22 miles from srinagar, and 4 miles from Patan, on the Srinagar-Rawalpindi road) has the ruins of an old temple, discovered in September, 1942, in the course of the excavations carried out by the Archaeological Department of the state. The temple appears to have been built in the 13th century, and dedicated to Vishnu. Some of the stones among the finds bear inscriptions in the old Sharda script—giving the name of the architect, and the time when it was built. The base of the temple, its court-yard, and the plinth of the enclosure wall, have been exposed till now. The temple is a square, the base of its sides being about 60 feet. It is 8 feet high from the level of the court-yard, and its walls are four feet thick. It is thus massively built of stone, but the dressing is simple. A number of interesting antiquarian remains also have been unearthed in the course of the excavations (which are still in progress), as also some stone inscriptions, inscribed in Sharda character, which throw interesting sidelights on its construction. From Sir Aurel stein's annotated translation of Kalhana's Rajatarangini, it seems that Taper is the ancient Pratapapura, a town built by Pratapaditya II, at the beginning of the 8th century. Though Kalhana is silent about the construction of this temple by Pratapaditya, the Persian historian, Hasan, clearly says (in his Tarikh) that the temple at Taper was built by Pratapaditya II, that it was destroyed by Sikandar "Butshikan", and that its material was used by Zain-ul-Abdin, his son, in constructing an embankment.

Lastly, the three charts which appear in Mr. R. C. Kak's book and which usefully supplement the information, are appended to this chapter for convenience of reference.

MONUMENTS IN SRINAGAR AND ITS VICINITY

From	To	Distance	Mode of Travelling	Remarks
Srinagar	Sankaracharya temple	2½ miles	By carriages to the Mission Hospital and thence on foot	
	Patthar Masjid, Shah Hamadan's Mosque	By boat to Badhas and thence by carriage to Jama Masjid, or	...	3 to 4 hours

	Zain-ul-Abdin's enclosure	throughout by carriage		
	Jama Masjid, Hari Parbat			
	Mosque of Madin Sahib			
	Vistar Nag ...			
	Chasma-i-Shahi	5½ miles by motor road from Srinagar		
	Pari-Mahal and back	1½ miles on foot Chasma-i-Shahi	...	Srinagar to Harwan by road is
	Nishat ...	2½ miles by motor road		11½ milles
	Shalimar...	2 do.		
	Harwan	1½ do.		

MONUMENTS ABOVE SRINAGAR

Srinagar to Pandrethan	3½ miles	Motor Road	
Do. to Avantipur	18 "	Do.	
Do. to Loduv	16 "	Road Partly unmetalled	Tents and necessaries
Avantipur to Payer and back	12 "	Bridle-path	must be taken.. Rest house at
Avantipur to Narastan	20 "	Do.	Matan; Dak bunglows at Achhbal.
Srinagar to Achhbal	39 "	Moror Road	
Do. to Martand	39 "	Do.	
Acchbal to Kother and back	6 "	Motor Road and bridle-path	

Martand to Mamal, two stages	30 "	Motor Road to Pahalgam, opposite to which, across the stream, is Mammal	
Martand and Bamzu and back	2 "	Motor Road	
Srinagar to Verinag	50 "	Do. Dak Bangalow at Munda within five miles	

MONUMENTS BELOW SRINAGAR

From	To	Distance	Remark
Srinagar	Parihasapura	14 miles by the Baramulla cart road, and 3 miles on foot or pony beyond	
Do.	Pattan	17 miles	Rest house at Pattan
Pattan	Baramulla and Ushkar	Do.	
Baramulla	Fathgarh	3 miles over the hill.	
Do.	Naranthal	3½ miles on pony.	
Do.	Buniar	14 miles	Dak at
Buniar	Bandi temple	9 "	Rampore.
Srinagar	Manasbal	18 " by motorable road, or by boat	
Do.	Wangath	33 miles, 18 milles by motorable road as far as Wayil, thence bridle-path.	

CHAPTER 3

MONUMENTS OF KASHMIR

By

G. L. Kaul

It is after the rise of Buddhism that Hindus began to build temples. the Kashmir classical style is fundamentally different from any other style of Hindu architecture. Writes Sir A. Cunningham, "The architectural remains of Kashmir are perhaps the most remarkable of the existing monuments of India as they exhibit undoubted traces of the influence of Gresian art. The Hindu temple is generally a sort of architectural pasty, a huge collection of ornamental fritters huddled together, either with or without keeping, while the Jain temples, usually a vast forest of pillars, made to look as unlike one another as possible by some paltry differences in their petty details. On the other hand, the Kashmirian fanes are distinguished by the graceful elegance of their outlines, by the massive boldness of their parts, and by the happy propriety of their decorations."

"They cannot indeed vie with the severe simplicity of the Parthenon nor with the luxuriant gracefulness of the monument of Lusicrates, but they possess great beauty, different indeed, yet quite their own."

"The Kashmirian architecture is characterised by its lofty pyramidal roofs, its trefoiled door ways, covered by pyramidal pediments, and the great width of its intercoluminations suited equally well to rainy and snowy climates. There is no doubt that the Kashmirian style was well-known to the Greeks. A

Kashmirian pillar has base, a shaft and a capital. The local architecture has also a stereotyped style. The trefoil arch of Kashmir is very original and interesting as may be seen from the remains of some old monuments."

Go wherever you may, you must met with some old wonder. One wonders when he beholds and ancient monument whose huge and massive constructions built in days of yore stand to this day as witnesses of a race of giants, un-equalled in the histories of chivalry, who once occupied this beautiful land. The reason is plain. The old architects built their temples solid. Their object was to construct imperishable abodes for their Gods to dwell in. They chose high ground as much as possible so as to avoid big floods. It must be remembered that in those days the river valleys were much more full of water than they are now and the forests also were very dense. Those ancestors have bequeathed a rich civilisation second only to the ancient Romans. A few such historical places are mentioned below with a short account that could be available.

Hari Parbat Fort

As traditions has it, Hari Parbat is the pebble which the sparrow goddess threw on the demon who had lived in Satisar. The demon was killed and water gave way to land. Akbar built the Hari Parbat Fort and the town of Nagar Nagar round it. Muslims later named it Kohe Maran.

Hari Parbat stands on the Dal Lake itself and is located in the centre of the city. Apart from its monumental value it is a symbol of secularism. Hindus, Muslims and Sikhs have shrines round it.

Shankaracharya Temple.

Ihe mountainous portal that opens,
Sublime from the Valley of bliss to the world".

The Temple on the top of Shankaracharya Hill once called Gopadri is supposed to have been built by Sandiman 2629-2564 B.C. and later on repaired by Gopaditya 426-365 B.C. and Lalitaditya 699- 736 A.D. According to another authority Jaloka built it in 220 B.C. Some assign to it the date 300 B.C., but this is generally considered inaccurate. Others mention the year 300 A.D., as the probable date of its construction. Tradition says that the Lingam was placed inside the temple by a goldsmith named Raja Hishti in the year 54 of the Hindu era.

An inscription quotes the name of Khwaja Rokm, son of Mirjan, in connection with its origin. Sikandar, The Iconoclast, did not raze it to the ground because he thought (erroneously) that Mahmud Ghazni might have read prayers in it. The temple commands a fine view of the city that lies prostrate at its foot. Even in such a land of precious stones of architecture the Shankaracharya remains a gem of the first water.

The Pari Mahal (Kash-i-Mah).

This is the 'fairy palace'. Tradition has it that Prince Dara Shikoh designed it for his tutor Mulla Shah and named it after his wife Pari Begum. Another authority says that it was once used for astronomical observations by the Moghul Kings. It stands on an isolated crag and with almost perpendicular sides towards the top. The Pari Mahal has stood for centuries, wheather-worn, sad, alone and untenanted which proves that the Paries (fairies) have it in their possession but where are they ?

Look on its broken arch ! Its ruined wall !
Its chambers desolate and portals foul :
Yes this was once Ambition's airy hall
The Dome of Thought, the palace of Soul.

—Lord Byron.

The massive building has a domed ceiling. The retaining wall is ornamented with a series of arches.

The Temple of Payech.

The sloping knoll on which it stands, the cool shade of a clump of walnut trees close by, the glimpses of a village seen through the trees behind and cheerful brook running at the foot of the slope, form a charming setting to a building which would be dwarfed by a scenery of a grander scale. The temple built of ten stones only, now in ruins, seems to be of long standing. Archaeologists do not definitely estimate its exact date. And who built it that also is not exactly known ?

The Temple of Pandrethan.

This temple has one of the largest moats. Cunningham says that it was probably built in 921 A.D. by Meru during the reign of KIng Partha. Round it once spread the old capital of Kashmir when none but the Aryans lived here. It was also once Asoka's Srinagar. The domed roof of the temple is fine piece of sculpture. There are series of arches in the retaining wall.

Avantipura.

The archaeologists are of opinion that the temples 174'148' here were built in the 9th century by King Avantivarman who had his capital 18 miles away from present Srinagar. The balconies alternate angular and rounded flutting set off the natural contrasts of massive stones of which they are built. Nothing sadder or more beautiful exists in India than this deserted city, the silent witness of a vanished dream. It still stands with its long circuit, its bastioned gates, its wonderful palaces, peerless in the whole Hindustan for its noble design and delicate adornment. Its carvings stand as they stood in Avantivarman's time but now a body without a soul. Ruinate it has remained ever since, desolate and abandoned. No later ruler of Kashmir has even aspired to dwell in Avantivarman's Versailles. The two temples known as Avanti Swamin and Avanti Sura were dedicated to Vishnu and Shiva.

Sumbal.

About one mile from the bridge over the Jhelum on the left bank is Andarkoth, the former capital of Jayapida, the grandson of Lalitaditya. Kuta Rani, the last Hindu Queen of Kashmir, is said to have committed suicide here (1339 A.D.).

The Temple of Martand.

The date of this temple is favoured to be 8th century by some Archaeologists. Cunningham places its date between 370-500 A.D. But Ferguson does not admit its foundation before the 8the century. Roughly speaking it is between 2,000 and 1,500 years old. The temple of Martand appears to be the ruins of a grand old temple 63 feet long enclosed in a quadrangle of columns and arches forming cloisters all round it. It is about 200 feet long and 142 feet broad. There are about 84 carved pillars many of which lie prostrate on the ground. Martand with its beauty in desolation has stirred the Poet's vision of a Heber and compelled the homage of the wisest critics of Indian art. It is a dream in stones designed by Titans and finished by Jewellers. It only needed a glass case. Its architecture is fairer than the site of the Parthenon, or of the Taj or of St. Peter, or of the Escurial. This temple with a mighty tradition behind it is now the lonely watcher on the mountain side. It alone had the strength to stand a huge blazing fire that could burn cities. The temple exists still but its designer and destroyer are no more. Certainly it is not less imposing than Persepolis.

Patan

There are ruins of two very fine temples attributed to King Shankaravarman 883-902 A.D. and his queen Sugandha who flourished in the 9th century.

Ruins at Wangat

"These are of steep wilderness whose airy sides
With thickets overgrown, grotesque and wild,
Access denied, and overhead up grew,
Inseparable height of loftiest shade, cedar, pine
and fir."

Distance lends enchantment to this place—an enchantment which baffles the novelist. Nothing precisely can be said as to the date of its origin or its founder.

Bijbihara

A high and isolated Kareva lies at a couple of miles from Bijbihara. Here is visible the site of one of the oldest and most famous temples of Kashmir which was occupied by crowds of refugees and soldiers during the civil wars of king Sussala's time. The wooden ramparts were set on fire by the besiegers from which ensued a terrible holocaust. This sacred place gets its name from the temple of Shivavijayeshwara. A bridge over the Jhelum was in existence here in the 16th century. A fine grove of chinar trees, the remains of a garden planted by the unfortunate prince Darashikoh, is till visible on each bank of the river.

Shah-e-Hamdan

Kutab-ud-Din Demolished the temple of Kaleshwari and built the present Sheh-e-Hamdan mosque (after Syed Ali Hamadani who came from Hamdan in Persia towards the end of the fourteenth century and converted a large section of the people to Islam) with its material. Hasan Shah and Barkat Ali rebuilt the mosque in 1479 A.D. and 1731 A.D. respectively. A spring dedicated to Kali is still believed to exist inside the mosque. The reputed walking stick of Christ Kept in this mosque is exhibited on rear occasions. The hall is 63'43'. Shah

Hamdan's death is given as 786 Hijri, corresponding to 1384 A.D.

Pathar Masjid.

Nur Jahan built this mosque for offering prayers in it. The Sunnis had abandoned it since because she belonged to Shia sect. It remained under the State control and was restored back to the Muslims in 1931.

Jamia Masjid.

Sikandar 1390-1415 A.D. demolished the temple built by Taradeva 693-697 A.D. and out of its material he constructed a huge mosque now known as Jamia Masjid. It was first built in 1404 A.D. and afterwards rebuilt in the year 1479, 1619, 1674, 1841 and 1912 A.D.

Hazrat Bal.

The Zairat at Hazratbal on the Dal Lake is visited by thousands of Muslims on Fridays. It is here that the famous feast of roses is celebrated every spring.

Badshah Dome.

Inside the dome there is a grave sheltering of the mother of Zain-ul-Abdin (1421-1472 A.D.). The plinth of the dome is the plinth of an old temple.

Harwan.

A temple and some tablets have been unearthed during recent excavations at Harwan which look like the oldest mountain monuments as belonging to the Kushan period when Kashmir was closely connected with Central asia. Nagarjuna, the philosopher, held Buddhist congregations here.

Tapar.

Archaeological finds were discovered at Tapar in 1942 revealing a temple 62'ā10' built by Pratapaditiya of the Karkuta dynasty. Certain inscriptions lead to the finding that repairs were made by a Brahmin named Gogga whose father Jagaraja lived in the reign of Pamanda, Jayasinha's son in (1157 A.D.).

Narasimha temple at Devasar.

This temple has a basement 30' square and nearly 3' high. The portico is 15'ā11'. It looks having been built in the 12th century.

Kshema Gaurishwara.

Kshema Gupta 850-858 A.D. is stated to have built this temple.

Didha Matha.

It is now the tomb of Malik Sahib. The queen of Kshema Gupta built a temple here.

Narpristan.

The edifice at Narparistan is attributed to Lahna Narendraditya 178-191 A.D.

Mahashri.

It is now a graveyard. Pravarsena II is supposed to have built temple here.

Skandabhawan.

It was probable built by Skanda Gupta, Minister of Yudhisthra 11—139-178 A.D.

Lokhrigar.

The shrine at Lokhrigar is attributed to Pravarsena II.

Sadahawashri.

It is now the Ziarat of Pir Haji Mohammad. Praversena II is supposed to have built a temple here.

Rameshwara

Rameshwara now the Ziarat of Madin Sahib is ascribed to Ranaditya 414-474 A.D.

Amritabhawana.

The shrine is attributed to Amritaprabha Queen of Meghvahana 22 B.C.

Vikrameshwara.

This holy place is attributed to Vikramaditya 521-553 A.D.

Bandi.

The temple at Bandi belongs either to the Hindus or to the Buddhists. It was built in about 700 A.D.

Bhunyar.

The temple at Bhunyar dedicated to the goddess Bhawani was built probably in the fifth century.

Fatehgarh.

The temple at Fatehgarh is of long standing. Maharaja Ranjit Singh built his Fort here.

Temples at Shri Narayantha, built by Narendraprabha, Queen of Prattapaditya II (634-684 A.D.), Tribhavana Swami built by Chandrapida (684-693 A.D.), Vikrameswara near Vicharnag built by Vikramaditya (521-563 A.D.), Vishnu Ranaswamin built by the Queen of Ranaditya, Sabhava Shri Pravarsena II, Khrew (Pampur) built by Padma, Ladhnu, Kuil, Payar built by Narendraditya (483-490 A.D.), Naristhan Lokbhavan built by Lalitaditya (699-736 A.D.) Bumzu, Mamal, Sangam near Amburhar built by Queen Suryamyti (1028-86 A.D.), Thiun Rarannag built by Jaluka (1394-34 B.C.), Narendraditya (308-273 B. C.) and Lalitaditya, Andarkot built by Jayapida (753-84 A.D.), Mosques of or Ziarats (I) Ali Masjid built by Ali Shah, brother of Zain-ul-Abdin, in 1397 A.D. (2) Akhun Mullah Shah (3) Hassanabad built by Shias in the time of Akbar (4) Pantachuk built by Hubba Khatun, wife of Yusuf Chak (1578-1584 A.D.) deserve only a brief notice.

CHAPTER 4

MEDIAEVAL VISNU IMAGES FROM KASHMIR AND SOME VISNUDHARMOTTARA PASSAGES

By

Jitendar Nath Banerjee

In the mediaeval temples of Kashmere, Viṣṇu is usually represented with four faces and four or eight arms; in the bas-reliefs, however, he is shown with three faces only, all of which are not human. Reliefs carved on the western walls of the ante-chamber in the Mārtaṇḍa temple built during the time of Lalitāditya, the great Kashmerian king of the Karkoṭa dynasty, depict the god with three faces, the left face being that of a boar and the right, that of a lion. Similar is the representation of Viṣṇu in the Avantisvāmin temple of Avantipur (modern Wāntipur). In both the places, the god is eight-armed, two of their hands being placed on the heads of the chauri-bearers who are, as will be presently shown, the Āyudhapuruṣas. Many of these reliefs are so mutilated that the emblems in their hands cannot be correctly identified. But the images of Viṣṇu which are fully in the round never fail to show the fourth head at the back. The fragmentary sculpture, No. Aa 21, in the Sri Pratap Singh Museum, Srinagar, has the front and side faces as in the above reliefs, the back face being that of a demon; its mutilated condition does not enable us to be sure about the attributes in all the four hands, but the front right hand undoubtedly holds a lotus.

The beautiful sculpture, fully in the round, illustrated by R. C. Kak in page 50 and described by him in pages 49-51, of his Handbook, however, supplies us with all the necessary details that must have been present in the other sculpture when it was whole. One other specimen of these four- faced images of standing Viṣṇu is known to me, which originally hailed from Benares. B.C. Bhattacharya discovered this image which is unfortunately very much mutilated; the four faces are, however, quite intact, all its hands and the portion below the waist being broken. The front face is human, placid in aspect, while the right and left faces are that of Narasiṃha and Varāha, the back face being horrid- looking with round protruding eyes, lolling tongue, jatas over the head, etc. Bhattacharya has rightly drawn our attention to the iconographic text as compiled by Hemādri from Viṣnudharmottara, which would partially explain this type of image; it says that "Viṣṇu, the god of the gods, should be shown on Garuḍa; he should have four faces and eight hands; the eastern face will be placid in form, the southern one that of Narasiṃha and the western (i.e., the back face) should be Kapila and the other face (i.e., the northern or left one, should be of Varāha". It should be noted that a text similar to the above must have been, followed in the carving of the Kashmerian four-faced images of Viṣṇu, as it is expressly mentioned by Kak that the back face is demoniacal in character. The Mārtaṇḍa temple specimens, as has been pointed out above, are eight-armed, but the objects in the hands are undistinguishable; the Avantipur ones, on the other hand, are four-handed and the Benares specimen also seems to have been so.

Some passages from the third book of the Viṣnudharmottara enable us to throw more light on the above types of Viṣṇu images. In the verses 2—14 of chapter 85 of the work (Book III), an elaborate description of the images of Vāsudeva are given; in verses 16—20 in the same chapter, an explanation about the real nature of the attributes in the hands of the god is supplied to us; then verses 21—26 describe the images of Saṃkarṣaṇa, Pradyumna and Aniruddha; again, in verses 29—37 are incorporated the names and real nature of the eight attendants of the four above- named deities; lastly the eight devagaṇas, viz. animā, laghimā, prāpti, prākāmya, īṣitva vasītva and kāmāvasāvitā (the eight yogic siddhis, the attainment of which is the desire of every yogin) are associated in batches of two with each of the four gods, in verses 39-41. After all this Mārkaṇḍeya tells Vajra that "what has been narrated to him is the Caturmūrti of the lord; but if the four are combined into one, the composite image should be called Vaikuṇṭha, and it should be four-faced—by making the god four-faced the one god becomes four-formed; the eastern (i.e., the central, because the deity faces east) face, the most important of the four, should be placid in aspect; the right face, of the lustre (form) of a lion, should typify knowledge; the western face should be terrific which is called (typifies) prosperity; another form of four-faced (image of the lord) is to be made as I have expounded". this interesting passage should be compared with the other description of the four-faced image of Viṣṇu from the same work noticed above (Bk. III, ch. 44, verses 9-13). The Varāha face is not explicitly mentioned here and the back face is named raudra in place of kapila (or kāpila). But there can be very little doubt that both descriptions fit in the case of the same types of images, as regards the number of the faces; in the case of the present text the god is named Vaikuṇṭha caturmūrti who is four-handed while in the case of the other, the deity is Viṣṇu, one of the triad (Trimūrti—Brahmā, Viṣṇu and Siva), but the number of his hands is given as eight. The Viṣṇudharmottara, while further describing the Kṛṣṇa (evidently Vāsudeva) form of the lord, explains the real nature of his four faces, eight hands, vanamālā, Garuḍa and other accessories. It is expressly mentioned there that "mind, which is in the body of all beings, is to be known as Garuḍa, than whom nobody is stronger or swifter, the eight hands of the wielder of Sārnga bow (i.e. Viṣṇu) are the eight quarters (four major and four minor), the four faces of the god are to be known (to typify) bala, jnāna, aisvarya and sakti (four of the six ideal gunas, associated with Vāsudeva, Saṃkarṣaṇa, Pradyumna and Aniruddha respectively); each two of the eight hands are to be associated with each of the four faces; in Vāsudeva's hands are to be known (placed) the sun and the moon; in Saṃkarṣaṇa's hands are a pestle and a ploughshare; in those of Pradyumna are known a bow and an arrow, while in Aniruddha's hands, a sword and a shield. The sun and the moon typifying Puruṣa and Prakṛti (appear as) a cakra and a gadā in the hands of Vāsudeva; the ploughshare should be known as time and the pestle as death, with which Saṃkarṣaṇa as Rudra ploughs this movable and immovable world. The bow and arrow in the hands of Pradyumna, the fire, are instrumental in piercing the highest target (reaching the highest goal) which is meditated on by the Yogins. The shield, in the hand of Aniruddha who is Brahmā, stands for the cloak of ignorance necessary for the creation of the world. The sword (in the other hand of Aniruddha) known as Nandaka, really passionlessness or indifference to the world, causes joy to the Yogins because it severs all their ties with the world."

It will be quite apposite here to take note of an essential doctrinal tenet of the Pāñcarātra system in order to understand the true significance of the images of the great god Vāsudeva Viṣṇu conceived in his four primary aspects, viz., Vāsudeva, Saṃkarṣaṇa, Pradyumna and Aniruddha and his twenty other secondary ones—totalling twenty-four forms in all (Caturvimsatimūrttayaḥ). The philosophy of the Pāñcarātrins, like the same of the various other religious systems, is inseparably bound up with the story of creation. The creation according to them takes place in gradual stages; in the beginning, Srī, the great sakti of Viṣṇu opens her eyes by his command (unmesa) and flashes up in her dual aspect of kriyā (acting) and bhūti (becoming), i.e., Force and Matter. Viṣṇu, the transcendent lord, himself inactive, indirectly acts through his consort in her two aspects and thus Viṣṇu, Kriyā Sakti (really the Sudarsana portion of Laksmi) and Bhūti Sakti are respectively the causa efficiens (efficient cause), causa instrumentalis (instrumental cause) and causa materialis (material cause) of the the world. Thus, in the Pāñcarātra system the transcendent aspect of Viṣṇu remains completely in the background, but still the motive force, while the one force (Lakṣmī) which as Bhūti appears as the universe and as Kriyā vitalises and governs it. The first phase of the manifestation of Lakṣmī is called suddhasṛṣti (pure creation) which consists of the creation of the six ideal gunas (gunonmesadasā). These gunas, the attributes of the highest god, are jnāna (knowledge), aisvarya (lordship), sakti (potency), bala (strength), vīrya (viṛility) and tejas (splendour) and are themselves aprākṛta (not belonging to Prakṛti, like the three gunas—sattva, rajas and tamas); they in their totality and by pairs are the material or instruments of pure creation. The first three of them connected with the Bhūti fall under one group called visrāmabhūmayaḥ (stages of rest) while the last three under the other, viz., sramabhūmayaḥ (stages of effort) and the corresponding gunas of each group join to form a pair connected with one to other of some special divine manifestation. In their totality the gunas make up the body of Vāsudeva, the highest personal god (Sādgunyavigraham devam), as well as that of his consort Lakṣmī. when, however, they begin to pair—one of the first group pairing with another of the second—begins that process of emanation, which appears as a chain, as it were, consisting of several emanations—each one excepting the first originating from an anterior one; thus, the favourite image of the process has, with the Pāñcarātrins, become that of one flame proceeding from another flame (any creation up to the formation of the Brahmāṇḍa, is imagined as taking place in this way). The first three—or including

Vāsudeva, four—beings thus coming into existence are called the Vyūhas which really denotes that the six gunas are shoved asunder into three pairs; and the Caturvyūhas (cf. the Caturmūrti of the Viṣnudharmottara passage) are Vasudeva (in whom all the six gunas are equally manifest), Saṃkarṣaṇa, Pradyumna and Aniruddha, the last three being the elder brother, the son and grandson respectively of Vāsudeva-Kṛṣṇa according to the epic and purāṇic tradition.

The above account of the Vyūha doctrine, one of the essential tenets of the Pāñcarātra system, read in connection with the Viṣnudharmottara passages, helps to explain the character of the mediaeval Viṣṇu images of Kashmir. It is not at all surprising that Kashmir, of all places in India, should particularise in these types of icons essentially associated with the Pāñcarātra doctrine. Schrader remarks that this system "must have originated in the north of India and subsequently spread to the south." He further observes, "The story of Svetadvīpa seems even to point to the extreme north and so do some Saṃhitas, among them Ahirbudhnya." This extreme north was most probably Kashmir, as the frequency of the above types of images there fully show.

(Indian History Congress Proceedings, 1940)

CHAPTER 5

AN OUTLINE OF THE HISTORY OF KASHMIR (BEING A CHAPTER OF 'A GUIDE TO KASHMIR MONUMENTS')

By

R. C. Kak

I

Of the long line of royal figures which fill the first three books of Kalhana's Rājatarangini we know little more than the names. The only kings of this period whose existence is corroborated by the contemporary historical records of India are Asoka, the great Buddhist Emperor of India (B.C. 272-232), Kanishka and Havishka, the Kushan kings of Gandhara whose sway extended from Patna to Kashgar and Yarkand (second century A.D.), Toramana and Mihirakula, the white Hun invaders who devastated northern India in the fifth century A.D. It is curious to observe that all of these great rulers, of whose possessions Kashmir formed only a small part, appear in Kalhana's chronicle as mere local Rajas who had, in certain cases, extended their conquests abroad. His attempts at arriving at their respective dates are hopelessly confused and entirely at variance with the accepted chronology of India. It is, however, interesting to note that the tradition from which Kalhana drew his information was substantially correct in its remembrance of the general character of their administration.

In Pravarasena II, who seems to have flourished sometime in the latter half of the sixth century, we meet, for the first time, a purely indigenous ruler possessing a truly historical character; but it is with the accession to the throne of the plebeian Kārkoṭa dynasty, about the middle of the seventh century A.D. that the authentic history of Kashmir begins. Considerations of space forbid the inclusion of an account, however brief, of each and every ruler who filled the throne of Kashmir for the next five centuries (the period for which Kalhana is our guide). A few names—those of Lalitāditya, Jayāpīḍa, Avantivarmā, Queen Didda, Sussala and Jayasimha— loom large over a crowd of petty princelings, the majority of whom did little to earn the gratitude, or merit the remembrance, of posterity.

Pravarasena II.—Among the kings of Kashmir, who preceded the Kārkoṭa dynasty, Pravarasena II is easily the most prominent. He seems to have spent the earlier portion of his life in exile, while the kingdom of his fathers was being ruled by Mātrigupta, a foreigner and a nominee of king Vikramāditya of Ujjain. Legend credits him with extensive conquests in Northern India and the replacement of Sīlāditya-Pratāpasīla of Malwa (cire A.D. 580) on the throne. But the chief historical interest of his reign is centred in his foundation of the city of Srinagar. He named it Pravarapura—a name which is still current among the learned—but the younger city soon assumed the name as it had already usurped the dignity, of the old capital of Asoka, which has since been called Purānādhishṭhana, the modern Pāndreṭhan, three miles above Srinagar. The new city can be proved to have occupied its present site and seems to have enjoyed an uncommon degree of prosperity during the reign of its founder, as can be gathered from the poetic description of Kalhana, who states that 'the city was once famous as containing thirty-six lakhs of houses. It was provided with regularly arranged markets and was at first only on the right bank of the Vitastā.'

'There are mansions which reach to the sky and ascending which one sees the earth, glistening in the rain at the close of the summer and covered with flowers in (the month of) Chaitra.'

Lalitāditya-Muktāpīḍa.—About a century and a half elapsed before another great and truly historical figure occupied the Kashmir throne. This was Lalitāditya-Muktāpīḍa who succeeded his vicious short-lived brother, Tārāpīḍa, and reigned gloriously for thirty-six years and about the middle of the eighth century A.D. was by far the most heroic ruler that Kashmir had ever produced. The popular tradition, still living, credits him with immense conquests stretching, in India, from shore to shore, and extending beyond the snowy mountain barrier to the parched ocean of sand in Central Asia. His march into Hindustan seems to have been more of the nature of a military raid than a permanent occupation of the country. Thus, he swooped with his army upon Kānyakubja, the modern Kanauj, and before the king Yasovarman had probably time to recover from his surprise he found his army annihilated and himself reduced to the necessity of suing for an ignominious peace. His further conquests bear a purely legendary character; but the fact of his sending an embassy to the Chinese Court, as stated by the Tang Annals, seems to show that he knew something of the power of that Empire by actual experience. It is, however, chiefly through his unstinting patronage of the arts and sciences, his erection of a number of magnificent structures, and his wise, though by no means mild, administration of the country that Lalitāditya still lives in the memory of prosperity.

Among the towns that he founded the chief are Parnotsa, the capital of the modern territory of Poonch and still a flourishing town, and Lalitapura and Parihāsapura, both of which have now dwindled into petty hamlets. The last named the chose as his capital in preference to the larger and more conveniently situated Pravarapura and embellished it with a group of temples, Chaityas, and monasteries—vestiges of which still remain to testify to the magnificence of their founder. But his greatest memorial is the superb temple of Mārtand, the most striking example of Kashmir architecture that now survives. He distributed even-handed bounty among the Brahmans and the Buddhists. Among his utilitarian works is mentioned the construction of a series of water wheels for irrigating the arid plateau of Chakradhara below Vijabror.

But Lalitāditya, though a great conqueror and ordinarily a just ruler, had yet certain defects of character, among which the most noticeable was hard drinking. It is related that in one of his drunken fits he commanded—like Alexander on a similar occasion—the city of Srinagar to be set on fire. His ministers, however, saved the city and satisfied his drunken whim at the same time by setting a large number of distant hay-ricks on fire. The king was far too tipsy to discriminate between a bonfire of hay and a burning town. But it must be said to his credit that next morning he showed the most profound contrition for his insensate conduct and directed his Ministers not to carry out any of the orders that he should issue in a state of drunkenness. Lalitāditya's last testament is an especially interesting document of Machiavellian wisdom, illustrative as much of the king's policy towards his subjects as of Kalhana's views on the administration of the country.

Jayāpīḍa-Vinayāditya.—Lalitāditya's grandson, Jayāpīḍa-Vinayāditya ruled for thirty-one years in the latter part of the eighth century A.D. At first he attempted to follow in the footsteps of his illustrious grandfather, but in the latter part of his reign he degenerated into a cruel, overbearing and exacting tyrant, and finally met an untimely end at the hands of the outraged Brahmans who had suffered the most by his rapacity. He founded the town of Jayapura-Andarkoṭ near Sumbal.

Jayāpīḍa was followed by a number of imbecile kings. Ministers rose to unprecedented power. For nearly the whole of the first half of the ninth century Utpala and his four brothers, the brothers of lowborn concubine of the lascivious king Lalitāpīḍa, held the reins of absolute power in their hands. They usurped all the offices and gave up the country to plunder and rapine, though at the same time they founded a number of towns and religious edifices, some of which still survive in name. Their career of lawlessness was crowned by an intestine war which culminated in the destruction of the four younger brothers. Utpala, the eldest and only surviving brother, acquired almost regal power which was consolidated by his son Sukhavarman who was the king in all but name. Even this pretence was dropped after Sukhavarman's death, when his son Avantivarman promptly dethroned Utpalāpīḍa and proclaimed himself king.

Avantivarman.—Avantivarman (A.D. 855-883) is one of the most lovable persons that we come across in the lengthy narrative of the Kashmir historian. The scion of a family of noblemen who had risen from a particularly low origin to the position of all- powerful king-makers, he possessed all the vigour of a self-made man who had graduated in the hard school of adversity. He was a rare combination of strength and gentleness, and the first and most conscientious servant of the State. But when he ascended the throne, he did not find it altogether a bed of roses. His powerful cousins were not disposed to submit to the inevitable as meekly as the roi faineant whom he had displaced. They had to be thrashed into submission, and they were. His next care was to give a much-needed rest to the country which had for nearly a century been distracted by feuds of the powerful barons and the rapacious administration of the Kāyasthas, 'clerks'. Avantivarman's wise rule of twenty-eight years gave the long- suffering people the necessary time to recover from their prolonged nightmare. His triumphs were essentially those of peace as the triumphs of his great predecessor, Lalitāditya, were those of war. His pacification of the country, though not described in as great detail as the other episodes of his reign, seems to have been no easy task. In his time we first meet a member of that turbulent class of Dāmaras, the feudal barons of Kashmir, who during the feeble rule of his successors inflicted untold misery upon the hapless kingdom by their constant and bloody warfare against each other and against the crown. But Avantivarman seems to have kept them in rigid check as is evidenced by the draconic judgement of his minister Sura upon the powerful baron, Dhanva, whom he killed first and—unlike the proverbial Jedwood Justice—did not try even afterwards. But though the curbing of the restless Ḍāmaras was essential to the stability of his own rule and to the peace of his subjects,it is mainly upon his public works which conferred a lasting boon on the country, and upon his munificent patronage of learning, that his claim for immortality rests.

The chief bane of the valley had for ages been the excess of its water and its liability to floods. A very considerable portion of the land was permanently submerged and even a moderate rainfall contributed to deluge the major part of what remained. The result was a chronic famine. The king, who recognized the necessity of taking prompt and effective action, engaged the services of an eminent Kashmiri engineer, Suyya by name, whose dredging operations at Baramulla were so successful that they resulted in an immediate and permanent fall of nearly 80 per cent in the price of paddy. The measure taken by him for confining the rivers and rivulets within their natural boundaries and the regulation of water-supply in the arid Karewas (plateau) which to-day are comparatively unproductive, are too numerous to detail here.

Among the king's religious foundations is that gem of architecture, the Avantiswāmi temple of Avantipura.

In his efforts to confer upon the country the benefits of peace, the king was ably seconded by his untiring lieutenant, the minister Sura, who had helped him to the throne and who in spite of the unquestioning obedience he accorded to his sovereign seems to have inspired him with such awe that the latter did not or could not reveal his real faith until his dying day. This minister was, like his master, a generous patron of learning and not only conferred upon the poets, philosophers, and rhetoricians of his day land and fortunes but, what is rather unusual, went so far as to give them seats in the king's council.

Sankaravarman (A.D. 883-902) and his Successors.—The disintegrating elements in the State, whose progress Avantivarman's strong arm had barely been able to check, broke loose again after his death. Sankaravarman earned lasting infamy by being the author of an ingenious system of exactions by which he reduced the country to misery and impoverishment. But even his cynical oppression was nothing to the gross misrule which followed his death. No less than ten sovereigns occupied the throne in the short period of thirty-four years which intervened between his death and the third restoration of Chakravarman. The power was entirely in the hands of the Tāntrins who in their close military organization resembled the Praetorian Guards of Rome and who, as might be expected, abused their strength in the same shameless manner. Kings and noblemen vied with each other in buying the favour of this formidable and fickle multitude. No sooner did the crown encircle the brows of one candidate than it was snatched away by another, who had paid a higher bribe and who in his turn was served in a similar fashion. No price was deemed too high to purchase the crown; ;kings squandered their revenues, queens bartered their honour, the son intrigued against his father and the father set assassins upon his offspring; all lost their sense of truth and dignity for the acquisition, however temporary it might be, of the fatal bauble. At last in A.D. 936 the deposed king Chakravarman invoked the aid of the Ḍāmaras, the feudal barons of the land, and succeeded with their powerful assistance in annihilating the Tāntrins who had so long held the crown as a pawn.

In getting rid of the Tāntrins by the arms of the barons, the country only passed from the devil to the deep sea. Henceforth for over two centuries the land lay at the absolute mercy of a class of hereditary freelances whose possessions enabled them to lie secure in their own demesnes, wherefrom they scoured the surrounding country for plunder and took away whatever they could lay their hands on. The king and the ministers he usually chose for the sole purpose of pandering to his pleasures were far too busy in levying imposts in order to find the means for defraying the cost of their debauchs, to think of restoring anything like order in the unfortunate country. Government there was none. The king was only remarkable for the extraordinary and, in modern times, unthinkable pitch to which he carried his license. A curious fatality seems to have always dogged the heels of the Kashmir rulers of this period. Princes who before their accession to the throne had given promise of a brave and virtuous career proved, as kings, even more dissolute, pusillanimous and tyrannical than their predecessors had been. For two long and weary centuries the court of Kashmir was the Pandora's-box of all the evils that afflict humanity, the home of assassins, stranglers and poisoners. Bawds as ministers of state, pettifogging functionaries as generals of armies, outcaste strumpets as reigning queens and kings, whose most innocent recreation was gross buffoonery—this was the administration under which the 'happy valley' was made so unhappy in those centuries. The state of Kashmir in the tenth and eleventh centuries forms a close parallel to that of Italy under Pope Alexander VI and Caesar Borgia. But the Italian popes and their satellites often differed from the Kashmir kings in that their evil lives were relieved by the display of commanding talents, while among the latter shameless vice and the most despicable imbecility were closely wedded.

HARSHA

This frightful misrule culminated in Harsha (A.D. 1089-1101) whose usually clouded intellect seems to have on rare occasions been illuminated by transitory flashes of intelligence during which he proved a liberal patron of learning and music. He appears to have possessed some skill in the composition of popular songs. But his neglect of state affairs was so outrageous that in his reign murders were committed on the highways in broad daylight and even the sanctity of the kings' own apartments was not respected by the daring robbers. Foodstuffs and other commodities rose to fabulous prices; famine and the plague committed such ravages among the people that few were left to cremate or bury the dead, and the river was swollen with floating corpses. To crown all this, the king himself assassinated his whole family and ordered a general massacre of the landed aristrocracy—an order which was partly carried out. But even the endurance of a Kashmiri has an end, though it usually takes a long time to awaken him from his sloth. When Harsha's nephews Ucchala and Sussala raised the standard of rebellion, soldier and priest, prince and peasant, all alike flocked to it with equal zeal. The palace was given up to flames, the queens burnt to death, the heir-apparent killed and the king who was deserted by everybody and had taken refuge in a beggar's hovel was hunted down and slain without mercy. With him ended the first Lohara dynasty.

UCHHALA

They Uchhala (A.D. 1101-1111) the eldest of the two rebel brothers ascended the throne. His first care was to disarm his troublesome allies, the barons; ;and this he effected more by diplomacy than by force. He kept firm control upon his government, overhauled the bureaucracy, rigorously punished official abuses, administered justice with a rare impartiality and insight into his subjects' character; listened to the grievances of his people and redressed them as far as lay in his power. He used to move about incognito, like the great Caliph Harun-al-Rashid, to discover the causes of distress and unrest among the citizens, and sold royal grain at cheap rates for the benefit of the famine-stricken inhabitants of the city. He was energetic in nipping rebellions in the bud before they could assume formidable dimensions. But his besetting sin was haughtiness which alienated all his dependants from him and eventually led to his murder.

SUSSALA

Ṣussala who was crowned king in A.D. 1112 wreaked a terrible vengeance upon his brother's assassins, and continued to rule peace-fully and well until 1120, when he was dispossessed by Bhikshāchara, the grandson of Harsha. After a few months' deposition Sussala regained his throne in 1121 and reigned until his murder in 1128. The latter part of his reign is disfigured by acts of oppression and cruelty, but it must be admitted that even in his worst days the administration did not degenerate to the low moral and political standard of his predecessors of the first Lohara dynasty.

Jayasimha (A.D. 1128-1155), his eldest son and successor. Jayasimha is a very remarkable figure in the history of Kashmir. Though by no means deficient in personal courage, he yet preferred to gain his ends by the safer and more secret methods of diplomacy and bribery. Where both craft and force had failed he did not shrink from having recourse to assassination. In gaining his ends he was absolutely without scruple in the employment of means. He was courteous to all who approached him, considerate to his servants and subjects, generous to his enemies when they had been deprived of their sting, relentless in the prosecution of his schemes, and possessed of a calm and smiling exterior which concealed a deep underlying purpose. His position on the throne was at first extremely precarious, and if he ultimately emerged triumphant over his numerous enemies and succeeded in giving peace and plenty to the country which he ruled, it was entirely due to his personal abilities, his extraordinary presence of mind and resourcefulness in the face of misfortune.

The first seventeen years of his reign are characterized by a long and bitter struggle with the barons who were chafing under the tight control which he attempted to exercise over them. To embarrass him further they set up no less than five pretenders to the throne, some of whom were actually crowned in the outlying district of Lohara. But his opponents were reckoning without their host. One by one both the pretenders and the barons succumbed to the intrigues and coercion which the king (at times so hard-pressed as to be almost a prisoner in his own house) incessantly employed against them, till in 1145 he was absolutely free from all the obstacles to his authority, and the people were free from a miltitude of pests who had made the valley a hell. Kalhana, his contemporary, sums up the account of his rule in the following appreciative verse : 'He restored to this land which, owing to the baseness of the time was like a decayed forest, wealth, population and habitations.' He was an enlightened despot who would have served as a model for Machiavelli's Prince.

After the death of Jayasimha the country again reverted to its chronic state of decrepitude. The two centuries that elapsed between the passing away of Jayasimha and the transfer of the throne to the Muhammadan condottieri, Shāh Mīr, produced no king possessing genius enough to consolidate his kingdom. If the valley escaped being annexed by the Muhammadan rulers of India, it was due to its natural isolation and the physical difficulties its conquest offered, rather than to its military strength and abundance of resources. But, at last, in the reign of Suhadeva (A.D. 1300-1 to 1319-20) the clouds began to gather thickly upon the horizon. Dulucha (Zulqadar Khān) who, according to Abul Fazl, was the chief commander of the armies of the king of Kandahār, penetrated into the valley and, though the king bought him off, the invader seems to have made a mental reservation when entering into the agreement; for, after he had accepted the money, he commenced to plunder, burn and slay with judicial impartiality and scientific accuracy. When at length the approach of the winter obliged him to leave the country, laden with immense booty, he left behind him not the flourishing home of teeming thousands, but a vast heap of smouldering ruins. But the Nemesis of his misdeeds overtook him were he was well out of the country which he had mercilessly put to fire and sword. The greater part of his army perished in the snow which surprised them in the passes as they were marching out.

RINCHANA'S INVASION

All the while that Dulucha was harrying Kashmir, Rinchana, the son of a Tibetan chieftain, was hovering upon the mountains ready to swoop down upon the prostrate country and pick up the leavings of Dulucha's orgies. Rāmachandra, a patriotic nobleman, offered an obstinate resistance. When the latter could not overcome his in open fight, he had resources to treachery in which he was entirely successful.

RINCHANA KING

Rāmachandra was murdered and the enemy forced his wife (or daughter ?) Koṭa to marry him. Rinchana's way to the throne was now clear. Suhadeva was promptly slain, the invader stepped into his place and ruled for three years : (1319-20 to 1322) with unexpected munificence and vigour. In the administration of justice he seems to have rigidly adhered to the principles of truth and equity. His desire to be admitted into the fold of the Hindu caste was thwarted by the blind prejudice of the Brahmans, who would have nothing to do with an outcaste Bhoṭṭa. Naturally then, he turned towards the more democratic Islam, and entrusted his infant son by Koṭa to the care of the Muhammadan Shāh Mīr, who had entered Kashmir in A.D. 1313 and taken service under king Suhadeva.

UDYANADEVA

The guardianship of the heir-apparent and the untimely death of Rinchana only three years after his accession, were turned by the needy adventurer to his own personal advantage. He did not crown Haidar, his ward, and as he was not yet powerful enough to usurp the kingdom himself he invited and enthroned Udyānadeva, a scion of the old Hindu dynasty, who since the invasion of Dulucha had been living as a refugee in Gāndhāra.

Curiously enough, the new king succeeded Rinchana not only to his throne but even to his bed; for he married the widowed queen, who bore an heir to him also.

But the part that Shāh Mīr took in the restoration of the old dynasty was not actuated by any sense of gratitude towards the family which had provided him with means of comfort when he was but a homeless wanderer. Since the very moment of his advent into Kashmir, he seems to have had an eye upon the throne, which he knew by experience was ready to be his who possessed the longest sword and the strongest arm. All authority was undermined by the dissensions of the nobles. Udyānadeva was too weak to curb their power and spent his time mostly in the performance of the duties prescribed by his religion. Moreover he was completely under the thumb of his domineering wife Koṭa.

Shāh Mīr gradually strengthened his hands by matrimonial alliances with the more powerful families. Many of the nobles who were needy, he subsidized, and those that remained he coerced into neutrality. He kept the king and queen in perpetual terror by threatening to raise Haidar, Rinchana's son, to the throne. By the year 1337-38, when Udyānadeva died, the extent of the king's authority was reduced to the precincts of the capital only. Shāh Mīr was the real ruler of the whole country.

KOTA DEVI

The Queen Koṭa now ascended the throne herself, but her triumph was short-lived. Her capable minister, Bhatta Bhikshana, was taken off his guard and assassinated by Shāh Mīr; and Koṭa, who at that time was in a position to bring the murderer to book, was dissuaded from taking vigorous action by her own councillors, who, dauntless, were in Shāh Mīr's pay. The opportunity thus let slip never occurred again, and the queen had afterwards to repent at leisure for what she had neglected to do promptly. Shāh Mīr now openly meditated treason and made himself master of the capital which the queen had left temporarily. He then proceeded to Andarkoṭ and besieged her in the fort there. Koṭa being now hopeless and helpless, surrendered herself on the explicit stipulation that she would share the throne with her conqueror. But her better nature seems to have revived at the last moment. When she entered the bridal chamber of Shāh Mīr, she stabbed herself with her own dagger in the presence of the husband who had till then been her servant and whose embrace she loathed more than the terrors of the grave.

Thus passed (1337-38) the last representative of the Hindu royalty of Kashmir. She died, though she had not lived, a worthy daughter of Lalitāditya and Avantivarman.

In her public capacity she made many mistakes, and in her private life she has much to account for, but her noble end throws a partial veil of oblivion over her many errors of omission and commission.

SHAH MIR-SHAMSU-D-DIN (A.D. 1337)

Shāh Mīr now ascended the throne under the title of Sultan Shamsu-d-Din. The most notable act of his reign was the lightening of the taxes which were telling very hard upon the prosperity of the country. He 'fixed the assessment on land at seventeen per cent of the gross produce.' Islam made much progress during the reigns of the first Muhammadan kings, but the change of masters was not accompanied by any change in the policy of the administration of the state. The same wearisome round of pleasures, the same petty politics and the same bickerings among the landed noblemen that had characterized the reigns of the later Hindu rulers, continued with unabated vigour in the time of their successors, the independent Sultans of Kashmir, who merely carried on the traditions which they had inherited. Sanskrit, corrupted, no doubt, by the infusion of numerous Persian and Arabic technical terms, was still largely used as the official language. The majority of the people were Muhammadans, but it was Muhammadanism of a type that would have astonished the orthodox Arab. The old places of worship still retained their sanctity, the only innovation being that the Hindu image had given place to the tomb of a muslim saint. Muhammadan Kashmir teems, to this day, with numberless little shrines and Ziārats which bear the unmistakable stamp of their Hindu origin. The conversion left the old manners, customs and even the superstitions of the people intact. As a rule the kings were far too busy with their own troubles and pleasures to bestow much thought upon their subjects who doubtless were content to plod their own way unmolested, happy if forgotten.

SHAHABU-D-DIN (A.D.1355-1374)

After Shāh Mīr, or, as he styled himself Shamsu-d-Din, the first king of mark in his dynasty was Shahabu-d-Din (A.D. 1355-1374). In the early part of his reign he made a brilliant raid on the North-Western India and overran the territories adjoining the upper course of the Indus (Ohind etc.), sacked Peshawar and seriously threatened Ghazni and Kandahār. The snowy barrier, Hindukush seems to have forced him to retrace his foot-steps to the plains. He marched eastwards as far as the Sutlej where he met and exchanged greetings with the Raja of Nagarkot who was returning from a similar expedition from Delhi. The year 1361, the sixth of his reign, was marked by a disastrous flood which deluged nearly the whole of the valley and forced the inhabitants to take refuge in the uplands and the hills. His indignation at the suggestion of Udayasri, his minister, to melt the brass image of the Brihat-Buddha and coin the metal into money, is eloquent of the tolerant character of these early Moslem rulers of Kashmir. The latter part of his reign was not a happy one for himself, chiefly because of the baneful influence which Lasa, the young niece of his queen Lakshmi, whom he had taken as a concubine, exercised upon his mind. She induced him to exile his three grown-up sons, and though he recalled Hasan, his eldest- born, when he felt his end was drawing near, he was not destined to see him again. In the absence of the legitimate heir, Qutubu- d-Din, the late king's brother, ascended the throne. In the annals of the Muhammadan rulers of most countries the maxim, 'first come, first served' finds frequent illustration. According to Ferishta 'This prince was remarkable for his attention to public business, which he transacted in person, and generally with justice and moderation.' In his old age two sons were born to him, the elder of whom, Sikandar, succeeded him while yet a minor, in A.D. 1390.

II

On Sikandar's accession to the throne, Islam adopted a more defined aggressive attitude. His predecessors had not been troubled with any scruples of conscience when expediency had urged upon them the necessity of stretching a point in favour of their Hindu subjects. Qutubu-d-Din performed a sacrifice and bestowed grants of land upon the Brahmans and other religious corporations, to avert an impending famine. The very birth of his son Sikandar was attributed to the efficacy of the magic pill of a Hindu ascetic. Sikandar himself was married to a Hindu lady Sri Sobhā, and during the earlier part of his reign, was content to follow in the foot-steps of his tolerant predecessors. But his liberal patronage of literature attracted a host of foreign scholars who, being uncompromising zealots, were naturally shocked at the amicable relations that existed between the believers and the non-Muhammadan infidels. That the influx of these foreign literati was not viewed without a good deal of misgiving by the Kashmirians, we perceive from the description of the incident by Jonaraja in the following verses : 'As the storms uproot the trees and the locusts annihilate the paddy crops, so the villainous followers of this religion destroyed the faith of the Kashmirians. Tempted by the honours and the riches which the king lavished upon them and by the beauty of the country, the Mlechchhas entered Kashmir as locusts in a goodly corn field.' 'As the fledgling pigeon is surrounded on all sides by crows, so was the king surrounded by Yavanas, who became his preceptors, his retainers, his servants, his favourites and even his relatives.' Among the foreigners was Mir Sayyid Muhammad Hamdāni, son of Mir Sayyid Ali Hamdāni (Shāh-i-Hamdan) who is said to have obtained complete mastery over the young king's mind and exercised it for the purpose of purging Kashmir of all heterodoxy.

But in spite of all the pressure that the Maulvis brought to bear upon him, the king persisted in keeping his hands clear of all religious persecution. Fate, however, had ordained otherwise for the unlucky inhabitants of the valley. The king reluctantly yielded at last to the specious arguments of his minister Suhabhaṭṭa, who had originally been a Hindu, but since his conversion to Islam hated his former co-religionists with the deep-rooted and implacable hatred which only a renegade can feel. All traces of king's reluctance, whether real or simulated, were washed away as soon as he had once given his consent. The die was cast; a gigantic campaign of persecution was instituted; temples were shattered to pieces; stone images ground to powder; idols of metal were melted and coined into money. The high-caste Brahmans were given the alternative of death or conversion. Even exile was denied to them. It is said of Charles IX of France when he ordered the massacre of St. Bartholomew that 'he who was hard to convince, was now hard to restrain. He rose, bade us to be silent, and with a face of fury, with great oaths (after his sort) said that as we found it good to kill the Admiral (Coligny), he wished it too; but that with him we must massacre all the Huguenots in France, lest one should be left to reproach him afterwards'. Charles himself took part in the massacre and is said to have taken a gun and fired at the flying wretches shouting, 'kill, kill' at the top of his voice. Sikandar seems to have undergone a similar mental convulsion. From the evil hour that he started on the inclined plane of persecution, his perpetual cry, hourly increasing in its vehement intensity was 'slay, burn, destroy'. No shrine was too sacred to be despoiled, no image too divine to be desecrated, and no man so old as to be respected, no woman so feeble as to be pitied, no Brahman so learned as to be spared if he refused to give up Hinduism. In Sikandar religion ran amok. Many bent before the storm but those who did not bend were ruthlessly broken. Cremation of the dead was interdicted; the wearing of caste-marks was prohibited, and orders were issued prescribing the residence of any but Muhammadans in the country. When the people began to leave the country in large crowds, the king and his minister permitted them to proceed to the frontier and then posed all passages of exit. There they were caught in a trap, driven back like cattle, and given the king's favourite alternative of death or conversion. The majority succumbed—but a number—more honour to them because they were so few—gave up their lives as willing martyrs to their cause. Kashmir was transformed into a fearful witches' cauldron. Fire and sword reigned supreme. Every hill and every dale resounded with wailing and lamentation when the poor panic-stricken people were not too benumbed with the fear of the awful shadow that clouded their lives, to give vent to their misery. There is not one religious edifice in Kashmir, whether Hindu or Buddhist, which does not bear some mark of Sikandar's handiwork. No consideration of sanctity or popularity or even significance, proved a sufficiently strong bulwark to ward off destruction. The great shrines of Chakradhara and Vijayesa were razed to the ground; Mārtāṇḍa and Avantipura temples so irreparably ruined that even the manner of their destruction is, to this day, a matter of conjecture. Jonaraja whose feelings would naturally be more embittered against the turncoat Suhabhaṭṭa, than against his master Sikandar, tells us that 'there was no city or town, no village or forest where an abode of the gods escaped destruction by Suhabhaṭṭa. All the images of the gods were broken (with no more consideration than if) they had been mere stones, but no misfortune was seen (to befall) the perpetrators (of the deed) as (had always been the case) of yore'.

The year A.D. 1398 is memorable in the annals of Hindustan for the invasion of Timur and his Tartar hordes. The empire of the Tughlaks had for many years been tottering to its fall. On the elevation, in 1394, of the minor Mahmud to the throne of Delhi, the provinces of Gujarat, Khandesh, Malwa and Jaunpore threw off the feeble yoke of the sultan of Delhi, and asserted complete independence. While the different chieftains were parcelling out the empire between themselves, the Tartar hurricane burst over their heads in one tremendous thunderclap and involved them all, princes and peasants, oppressors and the oppressed, in one common ruin. Kashmir was not an indifferent spectator while this tragedy was being enacted. Timur rewarded Sikandar for his neutrality with the gift of a couple of elephants, whose uncouth shape and extraordinary bulk seem to have considerably exercised the imagination of the simple Kashmiris. On Timur's return from Delhi, Sikandar marched out to meet him, but hearing that he was expected to make a present of 'three thousand horses and one hundred thousand pieces of gold as an offering' he quietly retraced his steps and contented himself by sending excuses.

Another expedition more creditable to his arms was his invasion of North-West India, in which he subdued the city or Ohind and married the daughter of its chief Firoz. This lady was the mother of Sikandar's illustrious son Zainu-l-Abidin. Both these ever as took place long before Sikandar had earned or deserved the title of Butshikan. The assistance he rendered to the Gakkhar freebooter Jasrat Khan who had been captured by Timur and taken by him to Samarkand and who had, on his captor's demise, made his escape to India, in obtaining possession of certain tracts of the country in the north of the Punjab, and his marriage of his own two daughters with the rulers of Sind and Ohind, belong to the latter part of his reign.

The reign of terror which Sikandar had inaugurated in Kashmir continued with unabated vigour even after his death in 1414 through the good offices of his minister Suhabhaṭṭa. This worthy was the de facto ruler until a virulent attack of consumption relieved him of his life, and the country of the blight which his life had caused. As he grew older and as the painful disease he was suffering from undermined more and more his sinking frame, his irritable nerves demanded greater and greater excitement. Innocent recreation is not for such as him. He had tasted blood and his demand was for more and more blood. The Hindus were mercilessly harrassed. When their sufferings grew beyond their power of endurance, many of them committed themselves to the flames, some took poison, some hanged themselves and many precipitated themselves down vertical cliffs and so found relief from the troubles of this world. By the execution of Laddaraja, a popular nobleman he put his own life into temporary jeopardy. For a time 'he went about in fear of the people like a bird fallen from his nest', but he soon tided over the storm, and resumed his butchery. 'Thus he passed three or four years in inflicting tortures on the Brahmans, in the defamation of their scriptures, in the contemplation of treason, and in taking physic', until death stepped in between him and his victims.

ZAINU-L-ABIDIN (A.D. 1421-1472)

Zainu-l-Abidin succeeded to the throne of his feeble brother Ali Shah in the year A.D. 1421 at the early age of seventeen, but his youth by no means stood in the way of his vigorously putting his heel upon all the abuses in the country. His one mission in life was to redress the wrongs and heal the wounds which his father and brother had inflicted upon the unhappy Hindus of the valley. In this he was entirely successful. But as his activities were extended to the over-hauling and readjustment of the entire administrative machinery, his character will be better understood, if we briefly mention his reforms under detailed heads, the place of honour being without question, reserved for his proclamation of 'peace and goodwill to all mankind'.

An idea of the complete barbarism to which Kashmir had been reduced by Sikandar will be gained from the fact that when Zainu- l-Abidin was suffering from a severe boil, no physician could be found willing or able to attend him. At last one Siryabhaṭṭa was induced, after promise of personal safety, to treat the king. Refusing to accept any reward for the successful treatment, except the boon of mercy for his co-religionists, he was made Chief Justice and High Treasurer, with injunctions to ameliorate the condition of the Hindus. This he did with a very natural enthusiasm. The destruction of Hindu scriptures was forthwith stopped. The Pandits who had fled were repatriated, their lands and property which had been usurped by Muhammadans were restored to them. The annual capitation tax of two palas of silver which weighed very heavily upon the Brahmans, was reduced to a nominal fee of a single masha and entirely abolished later on. Sacrifices and pilgrimages were again permitted to be resumed. Prohibition against cremation was removed. The Pāṭhashālas were reopened and Hindu boys allowed to study their own scriptures. The king carried his predilection for Hindu religion much farther than the mere toleration of it. He himself attended Hindu shrines, performed sacrifices, built monasteries, and not only acquired a thorough knowledge of Sanskrit but employed all his available time in the study of its sacred books. In his last years which were rendered unhappy by his own infirmity and the intestine feuds of his sons, he found his only consolation in the study of the transcendental philosophy of the Yoga Vasishta.

In the administration of justice he showed a remarkable combination of mercy and sternness and shrewd common sense. He thoroughly purged the law courts of corruption and bribery and anticipated the prison reforms of the nineteenth century by instituting a system of prison industries, pottery being one of them. Thieves and other criminals who formerly would have suffered instant execution were now made to work as labourers on the public works, this being the chief reason probably why his reign was so prolific of works of public utility which lasted down to recent times. The assessment of land was fixed at a reasonable rate and in the newly irrigated area of Zainagir near Sopor the rate was as low as one seventh of the gross produce. The prices of imports which then were arbitrarily fixed by the vendors thereof, were now regulated, with one consideration in each case of the carriage and other charges. The prices of commodities were also regulated by monthly notifications. This was a great boon in Kashmir where, owing to want of communications, profiteering has many attractions and immediate chances of success. The system of having the deeds of the sale of property stamped with the king's seal, the absence of which was the cause of much forgery, was instituted. In the distracted times of his two immediate predecessors the criminal classes had gathered much strength. Even during the long reign of Zainu-l- Abidin, thefts seems to have been by no means rare, and the means of tract-ing them were not many. The king hit upon a plan which seems to have met with an appreciable amount of success, though in some cases the innocent must have been involved with the guilty. The plan was to make the villages and the forest communities among whom the traveller sojourned for the period during which he was robbed, responsible for the loss. For the convenience of travellers rest-houses were built at many places on the principal roads. As the chronicler says 'the king administered punishment and reward to his subjects with due regard (to their merits) and watched over them as the hus-bandman watches over his crop, supplying water or keeping the field dry as might seem suitable.'

His patronage of merit, irrespective of caste or creed, is il-lustrated by the choice he made of his important officials among whom were the Buddhist Tilakāchārya, Prime Minister, the Brahman Siryabhaṭṭa. Chief Justice, and the Muhammadan Danya Khan who eventually succeeded Tilaka in the Premier-ship. The king's own predilections and they encouragement given to men of learning by his minister Siryabhaṭṭa induced a large number of scholars to flock to the Kashmir court. This was the period when the Kashmiri-Persian literature, which until the inclusion of the valley within the genial fold of the Pax Britanisica occupied an almost exclusive place in the educa-tion and culture of the official of Karkun class of Kashmiri Pan-dits, began to grow. The king was personally interested in the movement and caused a number of the more important Sanskrit works to be translated into Persian. The growth of the indigenous Kashmiri literature was given a strong impetus. Utta-Soma and Yodhabhaṭṭa wrote biographies of the king in vernacular and Bhaṭṭāvatāra who is said to have studied the Shāh Nama wrote the Jainavilasa. The king himself composed two works in Persian, the first being a treatise in the form of questions and answers on the manufacture of fireworks, and the second, entitled Shikāyat, 'the Plaint' a poem which he wrote in his old age when he had been completely disillusioned by his misfortunes, when the death of his minister and companions had left him lonely and world-weary, and when he saw his life-work undone by the mutual animosity of his worthless sons. This poem may have been a sort of 'Vanity of Human Wishes'.

But his favourite literary pursuit was undoubtedly the study of Sanskrit, to which as has been said above, he devoted a considerable part of his time. Without counting the historians Jonaraja and Srīvara the most notable scholars who attended his court were Karpūrabhaṭṭa, the physician Ruppabhaṭṭa, the astronomer, Ramānanda who wrote an exposition of the Mahābāshya, and Yuddhabhaṭṭa who, having during Subhabhaṭṭa's regime gone to Mahārāshṭra, and having studied there the Atharva Veda which until then seem to have been unavailable in Kashmir, returned at the invitation of Siryabhaṭṭa and promulgated the study of that Veda in his native land. A copy of the Atharva Veda was also presented to the king himself who, further to increase its popularity, established schools in which the scholars were fed, lodged and taught at the expense of the State.

Altogether, Zainu-l-Abidin's reign was the Augustan era of the later Kashmiri-Sanskrit literature.

The maintenance of a magnificent court and a galaxy of brilliant scholars must have meant much expense, which the revenue of the depopulated valley was ill prepared to provide. Zainu-l-Abidin, therefore, hit upon the working of copper mines, the collection of gold dust in the Ladakh rivers, and the construction of an extensive system of canals which irrigated very large tracts of heretofore arid land, and yielded a considerable revenue, as methods by which to increase his wealth without imposing additional taxes upon the already much-taxed people.

A prominent feature in the landscape of the Kashmir valley are the large waterless alluvial plateaus, locally called Wudar, which occupy a considerable part of its area. Unlke the lower parts of the valley which are irrigated by the numerous rivers and rivulets with which the country abounds, the productivity of these Wudars is wholly dependent upon the treacherous rainfall. The crops they usually yield are, therefore, naturally fitful and meagre, the harvest often being absolutely nil. Zainu-l-Abidin's keen eye was struck with the immense possibilities of these plateaus if they could be permanently irrigated. Fortunately, Kashmir, surrounded as it is on all sides by high mountains capped with everlasting snows, in whose ravines are huge glaciers which feed innumerable perennial streams, offers peculiar facilities for artificial irrigation as was demonstrated by the large network canals which nearly doubled the arable land of the valley in Zainu-l-Abidin's time. Most of the canals fell into disuse in the troublous times when the country lay writhing under the iron heel of the Pathan Viceroys of the Durrani rulers of Kabul, but one or two have been renovated during the last two decades. Chief among these canals were (1) the one which irrigated the lands round Kakapur; (2) the Tsakadar canal brought from Nandamarg; (3) the Karala canal which drained the plateau between Shupayan and Romuh where a colony of Brahmans was settled; (4) the canal to Avantipur, which is extant to this day but runs only as far as Miḍur and Rājpur; (5) the Shāh Kul, which branches off from the Sindh near Wusan and runs through the Pargana of Lār, to Mānasbal. The town of Saphala modern Safāpor, was built near its termination; (6)another canal branching from the Sindh brought to the capital where it supplied water to the Jāmī Masjid and emptied itself in the Mār Canal. This used to run as late as twenty years ago and was known as the Lachma Kul; (7) the canal from the river Pohur to irrigate the highlands of Sopor;

and (8) the most important of all, the Shāh Kul of Mārtand, whose renovation fifteen years ago has converted the arid burning plains which stretch for miles and miles on three sides of the temple into a smiling garden of waving corn.

His public works were not limited to the excavation of canals only. He was an enlightened promoter of the architecture and arts of the country. His name is to this day associated with the erection of the bridge, Zaina Kaḍal, still the most important commercial thoroughfare of Srinagar, the town of Zaina Pur and the island of Zainalank in the Wular lake. But the largest part, by far, of his secular and religious foundations have perished.

He gave a strong impetus to the manufacture of paper, shawls and embroidered tapestry for which Kashmir has always been famous. He promoted the silk industry by inviting weavers from Khurāsān and settling them in the country. It was in his reign (to be exact in the year A.D. 1466) that firearms were first introduced into Kashmir.

His relations with foreign powers were by no means restricted to the pretty principalities bordering on Kashmir. He himself conquered Sindh and Tibet, occupying the latter country permanently. According to Abul Fazl, Sultan Abu Said Mirza sent him presents of Arab horses and dromedaries from Khurāsān, and Bahlol Lodhi, king of Delhi, as well as Sultan Mahmud of Gujrat were in friendly relations with him. The contemporary chronicler reports that he exchanged presents with the kings of Misr, Egypt and Mecca, and that he exercised control over the rulers of Gandhāra, Jammu and Rajauri and the Gakkhar tribes of the northern Punjab. It is certain that he assisted Jasrat Khān Gakkhar in spreading his authority over the greater part of the Punjab.

To estimate the abstemiousness of Zainu-l-Abidin's character and the extent to which the transcendental philosophy of

Vasishṭa had tinged his mind, it is only necessary to say that he, a Muhammadan ruler, married a single wife, and remained faithful to her throughout his life. This may not sound a very extraordinary achievement to modern ears but those who know the numerical strength of the harems of the oriental potentates will appreciate the fact better. But, as Solon said, no man can be considered happy till he dies; Zainu-l-Abidin's last years were embittered by the mutual jealousy of his factious and dissipated sons, which on more than one occasion, broke into actual warfare and necessitated the exile of the one or the other. The king was moreover crushed with the bitterest course that can ever befall a human being, much more, an autocratic king,—'outliving one's age'. He had outlived his wife, his friends, his colleagues and his usefulness. He felt his authority slipping away from his hands, his sons were openly rebellious, his personal attendants were daily deserting him, everybody was waiting expectant for him to make his exit from the stage which he had filled so long. The mighty monarch, the benefactor of humanity, the patron of arts and sciences, was forgotten in the presence of this decrepit old man whose aged limbs shook at every sound and who spoke in a hesitating and apologetic treble. He refused to see anybody, shut himself up in a room, spent his few remaining days in hearing from Srīvara the Mokshopāya 'the way to salvation', that panacea of Hindus for all the physical evils and mental worries. At last, after a long eventful reign of more than half a century, merciful providence relieved him of the life which had grown a burden to him. While yet a beardless boy, he had fought his way to the throne; before he had reached the prime of his life he had seen nearly all his aspirations crowned with the most unprecedented success; and ere he felt old age creeping upon him, he had drained the cup of disappointment to its dregs. There are few more pathetic figures in the annals of India that this solitary old man refusing to be consoled for a life of earnest endeavour, splendid achievement and irremediable failure. No wonder that he wrote a Shikāyat accusing his destiny of flirting with him with a false show of happiness which he had, Tantalus- like, been ever persuing and never quite overtaking. Still less wonder is it that he flew for refuge to a philosophy which taught that life was vanity and the world an illusion.

So died Zainu-l-Abidin, commonly called 'Bad Shah','the great king', par excellence, of Kashmir.

HAIDAR SHAH

After his death in 1473 the dynasty of Shāh Mīr did not produce any sovereign of outstanding ability. Haidar, the son and successor of Bad Shah whose disgraceful behaviour had precipitated the declining king to his grave, was a habitual drunkard, and an unfeeling tyrant. He started anew the cruel persecution of the Hindus which his father had taken such pains to abolish. His administration of justice was whimsical and arbitrary to the extent of making children suffer for the sins of their fathers. Notwithstanding his drinking and his cruelty the king was not uncultured, at least when he had slept off the fumes of liquor. Indeed he is said to have had a great fondness for fiddling; and when a great conflagration broke out which reduced a considerable part of the city to ashes, Nero-like, he 'ascended the palace to see his own five chambered house in flames, and felt happy and sank into the pleasure of drink.'

HASAN SHAH

He was succeeded by his son Hasan who opened his regime by the establishment of the laws of his grandfather and the release of all political prisoners. He also, imitated his grandfather in the erection of numerous public buildings and is said to have issued a new and peculiar kind of coinage. But the bane of his life was his Sayyad wife, who subjected him completely to her will, and used her power in forwarding the interests of her numerous kith and kin who rose to such predominance that Malik Ahmad, the Chief Minister, was forced to expel the whole gang of them from Kashmir. They were, however, soon recalled and after bringing about disgrace and imprisonment of the minister, assumed absolute power, which they misused frightfully. The king's death occurred shortly after, not without a suspicion of the Sayyids' foul play.

The accounts that we have of the century which intervened between the first enthronement of Muhammad Shah, the infant son of Hasan, and the annexation of Kashmir to the Mughal empire, are dreary and profitless to a degree. The bewildering rapidity with which the kings were raised to the throne and deposed, reminds one or more of the shifting, scenes of a bioscope than of the course of every-day life. No less than twenty sovereigns, including the usurper Mirza Haidar of Kashgar ruled during this period. Of these Muhammad ruled four times, Nazuk Shah thrice and Fath Shah twice. Before the dethroned prince was well out of the country he was recalled and reinstated. There was no rule and there was no ruler except in name. The country was a pandemonium in which all the forces of disorder and lawlessness celebrated a mighty and prolonged carnival. Every person was a manat-arms and ready to hire his sword to him who had the longest purse. The only real national movement was the resistance offered to the Sayyids in the first year of Muhammad Shah's first reign. These foreigners had woefully wronged the Kashmiris who considered their very existence in the country as a standing affront to their self- respect. All united in the common cause. The Raja of Jammu lent them his aid and the Sayyids, though they had invoked the aid of Tartar Khan, the Lodhi Governor of the Punjab, were mercilessly slaughtered. But no sooner was the motive for union removed than the Kashmiri noblemen fell out among themselves regarding the distribution of the loot.

The names of Magre and Tsak loom large over a crowd of tribes and clans who exercised arms as a profession and who contended for the possession of supreme power. Magres were native while the Tsaks were foreigners,probably of Darad origin, who had become neutralized in Kashmir. Gradually all the parties were merged into these two fractions and there ensured a tug-of-war which ended only with the Mughal occupation of the country, though the Magres were playing a distinctly losing game from A.D. 1560, when Ghazi Tsak outside the pageant prince Habib Shah and occupied the throne himself.

The first reign of Fath Shah is notable for the introduction into Kashmir of the Nurbakhshi sect of Islam by one Shams-ud-din of Iraq. They were vigorously put down by Mirza Haidar. This celebrated Mughal condottieri conquered Kashmir twice and ruled it from 1541 to 1551. His first invasion was from the side of Ladakh, to which country he had accompanied Sikander Khan of Kashgar on a crusade against the infidels in A.D. 1533. Though he penetrated into Kashmir and occupied the city for a time, during which his soldiers behaved with ruthless barbarity, he was eventually compelled to come to terms and make his retreat towards Tibet. His second invasion was effected at the time when Sher Shah was chasing Humayun out of Hindustan. This time he conquered Kashmir on behalf of Humayun and struck coins in the latter's name. Among other things he occupied his time in writing his valuable Tarikh-i-Rashidi which is a history of the Mughals of Central Asia and which also gives an account, unfortunately very meagre,of the Kashmir of his day.

Of the dynasty of Tsaks little need be said except that 'they were fit for the gallows here and hell hereafter'. The inhuman ferocity of Ghazi Shah the first ruler of this dynasty cannot be explained except on the supposition of his being subject to fits of mental aberration. He is said to have killed a hundred men daily. This may be an exaggeration, but it is a fact that he not only slaughtered his own son and eighteen grandsons for an alleged attempt at murder, but even had a small urchin of seven killed for stealing a fruit. His sins, however, soon brought their own retributions; he was attacked by a virulent form of leprosy which spread all over his body and innumerable worms were seen eating away his flesh.

Yusuf Shah, the last independent sovereign of Kashmir, or perhaps it would be more correct to say the last but one, was anxious to make his submission to Akbar, but his ministers stood in the way and openly defied the Emperor's envoy. The first Mughal invasion under Raja Bhagwan Das resulted only in a treaty by which the Kashmir king bound himself to pay tribute to the Emperor. But Akbar, who had set his heart upon the full and unqualified conquest of the valley, refused to ratify the terms. A second army was set on foot. Yusuf was taken prisoner and endowed with a small jagir in the distant province of Behar. His son Yaqub fought hard and persistently for the throne of his father but was at last compelled to the yield, and made to join Yusuf Shah in his inglorious retreat.

The advent of the Mughals in 1586 ushered in the modern age of Kashmir. The conditions of the new rule were entirely different from that had obtained at any time in the mediaeval age. The country now formed part of a mighty empire and became for more than a century the pleasure garden of the most magnificent court that India has ever seen. The Subhadars having learnt the art of government at the seat of an empire which was made up of a vast aggregate of nations and countries, possessing diverse languages, manners, customs and religions, naturally displayed far greater breadth of vision, and statesmanship in the conduct of their administration than was the case with indigenous rulers and their ministers whose limited power and narrowness of jurisdiction only served to increase their rancourous animosity against one another. The realignment and construction, by Muhammad Kasim Khan, Akbar's Engineer-in-Chief, of the great empire-route via Gujrat, Bhimber and Shupayan, which ensured the regularity of communication and safety of traffic and transit, with the mainland of India, marks a revolution, scarcely less far reaching in its results than the opening of the Jhelum Valley Road in our own day. Kashmir was brought in touch with the current which permeated the policy and administration of an extensive empire, and in the presence of far mightier issues forgot its own petty jealousies. Its people, the most impulsive in the whole of India, basked in the sunshine of Akbar's benign rule, whom they almost deified, and with the characteristic inconsistency of a mob sang hallelujahs over the extinction of cruel tyranny, to the existence of which they themselves had in no small measure contributed. The Emperors themselves bestowed paternal care upon the valley and its inhabitants. To be sure, I must not be understood to say that this period of a century and more was for Kashmir a long round of unqualified pleasure. There were governors who in their eagerness to amass fortunes were not always scrupulous in the employment of righteous means only; but they were not many, for the Emperor's punishments of such delinquents were sharp and severe. But what I really do mean to say is that this century was, on the whole, one of the happiest periods in the history of the country.

Among the writers to whom we owe our knowledge of this period Abul Fazl the 'guide, philosopher, friend' and chronicler of Akbar, and the Emperor Jehangir himself are the most important and exalted. The former tells us that 'the country is enchanting and might be fittingly called a garden of perpetual spring surrounding a citadel terraced to the skies and deservedly appropriate to be either the delight of the worldling or the retired abode of the recluse. Its streams are sweet to the taste, its waterfalls music to the ear, and its climate is invigorating. The lands are artificially watered or dependent on rain for irrigation. The flowers are enchanting. Its spring and autumn are extremely beautiful. The houses are all of wood, and are of four stories, some of more, but it is not the custom to enclose them. Cattle and sundry stores are kept in the lower storey, the second contains the family apartments, and in the third and fourth are the household chattels. On account of the abundance of wood and the constant earthquakes, houses of stone and brick are not built, but the ancient temples inspire astonishment. At the present day many of them are ruins. Woollen fabrics are made in high perfection, especially shawls which are sent as valuable gifts to many climes. But the bane of this country are its people. Yet strange to say, notwithstanding its numerous population and the scantiness of the means of subsistence, thieving and begging are rare. Besides plums and mulberries, the fruits are numerous. Melons, apples, peaches, apricots are excellent. Although the grapes are in plenty, the finer qualities are rare; and the vines bear on mulberry trees. The mulberry is little eaten, its loaves being reserved for the silkworms. The eggs are brought from Gilgit and Little Tibet. The food of the people is chiefly rice, wine, flesh and various vegetables,—and the last mentioned, they dry and preserve. Rice is cooked and kept overnight to be eaten. Apparel is generally of wool. There are artificers of various kinds who might be deservedly employed in the greatest cities. the bazar system is little in us, as a brisk traffic is carried on at their own places of business. The people take their pleasure in skiffs upon the lakes, and their hawks strike the wild fowl in mid-air and bring them to the boats; and some times they hold them down in the water in their talons and stand upon them, presenting an exciting spectacle.

...The carriage of goods is effected by boat, but men also carry

great loads over the most difficult country. Boatmen and carpenters drive a thriving trade. The Brahman class is very numerous. 'Although Kashmir has a dialect of its own, their learned books are in the Sanskrit language. They have a separate character which they use for manuscript work, and they write chiefly on Tuz, which is the bark of a tree. . . . The majority of the narrow-minded conservatives of blind tradition are Sunnis and there are some Imams and Nurbakshis who are perpetually at strife with each other. They are chiefly from Persia and Turkestan. . . . The most respectable class in this country is that of Brahmans, who, notwithstanding their need of freedom from the bonds, tradition and custom, are true worshippers of God.

'They do not loosen the tongue of calumny against those not of their faith, nor beg nor importune. They employ themselves in planting fruit trees, and are generally a source of benefit to the people. . . .

'Srinagar is the capital and is 4 farsakhs in length. The rivers Bihat, Mar and Lachma Khul flow through it. This has been a flourishing city from ancient times and the home of artificers of various kinds. Beautiful shawls are woven, and they manufacture woollen stuffs extremely soft. Durmah, Pattu and other woollen materials are prepared, but the best are brought from Tibet. . . 'In the village of Pampur, one of the dependencies of Vihi, there are fields of saffron to the extent of ten or twenty thousand bighas, a site that would enchant the most fastidious.

'Adjoining (the city) is a large lake called Dal . . . on its surface numbers of floating islands are constructed which are cultivated, and fraudulent people will at times cut off a piece and carry it away to a different position. . . . Saffron is also cultivated in Paraspur.

'The system of revenue collection is by appraisement and division of crops, assessment for crops having special rates and cash transactions not being the custom of the country. Some part of the Sair Jihat (miscellaneous taxes other than land revenue) cesses, however, are taken in cash. Payments in coin and kind were estimated in Kharwars (Shali) rice. Although one-third had been for a long time past the nominal share of the state, more than two shares were actually taken out. Through His Majesty's justice, it has been reduced to one-half. . . . The revenue, therefore, amounted to seven crores, forty-six lakhs, 70, 411 dams (Rs. 18,66,760-4-5). . . .' Ain, Book VII, ii, pp. 347-371.

Akbar himself visited Kashmir thrice and was so enamoured of it that he designated it his 'private garden'. His abolition of the capitation tax on the Hindus, the restoration of their lands and the permanent land settlement, are still remembered with gratitude by the people of the valley. His most notable monument in the country is the magnificent rampart of the Hari Parbat fort, or as it was then called, the fort of Nagar Nagar, which he made the military cantonment of Srinagar. But it was in the time of Jahangir and Shah Jahan that Kashmir became the real pleasure garden of the empire. Jahangir himself states that he considered it 'bad taste' to stretch carpets on the green sword of the valley.

The best account we have of the visit of a Mughal Emperor and the condition of Kashmir in the latter part of the seventeenth century, is from the pen of Francois Bernier, the celebrated French physician-traveller, who accompanied Aurangzeb to Kashmir in 1664. I have summarized his account below :—

'That scarcity of provisions may not be produced in the small kingdom of Kachemire, the king will be followed by a very limited number of individuals. Of females he takes only ladies of the first rank, the intimate friends of Rauchenara Begam, and those women whose services cannot be dispensed with. The Omrahs and military will also be as few as possible. . . . The king has a few of the choicest elephants for his baggage and the women of the Seraglio . . also a few mules. . . . Porters supply the place of camels. . . the king alone has no fewer than six thousand . . and it is calculated that there are at least fifteen thousand porters already collected at Bhimber; some sent by the Governor of Kachemire and by the neighbouring Rajas, and others who are come voluntarily in the expectation of earning a little money. A royal ordinance fixes their pay at ten crowns (Rs. 20) for every hundred pounds weight. It is computed that thirty thousand will be employed; an enormous number, when it is considered that the king and Omrahs have been sending forward baggage, and the trades-people articles of every sort, for the last month.

'The whole kingdom wears the appearance of a fertile and highly cultivated garden. Villages and hamlets are frequently seen through the luxuriant foliage. Meadows and vineyards, fields of rive, wheat, hemp, saffron and many sorts of vegetables, among which are intermingled trenches filled with water, rivulet, canals and several small lakes vary the . . enchanting scene. The whole ground is enamelled with our European flowers and plants, and covered with our apple, pear, plum, apricot and walnut trees, all bearing fruit in great abundance. The private gardens are full of melons, pateques or water-melons, water parsnips, red beet, radishes most of potherbs and others with which we are unacquainted.

'The capital of Kachemire bears the same name as the kingdom. It is without walls and is not less than three quarters of a league in length and half a league in breadth . . . . In the town there are two wooden bridges thrown over the river; and the houses although for the most part of wood, are well built and consist of two or three storeys. . . . Most of the houses along the banks of the river have little gardens, which produce a very pretty effect, especially in the spring and summer, when many parties of pleasure take place upon the water. Indeed most houses in the city have also their gardens; and many have a canal, on which the owner keeps a pleasure-boat thus communicating with the lake.

'In truth the kingdom surpasses in beauty all that my warm imagination had anticipated. . . . Jehan-guyre became so enamoured of this little kingdom as to make it the place of his favourite abode, and he often declared that he would rather be deprived of every other province of his mighty empire than lose Kachemire.

'I was quite prepared to witness the emulous contest between the Kachemire and the Mughal poets. We were no sooner arrived than Aurangzeb received from the bards of both nations poems in praise of this favoured land, which he accepted and rewarded with kindness. . . .

'The Kachemires are celebrated for wit, and considered much more intelligent and ingenious than the Indians. In poetry and science they are not inferior to Persians. They are also very active and industrious. The workmanship and beauty of their palkeys, bedsteads, trunks, inkstands, boxes, spoons and various other things are quite remarkable, and articles of their manufacture are in use in every part of the Indies. They perfectly understand the art of varnishing, and are eminently skilful in closely imitating the beautiful veins of a certain wood by inlaying with gold threads so delicately wrought that I never saw anything more elegant or perfect. But what may be considered peculiar to Kachemire and the staple commodity, that which particularly promotes the trade of the country, and fills it with wealth, is the prodigious quantity of shawls which they manufacture, and which gives occupation even to little children. . . .

'The people of Kachemire are proverbial for their complexions and fine forms. They are well made as the Europeans, and their faces have neither the Tartar flat nose nor the small pig-eyes that distinguish the natives of Kacheguer, and which generally mark those of Great Tibet. The women especially are very handsome; and it is from this country that nearly every individual, when first admitted to the court of the Great Mogol, selects wives or concubines, that his children may be whiter than the Indians, and pass for genuine Mogols . . . .' et seq.

The decline in the fortunes of the Mughal Empire was accompanied by the decline in the prosperity of the valley. The rois faineants who succeeded Aurangzeb lost all hold of their distant possessions. In 1739, Kashmir was annexed to the kingdom of Kabul by the terrible Nadir Shah, and it remained subject to the dominion of the Afghans until Ranjit Singh wrested it from the Amir Dost Muhammad in 1819. In 1846 on the defeat of the Sikhs it was transferred to Maharaja Gulab Singh by the British Government. Since then it has been under the Dogra rule.

(Journal of Indian History, Dec. 1925 & Apr. 1926)

CHAPTER 6

ANCIENT MONUMENTS

By

S.N. Dhar

The "Paradise of the Indies" is full of archaelogical interest. Throughout the length and breadth of the Valley, a network of ancient monuments is spread. Most of them are in ruins. The pathetic sight of broken columns, fallen pillars and dilapidated arches of temples and shrines, dating back to hundreds of years, is touching as well as charged with a romantic beauty. Buddhist Gandhara art influenced the early architecture of Kashmir. Many Buddhist edifices and stupas survive to this day. Later on, strong Greek influences, which persisted for centuries even after the mediaeval period, are evinced in colonnades, porches and pediments of the Hindu temples.

Kashmiri Hindus had a wonderful gift of choosing fine and high sites for their temples and shrines, so to command spacious views of the valley as also to ensure safety from the ravages of floods and denudation. The characteristic features of the architecture of Kashmir are : lofty pyramidal roofs—safeguard against snow and rain—trefoiled doorways, covered by pyramidal pediments and great width of indvidual columns in colonnades of imposing dimensions. It is quite distinct from the Hindu architecture of the rest of India.

The larger temples have rectangular courtyards walled in by massive masonry and their enclosed spaces served as so many forts in times of siege.

1. MONUMENTS IN AND NEAR SRINAGAR

(i) Shankaracharya

A mediaeval massive stone temple on a hillock in Srinagar. Its high octagonal plinth, the stone staircase of massive slabs with arched gateway, wherein no mortar was used, the low parpapet wall with niches round it and a stone tank nearby, are worthseeing.

An excellent view of Srinagar, the lakes and the mountain-girt valley, are obtained from the temple : it is indeed one of the finest sights of the world.

(ii) Shah Hamdan

On the riverside in the city, it is a rectangular mosque, built chiefly of wood, on the site of an old temple dedicated to Kalishwari whose shrine still exists on the bank. Wood carving on windows and doors and the pannelled wood-work of the rooms are remarkable.

(iii) Pathar Masjid—(Stone Mosque)

On the river bank, opposite to Shah Hamdan. It was built by Nur Jahan. the plinth is underground. Its stone facade, due to the compactness of massive blocks and the stone arches, is imposing.

(iv) Tomb of Zain-Ul-Abdin's Mother

Between fourth and fifth bridge, on the riverside. It is wholly made of brick. The brick masonry of the five domes, ornamentally decorated with blue bricks, is interesting. A wall, made from massive, sculptured stones of some temple, surrounds it.

(v) Jama Masjid

The Biggest mosque in Kashmir—half a mile from the f-Fourth Bridge. Its chequered past epitomises the history of Muslim rule in Kashmir. The for tall minars have pyramidal roofs. Its many halls have a large array of lofty pillars, 378 in number, which support the roof. Runs of an ancient temple are found in its outer compound.

(vi) Peri Mahal (Fairy Palace)

It is situated on the spur of mountain slopes to the west of Chashma Shahi. It occupied a school of astrology built by the ill-fated Dara Shikoh—killed by his brother, Aurangzeb, in the prime of his life—for his tutor, Mulla Shah.

An ill-preserved terraced Moghul Garden, a water reservoir in ruins, arched retaining walls of sidestairs, running through big rooms having domed ceilings, form its attractions. It commands an excellent view of the Dal Lake and is well worth a visit.

(vii) Harwan

11 miles from Srinagar. Here there are the very interesting excavations of a Buddhist monastery, whose tiles, frescoes and ancient masonry are worthseeing.

(viii) Pandrethan

4 miles from Srinagar, on the site of the former capital of Kashmir. It is well-preserved mediaeval temple. The ceiling of the domed roof, showing classic sculpture of the early 10th century A.D., is worthseeing. The temple is 17'6" square with

projecting stone portico on either side and string-course of elephants runs round it.

2. AVANTIPUR

13 mile above Srinagar, on the right bank of the Jhelum. Height : 5,225 ft. It was the site of the capital of a famous King of Kashmir, Avanti Varman, who built two magnificent temples, Avant Swami and Avant Sura which have been excavated by the Government.

(i) Avant Swami

This temple, dedicated to Vishnu, was built by Avanti Varman, in his youth, before his accession to the throne. The stone gateway, profusely sculptured, is very impressive. The spacious quadrangle is enclosed by a colonnade of great architectural beauty. It is one of the gems of architecture in Kashmir.

(ii) Avant Sura

This temple comes first on the left side of the road from Srinagar to Anantnag. Avant Varman built it after his accession to the throne and dedicated it to Siva. It is less ornate in sculpture and less preserved than the other temple.

3. MARTAND

The reputed Temple of the Sun, 3 miles from Anantnag.

The far-famed temple of Martand, situated on a unique, commanding sight over an upland plateau, has been styled as "the architectural lion of Kashmir". This most finished of the temples of Kashmir has very imposing dimensions, the total length of the temple being 63 feet; the dimensions of the flute-pillared quadrangle are 220 by 142 feet. A graceful colonade of 84 columns, most of which lie prostrate with intervening trefoil-arched recesses, flank the temple on either side. Carving on the pediments, arches and on walls, is fine and delicate.

4. BAMUZU

Situated on mile to the north of the sacred springs of Bhawan, there is an interesting group of excavated caves, cut into the lime-stone along the foot of the hills. These form the only important group of artificial caves in Kashmir. The passage of one of these caves and leads to a small temple in the interior, flanked by two arched recesses.

5. PAYECH

18 miles from Srinagar. This small, pyramid-roofed temple, set in a picturesque setting, is the most beautiful of ancient shrines. In its design it is like Paudrethan temple but is more solid, being built out of only 10 stones. The central chamber is 8′ square. It is rightly termed an "architectural gem".

6. ACHADAL

39 miles from Srinagar. There are the ruins of a Moghul pavilion. the underground earthen pipes that fed the royal hammam of Jehangir with water from the spring, are remarkable.

7. VERINAG

50 miles from Srinagar. The water of the spring was enclosed by Jehangir in an octagonal basin. 24 arches were raised by Shah Jahan who completed the work of his father.

8. MAMAL

This small masonry temple in Pahalgam is well worth a visit. There is a string of pure water at its base and a rubble—stone wall round it.

9. MANASBAL

18 miles from Srinagar. there are ruins of a Moghul Garden laid out by Nur Jahan. An old Hindu temple, made of stone and partially submerged in water, is another monument.

10. PATTAN

17 miles from sRinagar. The ruins of two temples, built by Shanker Varman and his consort, Suganda, are found here. Its architecture is after the style of Martland, but much less ornate, though its carving is in a better state of preservation. The gateway and trefoiled niches are remarkable.

11. PARIHASPURA

14 miles from Srinagar. the ruins mark the site of the capital of Lalitaditya. There are the Buddhist edifices of stupa and a monastery. Some of the most massive blocks of grey limestone use in Kashmir, can be seen here.

12. WANGAT

Approached from Kangan—on the road to Sonamarg. There are ruins of two group of mediaeval Naran Nag temples which stand on a height at the mouth of a gorge in the Wangat Nala. These cloisters were the far-famed abode of Sanskrit learning of yore in Kashmir. They formed the sacred gateway to the holy Gangabal Lake, 5,000 feet further up from Wangat.

13. BUNIYAR

Near Ramput, on the Jhelum Valley Road. It is the best preserved of the larger stone temples of Kashmir. The gateway is impressive.

(1945)

CHAPTER 7

ANCIENT MONUMENTS

Shankaracharya Temple: The Shankaracharya Temple is situated on the summit of the Takht-i-Sulaiman hill, to the south-east of Srinagar. It commands one of the finest views in whole of Kashmir. The view of the city with its green turfed roofs is without doubt unique. Neither the temple nor the hill preserves its ancient name. In ancient times the hill was called Gopadari and the shrine, probably some earlier structure which occupied its place, the Jyeshthesvara.

The date of this temple has been a source of controversy among archaeologists. General Cunningham and, after him, Lieut. Cole assigned it to the times of Jalauka (whom they date 220 B.C.) on the strength of local tradition. This theory has been rejected, firstly, on architectural grounds, and secondly, because of the doubtful character of the tradition. Another theory, advanced by Fergusson, is that the temple was built in the reign of Jahangir.

Kalhana in his Rajtarangini, definitely states that King Gopâditya built a shrine of Jyeshthesvara on the Gopadari, but it cannot be asserted with certainty that the present temple is the same as that was built by Gopaditya. It appears, however, probable that that shrine occupied the same position. Gopaditya's date, and consequently that of his buildings, is uncertain. But the conjecture that the present temple must be at least a century or so earlier than that highly finished example of Kashmir architecture, the Martand Temple, seems plausible.

Khanqah of Shah Hamdan: Between the third and fourth bridges on the right bank of the river Jhelum in Srinagar City stands the Khanqah of Mir Sayyid Ali Hamdani popularly known as Shah Hamdan. Tradition ascribes his origin to the city of Hamdan in Persia.

It is difficult to determine the date of the present structure, but it is practically certain that it does not belong to the time traditionally ascribed to the migration of Sayyid Ali Hamdan to Kashmir i.e. prior to 786 Hijra (A.D. 1384). Baron von Hugal, who visited Kashmir in 1835, speaks of it as a modern-looking building. But there is no doubt that mosque or some such religious edifice stood here at least as early as the reign of Akbar; for Abul Fazal in his Ain-i-Akbari says that "Mir Sayyid Ali Hamdani resided for some time in this city (Srinagar), and a monastery by him still preserves his name".

Pather Masjid: Of the Moghul mosques in Kashmir, the Pather Masjid is the largest surviving example. Its facade consists of nine arches including the large arched portico in the centre. The arched openings are enclosed in shallow decorative cusped arches, which in their turn are enclosed in rectangular frames. The horizontal construction of these arches is remarkable. All of them have recently been closed up with rubble stone masonry. This is said to have been built in A.D. 1632 by the Empress Nur Jahan.

Tomb of Zain-ul-Abdin's Mother: The most attractive chapter of Muslim rule in Kashmir is the reign of Zain-ul-Abdin (1421-1472). He was a great patron of art, literature and industries. He was tolerant to his Hindu subjects and his this nature is also apparent from the plinth of the tomb which with its filleted torus cornice is entirely in Hindu style. Similar is its trefoiled entrance and its still undistrubed massive jambs.

Near Sri Ranbir Ganj, the busiest and the most important trading market in Srinagar, is seen this great historical monument with its high and massive domes. Its superstructure alone was erected by the King. Its enclosure has been used as cemetery since the days of Zain-ul-Abdin and many of the notabilities of Muslims of Kashmir are interred here.

Jama Masjid: The original conception and erection of the Jama Masjid of Srinagar are ascribed to Sikandar Butshikan, who reigned in Kashmir from A.D. 1390-91 to 1414-15. He is said to have laid its foundation in A.D. 1398 and completed it in 1402. His illustrious son, Zain-ul-Abdin, is reported to have greatly exerted himself in adding to its aesthetic attractions.

The Hari Parbat Fort: The hill of Hari Parbat, crowned by the Pathan fort which is visible from every part of the city, has from times immemorial been a palce of great sanctity in Kashmir. The name is the Kashmiri equivalent of the Sanskrit Sarika-Parvata, "the hill of Sarika". It is said that the valley was, in prehistoric times, a vast lake, one of the most beautiful in the world. In this lake dwelt the water-demon Jalobdheva. This demon wrought havoc among the mountains of the adjacent districts, but being invulnerable in his own element, and declining to fight at a disadvantage on land, continued his life of depredation in impudent security for a long time. The gods fumed and stormed in impotent rage, and finally resolved to lay the matter before the Almighty Mother Sati—the controller of the titanic forces of Nature. At the pressure of the gods she assumed the form of a Sarika bird (Maina) and taking a pebble in her beak dropped it at the spot where she knew the demon was lying and finally the pebble swelled into gigantic proportions and crushed the demon by its weight. This pebble to this day survives under the name of Hari Parbat. A depression in the ground outside the Sangin Darwaza of the fort wall is pointed out as the spot wherefrom the parting breath of the demon forced its way out. The legend adds the gods in grateful memory of their deliverance took up their abode here. Since then every individual stone on this hill is reverenced by the orthodox Brahmins. In modern times, both Hindus and Muslims have appropriated parts of the hill for their shrines, but none of the shrines possesses any architectural interest. The fort's rampart and gates particularly Kathi Darwaza and Sangin Darwaza, and the mosque of Akhun Mulla Shah are well worth a visit.

Pari Mahal: Upon the mountain slope to the west of Cheshma Shahi is Pari Mahal, "the fairies' abode", a ruined garden palace, the construction of which is ascribed by tradition to the ill-starred prince Dara Shikoh, who was beheaded in 1659 by Aurangzeb. The garden consists of six terraces, with a total length of about 400′. The width of the terraces varies from 197′ to 205′.

In the uppermost terrace are the ruins of two structures, a barahdari facing the lake, and a water reservoir built against the mountainside. The reservoir was fed from above by a spring, which has since gone dry. In the middle of the second terrace exactly in front of the barahdari is a large tank with brick sides measuring 39′-6" by 26′-6". The facade of the retaining wall is ornamented with a series of twenty-one arches, including two of the side-stairs. The arches are built in descending order of height from the centre. Each of them is surmounted by a niche, the height of which increases in proportion to decrease in the height of the arch.

The third terrace is, architecturally, the most interesting portion of the garden. The entrance, which is of the usual Mughal type, arched in front and behind with a central domed chamber, is in the middle of the east wall, and is covered with a coat of fine painted plaster. On either side of it are a series of spacious rooms: the one to its north seems to have been a hammam. Fragments of the water-pipe are still to be seen projecting from a corner of its domed ceiling. Its interior is the most highly decorated of all the rooms in Pari Mahal. On the south of the entrance are two other chambers, but it is difficult to say what use they were put to.

Nishat Bagh: Returning from Chashma Shahi to the main road, the visitor proceeds 2½ miles to the north to reach Nishat Bagh. This is the most favoured resort of pleasure-seekers in Kashmir. Its twelve terraces, one for each sign of the zodiac, rise dramatically higher and higher up the mountain side from the eastern shore of the Dal Lake. The stream tears foaming down the carved cascades and fountains play in every tank and water-course, filling the garden with their joyous life and movement. The flower beds in these sunny terraces blaze with colour roses, lilies, geraniums, asters, gorgeous tall-growing zinnias, and feathery cosmos, pink and white. Beautiful at all times, when autumnlights up the poplars in clear gold and the big chenars burn red against the dark blue rocky background. There are few more brilliant, more breathlessly entrancing sights than this first view. The garden was laid by Asaf Khan, Prime Minister of Emperor Shah Jehan.

The lowest terrace has unfortunately been cut off by the modern road, which has likewise shorn Shalimar of part of its length. The two wooden doorways as well as gaudily painted barahdari on the third terrace are innovations which date from the time of Wazir Punnu's governorship of Kashmir in the reign of the late Maharaja Ranbir Singhji. These Mughal gardens of Kashmir owe a heavy debt of gratitude to this gentleman for arresting their decay.

There is a story that the Emperor Shah Jehan, who visited Kashmir in 1633, "decided that the garden was altogether too splendid for a subject, even though that subject might happen to be his own Prime Minister and father-in-law. He told Asaf Khan on three occasions how much he admired his pleasure-ground, expecting that it would be immediately offered for the royal acceptance. But Asaf Khan could not bring himself to surrender his cherished pleasurance to be a 'garden of herbs' for his royal master, and he remained silent. Then as now, the same stream supplied water both to the Royal Garden

(Shalimar) and Nishat Bagh. Shah Jehan in his anger ordered the water supply to be cut off from Nishat Bagh.

The stoppage of water made the garden desolate, dry and empty. Asaf Khan, who was staying in his summer palace at the time, could do nothing except feeling grief and bitter disappointment. One day, lost in a melancholy reverie, he at last fell fast asleep in the shade by the empty water-course. At length a noise aroused him; rubbing his eyes, he could hardly believe what he saw, for the fountains were all playing merrily once more and the long carved water-chutes were white with foam. A faithful servant, risking his life had defied the Emperor's orders, and removed the obstruction from the stream. Asaf Khan rebuked him for his zeal and hastily had the stream closed again. But the news reached the Emperor in his garden Shalimar; whereupon he sent for the terrified servent and, much to the surprise of the Court, instead of punishing him, bestowed a robe of honour upon him to mark his admiration for this act of devoted service, at the same time granting a sanad which gave the right to his master to draw water for the garden from the Shalimar stream.

Shalimar: Of all the Mughal gardens in Kashmir, Shalimar, the summer residence of Empress Nur Jehan and Emperor Shah Jehan, is one which has received the greatest attention from the later rulers of the country. The Pathan and Sikh Governors occasionally used it as their pleasure resort, and when, from the reign of Ranjit Singh, Europeans began to visit the Valley with comparative freedom, its marble pavilion was often assigned to them as residence.

The garden originally consisted, as now, of three enclosures, the lower one of which, however, has been considerably curtailed by the intrusion of the cart-road. The outermost enclosure was used as the public garden, and its barahdari was the Diwan-i-Am (The Hall of Public Audience). The second enclosure is slightly broader, consisting of two shallow terraces with the Diwan-i-Khas (The Hall of Private Audience) in the centre. The buildings have been destroyed, but their carved stone bases are left, as well as fine platforms surrounded by fountains. On the north-west boundary of this enclosure are the royal bathrooms. The little guard rooms that flank the entrance to the ladies'garden have been rebuilt in Kashmiri style on older stone bases. Around the beautiful black marble pavilion built by Shah Jehan, which still stands in the midst of its fountain spray, the whole colour and perfume of the garden is concentrated with the snows of Mahadev for a background.

Avantipur

Avantisvara Temple: The village of Avantipur, situated at a distance of 18 miles from Srinagar on the Anantnag cart-raod, represents the town of Avantipura, founded by Avantiverman, who reigned from 855 to 883 A.D. Its chief interest centres in two magnificent temples with which its founder embellished it. The first and larger is the temple of Siva-Avantisvara, whose massive walls rise in forlorn grandeur outside the village of Jaubror, half a mile below Avantipur. The temple which has been sadly mutilated, is situated in a courtyard enclosed by a massive stone wall, the western face of which is adorned externally with a row of fluted columns, but without any recesses behind. The gateway is in the middle of this wall, and is divided into two chambers by a cross wall. Its walls are not decorated with figure sculpture. The niches and the panels are quite plain.

The base on which the shrine in the centre of the courtyard stands is 76'-4" square and 10' high. To each of its corners was attached a platform about 16' square, which must originally have supported a small subsidiary shrine. It has a stair on each of its four sides. The stairs have a width of 28½' and are supported on either sides by flank walls 17½' in length. The sanctum has been reduced to a "confused mass of ruins".

There is a large assortment of architectural fragments strewn about in the courtyard, the most interesting of which are (1) the spandrel of an arch in front of the southern stair, (2) the flower-and-vase capital of a dodecagonal pilaster, (3) the spandrel of another arch by its side, and (4) the base of a pilaster decorated with two seated rams and a dancing girl who plays upon a damaru (small hand-drum) standing on a throne ornamented with two lions at the sides and an elephant, facing in the middle.

Martand Temple: The temple of Martand is situated at a distance of 5 miles form the town of Anantnag. Being on the top of a lofty plateau, at whose stretch the broad verdant plains of Kashmir intersected by a network of rivers, lakes, and canals, thickly dotted with clusters of busy villages nestling like beehives in closely planted groves of trees, and encircled by snow-clad mountain ramparts — the temple of the Sun, as Martand originally was, commands a superb view, such as the eye rarely lights upon. It is this beauty of situation that contributes so largely to the sense of grandeur with which the sight of these ruins always inspires even the most unimaginative visitors.

There is some uncertainty regarding the exact ascription of this temple. But the most probable assumption, which is strengthened by the architectural style, the that the temple as it exists today was built by King Lalitaditya in the middle of the eight century A.D.

So far little attention has been paid to archaeological remains of the Jammu Province by scholars of the subject. The forts of Reasi, Ramnagar, Bhaderwah, Gajpat, Basholi and the temples of Babore, Purmandal, Billawar, etc. are magnificent monuments that deserve notice and careful study.

(Kashmir Today)

CHAPTER 8

ANCIENT TEMPLES OF KASHMIR

By
C.G. Bruce

Every country of importance has had a religious past, and even if the present finds ruined temples, the fact remains that those lofty arches and massive blocks of masonry were quarried and erected, bit by bit, by a people who expended their best on a building which was to be set aside for worship.

The ruined temples of Kashmir are solid, and simple of design, and yet they have fluted pillars and trefoiled arches which trace their origin to an artistic source. The keynote of some of these old temples is decidedly Grecian in character, which would be accounted for, as we have seen, by their erection by so gifted and widely informed a person as Akbar.

The best situated of the present ruins, though not the best preserved nor the finest, is the temple dome crowning the summit of the hill above Srinagar. The Takt-i-Suleiman, as it is named, is an object for an early morning ride, well worth the trouble of such a climb as it entails. Paving-stones mark the winding way, which zigzags up the face of the hill, and presently you emerge on a platform 1000 feet above the plains, while Kashmir and its surrounding mountain ranges lie spread out beneath you in a wide bird's-eye view.

There was an older temple still on the same site, which was built by the son of the great Asoka, of which very little is left;

but the present one is hoary enough to command our respect and to form a link with the past, as the date of this one even is said to be about A.D. 250.

Another temple ruin is in the Lidar valley at Bhaumjo, about the same date; there is also a great column standing on the road to Islamabad, 24 miles from Srinagar, and several others in various parts. But the best remains of all are to be found at Martand in the Lidar valley. This temple was built on a superb site: a gentle slope of grassland, with snowy mountains as a background, and close at hand are stretches of fertile valley, fine trees, and streams of cool water under their shade. This is the only temple which possessed what we name, in our cathedrals, chancel, choir, nave, and transepts. Although it is in ruins, we can still see what a grand pile it must once have been. The height is reported to have been 75 feet.

There was a wide flight of stone steps up to a splendid trefoil arch. On each side was a small chapel with lofty arch. On each side was a small chapel with lofty arches, said to have been built by the queen of King Ramaditya, who lived, we believe, in the beginning of the sixth century. This was over four hundred years before the battle of Hastings, and the temple was mentioned in the records of the King of Kashmir, Lalitaditya, who reigned from 693 to 729. There was also a wide quadrangle, 220 feet by 142, supported by carved pillars, and eighty-four columns carried the roof, which no longer exists.

If the outside influence which was great enough to raise such temples as these in a strange country hundreds of miles from the seat of rule, had only been as practical and benevolent as it was powerful, the story of Kashmir would have been very different. The origin of these temples was not based on any specially religious turn of mind of the people themselves, and the rulers succeeding Ashoka were not filled with his religious zeal, though Lalitaditya revived it. After his death the succession of his worthless son brought another sad period, which only served to make his reign stand out as a vivid contrast.

In 1586 the best thing possible happened for Kashmir in its conquest by the great Akbar, who lived at the same time as our Queen Elizabeth, and for two hundred years Kashmir remained part of the Mogul dominions.

The fort outside Srinagar, Hari Parbat, which is still used as quarters for troops and stores, was built by Akbar on one of his three visits to Kashmir.

As the power of the Mogul emperors declined the old evils in Kashmir revived, and became even worse. Once more it was the scene of cruelty, oppression, and poverty. The worst time of all was when it was dominated by the Afghans. As under the imperious Duchess in Alice in Wonderland, the standing order of the day was "Off wiuh their heads." The unfortunate people were even sewn up in sacks by twos and threes and sunk in the lake. They were even spiteful enough to spoil the beautiful Mogul gardens on the Dal lake.

At last, in their despair, they besought the help of the great Sikh ruler of the Punjab, Ranjit Singh. This was in 1819, and Kashmir was once more annexed by a foreign power.

As rulers of other religious beliefs came to Kashmir they generally destroyed to a certain extent the buildings they found, and as the religious fervour melted, the temples, no longer protected from any destructive influences, gradually crumbled to ruin. It has often been noticed that the decay of religion marks the decay of a country, and Kashmir, though she had been given a good chance, lost her place in the race of human prosperity.

With the decline of Buddhism the Hindu religion took its place about the eleventh century. Again it was changed about two hundred years later for Mahomedanism, and back again to Hinduism, and so on. The country-people are now chiefly of the religion of Mahomed, but the Maharajah and townsfolk are Hindus by faith. They all seem to pull along, however, possibly because their religion is more inspired by the letter than by the spirit.

The religion of Kashmir in these days is just about as mixed as possible, partly Mahomedan, partly Hindu, with the worship of saints and the fear of demons still prevalent. This is not surprising, considering the many changes of faith forced upon the people by changes of rule.

The most ancient of all worship, even before Buddhism was brought in, was Nag or snake worship. The people imagined that huge snakes lived in every mountain, and especially near the springs at their foot. They used to build tanks at these spots, which the snake god was to occupy at his pleasure. Their veneration for snakes was no doubt dictated more by fear than reverence; but fear lessened by degrees, and a regular worship grew out of the ideas produced by old legends.

The syllable Nag, which is part of the names of many places in Kashmir, has been given from the place being dedicated to one of these snake gods. We find Vernag, "the place of many springs and the snake," Nagmarg, the alp of the snake, and so on. We know that in our own old Bible history the people of Israel were healed by worshipping the form of a serpent, even though it was the faith which really pulled them through. Then there is the serpent of the garden of Eden, a demon much feared. The origin of the Chinese dragon may possibly be traced to Nag worship, though it is also supposed to have been from the legends of terrible prehistoric monsters which have been handed down. Our own dragons, too, show that our ancient history was much like any other. The strange thing about Kashmiris is that they seem to know nothing about their fine old temple remains. If we question them, the answer will probable be that they are just "old praying-places " built in the old days; but even the Pundits, or educated people, seem to care nothing for their antiquities, as, for instance, our old country-folk care for our Druidical or Roman remains.

It is a pity to see the Kashmir ruins going from bad to worse. A special department is much needed, so that there may be some one to preserve them from further ruin. Very likely many interesting relics of the old cities might be found buried in their ruined sites.

On one of the many tablelands or flat part of the valley where the lower hills slope up to the mountains, there are some curious old stones firmly imbedded in the ground, from which they project about four feet. They are shaped something like blunt arrowheads, and the people will tell you that they are arrows which were shot from the bows of the gods in defence of the men of the valley at a time when they were preyed upon by huge giants, who devoured them by way of refreshment after their huge wrestling bouts. The undulations of the grassy ground are said to be the result of the pommelling of great knees and elbows.

Saint worship is very popular in Kashmir, especially among the boatmen, and the chant we heard as one of those dredging barges passed us on the Dal lake was an invocation to some special saint.

Every village has its shrine or miniature temple. But that their religion consists in keeping the outside of the platter clean is proved by the fact that most villagers in any position of trust will keep three accounts: one for the eye of his superior, one for his subordinates, while the correct one, showing real returns, is the one which lives in his own pocket and is consulted by himself alone.

The contrast between temples ancient and modern is amazing, and yet it is in accordance with the history of the people. They did not of themselves build the solid shrines of worship which continue even now to attract veneration, and we have only to visit Srinagar to see how true this is. The principal mosque is built of wood, and has beautifully carved cedarwood pillars. Among the temple roofs we can see, both Hindu and Mahomedan, is one called the Golden Temple. Its burnished roof of gold lacquer is still preserved, but other domes glint silver in the bright sunshine. Alas, some of them are only plated with old kerosene tins!

There is another temple, the daintiest and prettiest thing imaginable. In the spring, on the edge of the river, it makes a vivid bit of colouring, though built of humble whitewashed plaster. Its roof is a garden of purple iris and pink and white tulips. Brass bells and an elegant spire complete the feminine appearance of this little mosque of the twentieth century.

In future times no one will visit the ruins of that fairylike mosque, for it is built of mud, and to mud it will return. No one surely will care to visit, in days to come, any but a small minority of the religious edifices of this or last century, whether East or West. We count the cost too carefully for one thing, and Time will not wait as he did, or seemed to do, in old days.

Missionary zeal is no less—we will hope the right kind is even greater than in past years—and no doubt there is a great deal of true Christian faith and endeavour among people who cannot as yet profess it openly. But most important of all is a spread of practical Christianity which shall alter the lives of people who have been accustomed to look on their religion as separate from their daily tasks and pleasures. We want to teach truth for the sake of goodness, not for any advantage it may produce. We want to teach true strength in place of tyranny and abuse of power. We also want to teach that cleanliness is next to godliness, and love for one's neighbour of more importance than prayers on the high road. The practical example of British men and women is the leaven which is gradually if slowly spreading, and this is as important, even more so, than teaching only the letter of our religion.

(1915)

CHAPTER 9

THE TEMPLES OF CASHMERE

The architectural remains of Kashmir are perhaps the most remarkable of the existing monuments of India, as they exhibit undoubted traces of the influence of Grecian art. The Hindu temple is generally a sort of architectural pasty, a huge collection of ornamental fritters, huddled together with or without keeping; while the "Jain" temple is usually a vast forest of pillars, made to look as unlike one another as possible, by some paltry differences in their petty details.

On the other hand, the Kashmirian fanes are distinguished by the graceful elegance of their outlines, by the massive boldness of their parts, and by the happy propriety of their decorations.

They cannot, indeed, vie with the severe simplicity of the Parthenon, but they possess great beauty—different, indeed, yet quite their own.

The characteristic features of the Kashmirian architecture are its lofty pyramidal roofs, its trefoiled doorways, covered by pyramidal pediments, and the great width of the intercolumniations.

Most of the Kashmirian temples are more or less injured, but more particularly those at Wantipur, which are mere heaps of ruins. Speaking of these temples, Trebeck says: "It is scarcely possible to imagine that the state of "ruin to which they have been reduced has been the work "of time, or even of man, as their solidity is fully equal to "that of the most massive monuments of Egypt. Earth—"quakes must have been the cause of their overthrow." In my opinion, their overthrow is too complete to have been the result of an earthquake, which would have simply prostrated the buildings in large masses. But the whole of the superstructure of these temples is now living in one confused heap of stones, totally disjointed from one another.

I believe, therefore, that I am fully justified in saying, from my own experience, that such a complete and disruptive overturn could only have been produced by gunpowder.

The destruction of the Kashmirian temples is universally attributed, both by history and by tradition, to the bigoted Sikander. (A.D. 1396). He was reigning at the period of Timur's invasion of India, with whom he exchanged friendly presents, and from whom, I suppose, he may have received a present of the villanous saltpetre.

As it would appear that the Turks had metal cannon at the siege of Constantinople in 1422, I think it no great stretch of probability to suppose that gunpowder itself had been carried into the East, even as far as Kashmir, at least ten or twenty years earlier—that is, about A.D. 1400 to 1420, or certainly during the reign of Sikander, who died in 1416.

Even if this be not admitted, I still adhere to may opinion, that the complete ruin of the Wantipur temples could only have been effected by gunpowder; and I would, then, ascribe their overthrow to the bigoted "Aurungzib".

"Ferishta" attributed to Sikander the demolition of all the Kashmirian temples save one, which was dedicated to Mahadeo, and which only escaped "in consequence of "its foundations being below the surface of the neighbour-"ing water."

In A.D. 1580, "Abul Fazl" mentions that some of the idolatrous temples were in "perfect preservation;" and Ferishta describes many of these temples as having been in existence in his own time, or about A.D. 1600.

As several are still standing, though more or less injured, it is certain that Sikander could not have destroyed them all. He most likely gave orders that they should be overturned; and I have no doubt that many of the principal temples were thrown down during his reign.

But, besides the ruthless hand of the destroyer, another agency, less immediate, but equally certain in its ultimate effects, must have been at work upon the large temples of Kashmir. The silent ravages of the destroyer, who carries away pillars and stones for the erection of other edifices, has been going on for centuries. Pillars, from which the architraves have been thus removed, have been thrown down by earthquakes, ready to be set up again for the decoration of the first Musjid that might be erected in the neighbourhood. Thus every Mahomedan building in Kashmir is constructed either entirely or in part of the ruins of Hindu temples.

TAKT I SULIMAN

The oldest temple in Kashmir, both in appearance and according to tradition, is that upon the hill of "Takt i Suliman, " or Solomon's Throne. It stands 1,000 feet above the plain, and commands a view of the greater part of Kashmir.

The situation is a noble one, and must have been amongst the first throughout the whole valley which was selected as the position of a temple. Its erection is ascribed to Jaloka, the son of Asoka, who reigned about 220 B.C.

The plan of the temple is octagonal, each side being fifteen feet in length. It is approached by a flight of eighteen steps, eight feet in width, and inclosed between two sloping walls. Its heights cannot now be ascertained, as the present roof is a modern roof is a modern plastered dome, which was probably built since the occupation of the country by the Sikhs. The walls are eight feet thick, which I consider one of the strongest proofs of the great antiquity of the building.

PANDRETHAN

This name means the old capital, or ancient chief town. The name has, however, been spelt by different travellers in many different ways. "Moorcroft" calls it Pandenthan, "Vigne" Pandrenton, and "Hugel" Pandriton.

The building of this temple is recorded between A.D. 913 and 921; and it is afterwards mentioned between the years 958 and 972, as having escaped destruction when the King Abhimanyu—Nero- like—set fire to his own capital.

As this is the only temple situated in the old capital, there can be very little, if any, doubt that it is the very same building which now exists. For as it is surrounded by water, it was, of course, quite safe amid the fire, which reduced the other buildings to mere masses of quicklime.

Baron Hugel calls the Pandrethan edifice a "Buddhist temple," and states that there are some well-preserved Buddhist figures in the interior. But he is doubly mistaken, for the temple was dedicated to Vishnu, and the figures in the inside have no connexion with Buddhism.

Trebeck swam into the interior, and could discover no figures of any kind; but as the whole ceiling was formerly hidden by a coating of plaster, his statement was, at that time, perfectly correct.

The object of erecting the temples in the midst of water must have been to place them more immediately under the protection of the Nagas, or human-bodied and snake-tailed gods, who are zealously worshipped for ages through Kashmir.

MARTTAND

Of all the existing remains of Kashmirian grandeur, the most striking in size and situation is the noble ruin of Marttand.

This majestic temple stands at the northern end of the elevated table-land of "Matan," about three miles to the eastward of Islamabad.

This is undoubtedly the finest position in Kashmir. The temple itself is not now (1848) more than forty feet in height, but its solid walls and bold outline towering over the fluted pillars of the surrounding colonnade give it a most imposing appearance.

There are no petty confused details; but all are distinct and massive, and most admirably suited to the general character of the building.

Many vain speculations have been hazarded regarding the date of the erection of this temple and the worship to which it was appropriated.

It is usually called the "House of the Pandus" by the Brahmins, and by the people "Matan."

The true appellation appears to be preserved in the latter, Matan being only a corruption of the Sanscrit Marttand, or the sun, to which the temple was dedicated.

The true date of the erection of this temple—the wonder of Kashmir—is a disputed point of chronology; but the period of its foundation can be determined within the limits of one century, or between A.D. 370 and 500.

The mass of building now known by the name of Matan, or Marttand, consists of one lofty central edifice, with a small detached wing on each side of the entrance, the whole standing on a large quadrangle surrounded by a colonnade of fluted pillars, with intervening trefoil headed recesses. The central building is sixty-three feet in length, by thirty-six in width.

As the main building is at present entirely uncovered, the original form of the roof can only be determined by a reference to other temples, and to the general form and character of the various parts of the Marttand temple itself.

The angle of the roof in the Temple of Pandrethan, and in other instances, is obtained by making the sides of the pyramid which forms it paralled to the sides of the doorway pediment, and in restoring the Temples of Patrun and Marttand I have followed the same rule.

The height of the Pandrethan temple—of the cloistered recesses, porch pediments, and niches of Marttand itself—were all just double their respective widths. This agreement in the relative proportions of my restored roof of Marttand with those deduced from other examples, is a presumptive proof of the corrcetness of my restoration. The entrance-chamber and the wings I suppose to have been also covered by similar pyramidal roofs. There would thus have been four distinct pyramids, of which that over the inner chamber must have been the loftiest, the height of its pinnacle above the ground being about seventy-five feet.

The interior must have been as imposing as the exterior. On ascending the flight of steps—now covered by ruins—the votary of the sun entered a highly-decorated chamber, with a doorway on each side covered by a pediment, with a trefoil-headed niche containing a bust of the Hindu triad, and on the flanks of the main entrance, as well as on those of the side doorways, were pointed and trefoil niches, each of which held a statue of a Hindu divinity.

The interior decorations of the roof can only be conjecturally determined, as I was unable to discover any ornamented stones that could with certainty be assigned to it. Baron Hugel doubts that Marttand ever had a roof; but, as the walls of the temple are still standing, the numerous heaps of large stones that are scattered about on all sides can only have belonged to the roof.

I can almost fancy that the erection of this sun-temple was suggested by the magnificent sunny prospect which its position commands. It overlooks the fine view in Kashmir, and perhaps in the known world. Beneath it lies the paradise of the East, with its sacred streams and cedarn glens, its brown orchards and green fields, surrounded on all sides by vast snowy mountains, whose lofty peaks seem to smile upon the beautiful valley below. The vast extent of the scene makes it sublime; for this magnificent view of Kashmir is no petty peep into a half-mile glen, but the full display of a valley sixty miles in breadth and upwards of a hundred miles in length, the whole of which lies beneath "the ken of the wonderful Marttand."

The principal buildings that still exist in Kashmir are entirely composed of a blue limestone, which is capable of taking the highest polish—a property to which I mainly attribute the beautiful state of preservation in which some of them at present exist.

Even at first sight one is immediately struck by the strong resemblance which the Kashmirian colonnades bear to the classic peristyles of Greece. Even the temples themselves, with their porches and pediments, remind one more of Greece than of India; and it is difficult to believe that a style of architecture which differs so much from all Indian examples, and which has so much in common with those of Greece, could have been indebted to chance alone for this striking resemblance.

One great similarity between the Kashmirian architecture and that of the various Greek orders is its stereo-typed style, which, during the long flourishing period of several centuries, remained unchanged. In this respect it is so widely different from the ever-varying forms and plastic vagaries of the Hindu architecture that it is impossible to conceive their evolution from a common origin.

I feel convinced myself that several of the Kashmirian forms, and many of the details, were borrowed from the temples of the Kabulian Greeks, while the arrangements of the interior and the relative proportions of the different parts were of Hindu origin. Such, in fact, must necessarily have been the case with imitations by Indian workmen, which would naturally have been engrafted upon the indigenous architecture. The general arrangements would still remain Indian, while many of the details, and even some of the larger forms, might be of foreign origin.

As a whole, I think that the Kashmirian architecture, with its noble fluted pillars, its vast colonnades, its lofty pediments, and its elegant trefoiled arches, is fully entitled to be classed as a distinct style. I have therefore ventured to call it the Arian order—a name to which it has a double right; first, because it was the style of the Aryas, or Arians, of Kashmir; and, secondly, because its inter-columniations are always of four diameters—an interval which the Greeks called Araiostyle.

Extract from Vigne's "Travels in Kashmir."

The Hindu temple of Marttand is commonly called the House of the Pandus. Of the Pandus it is only necessary to say that they are the Cyclopes of the East. Every old building, of whose origin the poorer class of Hindus in general have no information, is believed to have been the work of the Pandus. As an isolated ruin, this deserves, on account of its solitary and massive grandeur, to be ranked not only as the first ruin of the kind in Kashmir, but as one of the noblest among the architectural relices of antiquity that are to be seen in any country. Its noble and exposed situation at the foot of the hills reminded me of that of the Escurial. It has no forest of cork-trees and evergreen-oaks before it, nor is it to be compared, in point of size, with that stupendous building; but it is visible from as great a distance. And the Spanish sierra cannot for a moment be placed in competition with the verdant magnificence of the mountain-scenery of Kashmir.

Few of the Kashmirian temples, if any, I should say, were Buddhist. Those in or upon the edge of the water were rather, I should suppose, referable to the worship of the Nagas, or snake- gods. The figures in all the temples are almost always in an erect position, and I have never been able to discover any inscription in those now remaining.

I had been struck with the great general resemblance which the temple bore to the recorded disposition of the Ark and its surrounding curtains, in imitation of which the Temple at Jerusalem was built; and it became for a moment a question whether the Kashmirian temples had not been built by Jewish architects, who had recommended them to be constructed on the same plan for the sake of convenience merely. It is, however, a curious fact, that in Abyssinia, the ancient Ethiopia, which was also called "Kush," the ancient Christian churches are not unlike those of Kashmir, and that they were originally built in imitation of the temple, by the Israelites who followed the Queen of Sheba, whose son took possession of the throne of Kush, where his descendants are at this moment Kings of Abyssinia.

Without being able to boast, either in extent or magnificence, of an approach to equality with the temple of the sun at Palmyra, or the ruins of the palace at Persepolis, Marttand is not without pretensions to a locality of scarcely inferior interest, and deserves to be ranked with them, as the leading specimen of a gigantic style of architecture that has decayed with the religion it was intended to cherish, and the prosperity of a country it could not but adorn.

In situation it is far superior to either. Palmyra is surrounded by an ocean of sand, and Persepolis overlooks a marsh; but the temple of the sun in Marttand is built upon a natural platform at the foot of some of the noblest mountains, and the most pronounce valley in the known world.

We are not looking upon the monuments of the dead. We step not aside to inspect a tomb, or pause to be saddened by an elegy. The noble pile in the foreground is rather an emblem of age than of mortality; and the interest with which we perambulate its ruins is not the less pleasurable because we do not known much that is certain of its antiquity, its founders, or its original use.

(Extract from "An Essay on the Asian Order of Architecture, as exhibited in the Temples of Kashmir", by Capt. A. Cunningham)

CHAPTER 10

ANCIENT ARTS

By

Sansar Chand Sharma

The Jammu Kalam has made a distinct contribution to the gallaxy of Pahari paintings, which constitute one of the richest chapters in the history of Indian art and have already been accorded a place of honour in the artistic heritage of the world. From sixteenth century to the dawn of the present century, Sivalik ranges had been the abode of art of painting in India. The art of sculpture is, in fact, many centuries older. Many known and unknown artists gave expression to the sprit of the age—the grandeur of the palaces of feudal chieftains, the unsophisticated beauty of flesh and nature, tales of battles and chivalry, mythological beliefs and eternal theme of love—through folk songs, sculptures and paintings on cloth, vessels, ornaments and hand made paper.

Plastic art was a fore-runner to painting in Jammu as it was in the rest of India, except that unlike elsewhere it did not recur after painting. The first evidence of the existence of terra cotta art in Jammu is believed to have been found in 1932, when some pieces were unearthed, by a mere chance, in Ambaran village in the vicinity of Akhnoor on the right bank of the river Chenab, about 25 miles from Jammu. Carried merely by curiousity, people rushed to the spot and collected many pieces of baked earthen pieces, queer naturalistic heads and limbs of men and animals. Most of them fell into ignorant hands, who passed them on to the children to play with. Only a few pieces chanced their way to art dealers who got them a place in the Lahore museum. Dr. Fabri who has made a thorough study of the terra cotta art of Akhnoor, dates them, in one of his articles in the MARG (March 1955) from 700 to 730 AD.

Gupta Influence on sculpture

Again, in 1949, the Indian army, while digging trenches, unearthed a few superb sculptural pieces. Two of them were triumvirates of Siva and Surja, made of greenish dark granite (2ft.). They are now preserved in the Dogra Art Gallery of Jammu. Mr. Ramachandran, Deputy Director of Archeology, dated them to the late Gupta period of 800 to 1000 AD. There were several more pieces of Siva and Parvati, all mutilated and measuring 12 to 14 inches in length.

We, in fact, find abundant traces of the Gupta influence in a large part of Jammu, below the Trikuta range, from Akhnoor in the west to Basohli in the east. A broken sculptural piece, with Siva and Parvati in a sitting pose, was, for instance, recently collected from Basohli for the Dogra Gallery. The temples, in the architectural ruins of Krimachi, near Udhampur reflect Chaulokiya pattern, resembling Bhuvneshwar temple of Orissa. But the decoration on the slopes is abstract and is like that on the Mahabodhi temple of Gaya, with the difference that corners have imitation small temples, one rising above the other. These temples have been dated by an expert to 1325 AD. But as he has based it on a date scratched on a slate, which might have been done by even a visitor, its authenticity is doubtful. Judging from other characteristics of these ruins, it is unlikely that they belonged to a period later than 1,000 AD. The statuary on some of the 'baulies'—springs—of Udhampur are perhaps older. Trimurti is common in this area also.

Yet another site of old monuments is in Babaur in Ramnagar Tehsil, where architectural variety. There are stone-blocks measuring 10'X2'X2½' raised to considerable height. The sculpture is grand and the decoration is equally matching. Here, again, we find Siva Trimurti. It also contains a piece of tandav, found for the first time in the State. The place is now being made accessible by the newly constructed Udhampur-Dhar road.

Unfortunately no systematic study of these ruins has been made and no final verdict about their antiquity is available. There is complete lack of historical record to built up an authentic link with the rest of India. The architecturai ruins of Sunara near Udhampur is still an enigma for the students of antiquities. Likewise the existence of Trimurti in Bhaderwah and Kishtwar—north east of Jammu—where Naga cult was rampant is not easily explicable. The vast sculptural treasures of Jammu pose a serious challenge to the archeologist and the historian.

Early Paintings of Jammu

By sixteenth century the artistic talent of the area found expression through painting. Jammu school of painting, which came to the notice of art critics and scholars rather late, has yet nor received due attention at their hands. Its antiquity has not therefore been finally ascertained. W.G. Archer, in his monumental book "Punjab Hill Paintings", divides this school in two phases viz pre-Kangra and post Kangra influence. He traces the former to the advent of the refugee artist. Pandit Sen, whose son Nain Sukh painted dozens of pictures for Raja Balwant dev of Jammu. He was a shrewd hand who stuck loyally to his patron and did not do a single portrait even for the brothers of the Raja. He imparted sobriety in colour and form to his figures. His compositions, drawings and portraits are admirable.

There is, however some evidence to indicate the existence of an indigenous Jammu Kalam, before Nain Sukh. Unfortunately, a lot of art treasure of Jammu has been sold as scrap.

Its whereabouts have still not been fully traced. It is, therefore, not possible to throw much light on the indigenous Jammu Kalam.

In any case, Nain Sukh was not the only artist in the courts of Jammu. Guranditta and Ganda, son and Grandson of Purkha and Didi were in the employ of the great art patron, Raja Balwant dev whose court was also adorned by another talented artist, Vajan. There were also artists in the courts of the brothers of the Raja. The many figures that are missing in the family portraits of Balwant dev have probably been dealt with by their own artists. The portraits of Ghansar dev and Surat singh definetely appear to be the work of the indigenous Kalam.

The indigenous art of Jammu which is quite distinct from Basohli Kalam is rustically vigorous with stunted but stable forms. It is virile but primitively harsh in colours. The technique is immature and figures often lack proportions. The decoration is minute and contrasting in colour. While the pre-Kangra phase referred to by Archer ceased to exist, the indigenous art survived even thereafter.

Mughal Influence

The Mughal influence shaped the Pahari art in two stages. Firstly, Mughal court, that used to be attended by rajas from all over the country, including Jammu, set a pattern of manners and royal behaviour which, in turn was reflected in the work of local artists. Secondly, when Aurangzeb took the reins of the Mughal empire, the artists lost the court patronage and started seeking it at smaller courts. Subsequent invasions from the north west further scared the artists and forced them to seek refuge with the Pahari chiefs. Quite a few of them were drawn to the court of Ranjeet dev of Jammu. But his incompetent son Brijraj dev failed to maintain peace and was soon overwhelmed by the rising power of the Sikhs. The Jammu art which had its break in these vicissitudes of history, recovered its continuity when Ranjit Singh restored order and stability in his regime.

It was a great day for Jammu when Gulab Singh, with another turn of history, not only got back the kingdom of Jammu from the Sikhs but also succeeded in carving out the modern state of Jammu and Kashmir. The fame of the Jammu Durbar spread far and wide and quite a few talent was attreated by it. Gulab Singh's son, Ranbir Singh was a great patron of art and learning. His marriage to the princess of Guler (Kangra) provided another link with the then great seat of Pahari Paintings. Many adventurer artists of Kangra school, which was at that time at its zenith, found their way to Jammu. Nandlal, a Kangra artist, had come to Jammu in the same golden period. His two sons, Chananu and Ruidoo had also accompanied him. But the credit goes to Hari chand, son of Chananu, who rose to reknown and won the favour of Ranbir Singh. He always accompanied his patron.

Kangra-Kashmiri impact on indigenous talent.

Then arose the necessity of constructing a huge building, the present Ajaibghar, to house the pieces of art. It was meant to commemorate the visit of the then Prince of Wales. It was designed and completed in haste. A hoard of decorators and floral designers were brought from Kashmir. They were called Kamgars. Whole of floral work on walls and roof was done by them. After the completion of their work, they settled permanently in Jammu. They helped the local artists, who were simply figure workers, to paint pattern on their paintings. Floral designs in Jammu may also be attributed to the Kangra influence, brought by the artists from Kangra. Jani, Indru and Pangu—the masters of floral painting—represent the kangra and Kashmiri influence on the genius of Jammu. Faqir Mohd., a descendant of jani and an employee of the State, had, alas, to leave Jammu, in his old age, at the time of the partition in 1947.

Jagat Ram son of Shri Ram was initiated as a pupil to Hari chand. But the former soon became a contemporary of his master. Thus Kangra Kalam implanted in Jammu continued to flourish for a quarter of the twentieth century.

The End

Hari chand was a great artist. His genial attitude attracted a large number of puplis. However, none survived him except Jagat Ram, who became the sole torch bearer of the ancient but languishing art. He continued to serve Maharaja Partap Singh, son of Ranbir Singh and learnt miniature (on ivory) and tried his hand on oil technique. During that period, Raja Ram Singh, brother of the Maharaja, employed a Guler artist, Narotam by name. He got a palace built at Ramnagar with murals of Kangra Kalam over the walls. Two rooms and hall, that still stand, speak of the taste of the owner. Pity, the building has not been looked after carefully.

At the fag end of his life, Jagat Ram could not find anybody interested in his art or even in preserving the works of his life's labour. For by that time the last knell of Pahari art had been sounded. When the great artist breathed his last in 1922, be had no money, no name and no peace.

The tragedy of his life was parhaps his appropriate tribute to the art, of which he had the privilege to be the last exponent. For it, too, died as unmourned as the artist.

The four century old Pahari art came to an abrupt end at the hands of upheavel of values following technological and political changes. The cheap Bombay prints, photography, commercial art and movies soon made painting an obsolete medium of expression.

No tears were shed at the death of the art, certainly not by its inheritors. The inherited treasure was squandered in no time till its value was pointed out by foreign connoiseurs. Hectic efforts were then made to preserve whatever was left. Some purchases, made at the close of a fair, formed the nucleus of what has now grown into the Dogra Art Gallery.

CHAPTER 11

KASHMIR—EDEN OF THE EAST

By
S.N. Dhar

I

THE ROAD TO KASHMIR

Natural beauties of the Vale of Kashmir have deservedly won high and even extravagant praise from visitors, ever since ancient times. The sparkling streams, the happy murmuring of myriad brooks, limpidity of its sheety lakes, the sublime splendour of snow-covered sunny summits, the idyllic picturesqueness of mountain hamlets, the thick woods pleasantly laden with fragrance and ozone, gorgeous tints of fruit blossoms, of wild flowers and of the chinars, one and all, combine to make Kashmir a veritable dream of loveliness—a most delightful dream that affords one communion with nature. Very justifiably did the Moghul lover of Kashmir, Jahangir, call it "Paradise on earth!"

The climate of Kashmir is not only temperate but bracing and invigorating—rendering it a popular and loved haven from the oppressive heat of the plains in India. It was spoken of by Elphinstone as "delicious climate." The unique and attractive feature of the climate is a large amount of sunshine combined with a low temperature. The New Year finds the Valley mantled with a few inches of snow in the midst of sleet and storm. February continues to be snowy. By the middle of March spring sets in with its pleasantly surprising suddenness. Willow trees are tinged with green. Wild flowers bloom and adorn whole hill-sides. Daffodils venture a first splash of colour against the fresh sward. April showers do not ruffle the almond blossoms which decorate orchards in the outskirts of Srinagar. Other fruit blossoms follow. May is not very warm. The chinars, arrayed in their dense foliage, provide excellent camping sites. River and lake banks, flanked with graceful willows, magestic chinars and tall poplars, are lined with gay and colourful rows of roored house-boats. The golden oriole, the flycatcher, the bulbul and other beautiful birds of Kashmir, provide nature sweet symphony. June, July and August find the hill stations, margs upland meadows and mountain lakes thronged with campers, trekkers and other tourists. Swimmers occasionally visit the Dal and other Valley lakes for bathing. September, heralds the autumn and visitors flock back to Srinagar, where September and October are very pleasant. From October to Christmas Kashmir has fine but cold weather. Then the winter, grim and severe, full of thrills only to those interested in skiing, sets in.

So the visitor to Kashmir sees nature in all her moods, gentle and beautiful as well as stern and sublime. The gorgeous loveliness of beautiful spring, the mountain attractions of flowery summer, the variegated tints of sunny autumn and the stern grandeur of snowy winter, bewitch the newcomer to the valley. He may be an artist and he can use his brush at every turn. If he is a botanist or a florist, the margs and hill sides will keep him delightfully busy. Amateur and professional photographers shoot artistic scenes. In the Valley and its environs, the sportsmen find excellent game. Anglers make full use of their rods. Invalids regain lost health. Clubs, golf, etc. at Srinagar and Gulmarg retain the precious links of sophisticated visitors with civilization. Herdsmen and other nomadic tribes feed their flocks on the rich pasturage of the margs. The archaeologists study the many interesting and impressive ruins of Kashmir. The geologists continue their researches with valuable results.

So does the linguist, thanks to the many languages and dialects prevalent in the Valley and the bordering districts. Others just give themselves to rest and amusement like so many lotus eaters, benefitting by the pleasant climate and lovely surroundings.

Two fine motorable roads lead to Kashmir from the railway terminuses of Rawalpindi and Jammu Tawi, called Jhelum Valley Road and Banihal Cart Road, respectively.

Jhelum Valley Road, so called as it runs along the river Jhelum, is a wonderful triumph of modern engineering. It is remarkable for its curious zigzag bends, small tunnels and the picturesqueness of its surroundings. It enters State territory from Kohala. The bigger stages from Kohala onwards, which have post and telegraph offices and dak bungalows, are Domel ; Garhi, Chinari, Uri, Rampur and Baramulla.

The Abbaotabad Road, which runs via Muzaffarabad, meets Jhelum Valley Road at Domel—the customs and toll bar station of this route. Apart from Abbotabad, this road has post and telegraph offices and dak bungalows at Mansehra and Garhi Habib Ullah.

Banihall Cart Road runs throughout in the State territory. Formerly it used to be His Highness' private route. Udhampur, Kud, Batote, Ramban, Upper Munda, Qazi Gund and Khannabal are the bigger stages which have dak bungalows. The road crosses the Banihal Pass tunnel at an elevation of 9,500 feet from the sea level. On the side of the Valley the Pass commands a panoramic view of the Valley.

There is a mountain route to Kashmir which crosses the Pir Panchal range over a height of 11,000 feet from the sea level. For grandeur and magnificence of scenery, this route is matchless, but only sturdy climbers, who are prepared to rough it, may take this route. It is closed from mid October to beginning of May. Moghul Emperors, Afghans and Sikhs used this route. There are some interesting ruins to be found. There is also a route via Poonch, which meets Jhelum Valley Road at Uri.

The road to Kashmir, on either of the bigger routes, permits easy and pleasant journey. Not only motor cars but lorries too travel from Rawalpindi or Jammu to Srinagar, in one day, during summer. Exquisite picturesqueness of these routes leaves a lasting impression on the visitor about the Eden of the East.

II

WHAT TO SEE IN KASHMIR

1. Ganderbal. 13 miles from Srinagar. Height : 5,220 feet. A pretty, small village on the bank of the Sind Stream—a thronged mooring place for visitors' houseboats. Base for treks to Ladakh and Baltistan. Visitors' Bureau Branch—to give assistance and information to visitors.

2. Sonamarg. 51 miles from Srinagar. Height : 8,750 feet. Excellent camping sites on crescent swardy terraces. Grass meadows, margs, spangled with alpine flowers—a speciality. Starting place for treks to Gangabal, Haramoukh, Ladakh etc. Camping season : mid-June to mid-September. A tourist hut at Thajiwas. Stores and provisions insufficiently available on spot.

3. Gangabal. 41 miles from Srinagar. Height : 11,720 feet. One of the most beautiful and largest lakes at the foot of Mt. Haramoukh towering 5,000 feet above its level.

Destination of a Hindu pilgrimage in August. A fair weather path leads to it. Trekkers' favourite resort. Fishing in the lake is prohibited.

4. Gulmarg. 28 miles from Srinagar. Height : 8,700 feet., i.e. 3,000 feet above the valley level. Most accessible of all hill sta-

tions in Kashmir. Golf links, polo-ground, hotels, well furnished "huts", church, club : Europeanised special attractions. Centre of skiing and other winter sports. Season : June to September.

Big bazar, cinema, P. O., T. O., Dispensary, Banks, Provision stores, Visitors' Bureau open for the season etc. modern specialities available. Commands excellent views of the Nanga Parbat and of the Valley, in the opposite direction.

5. Pahalgam. 58 miles from Srinagar. Height : 7,000 ft. Popular camping site in the Liddar Valley at the confluence of the two streams, the Liddar and the Tanin. Camping season : July to September. Amenities available : P. O., T. O., Indian Club, Hotels, Church, Visitors' Bureau Branch, Provision stores and regular transport service.

An important stage in the all India Hindu Pilgrimage to the cave of Sri Amar Nath (12,729 ft.) during August. Base for treks to Chandanwari, Aru, Shishanag, Mt. Kolohai, the Tar Sar lake, etc.

6. Verinag. 50 miles from Srinagar. Height : 6,100 ft. Bluewater spring, 30 yards across, enclosed within octagonal stone paved walk—the source of the river Jhelum. Fishing prohibited. An excellent camping ground.

7. Achabal. 39 miles from Srinagar. Moghul garden with usual watercourse, cascade and fountains. Rest House with catering arrangements.

8. Kokarnag. 48 miles from Srinagar. Reputed for ice-cold and very digestive water that gushes out from a line of springs near the foot of a ridge of mountains.

Attractions. Trout fishing, camping ground, accommodation available for anglers and tourists and base for short trips and treks.

III

VALLEYS OF KASHMIR

"A Vale of purple glens and snow-cold streams,
Broad meadows lush with verdure, flower and fruit,
The broad-leafed maple towering in his pride,
The temple's noble ruin, on the height;
The poplar lines that mark the homestead there,
Calm lakes that bear the lotus on their breast."

—C.R. Tollemache.

The mountain barrier of Pir Panchal range, extending over 120 miles in three chief divisions, separates the Valley of Kashmir from the plains of Northern India. The range bears summits of great beauty which command magnificent views of the Valley, whose size is 84 miles long and 20 to 25 miles broad. The beautiful Valliy is indeed "an emerald of verdure enclosed n a radiant amphitheatre of virgin snow". The Jhelum intersects the Valley in the middle through green alluvial plain, studded with orchards, gardens, rice and other fields, intersected by streams and brooks. Though mountainous and full of plateaux, called Karewas, for the most part, the entire Valley gives the total effect of an immense oval amphitheatre, justifiably characterised as Sub-Alpine Region of asiatic Italy. Spring embellishes it with a riot of colour. The summer clothes hill and dale in green. The autumn finds it pleasantly sunny. The winter spreads a mantle of snow over its entire area. Actually there are many smaller valleys in Kashmir, opening out into the big Valley, formed by alluvial deposits around the Jhelum. The more prominent among them are : Liddar, Sind and Lolab.

The Liddar Valley is one of the finest valleys in the Himalayas though it is less picturesque than the Sind Valley. Yet it is noted for the flowery spring, cool summer and autumnal foliage. it is drained by the Liddar and a few smaller streams, which originate from large glaciers and have a lot of swardy margs on their banks. Many cataracts also cut through rocky ridges and pine forests and widen into the beautiful valley below Pahalgam and Eishmukam, the latter affording one of the most beautiful and spacious views of the Liddar Valley.

Two streams meet at Pahalgam, where the Valley bifurcates towards the mountains, the north-eastern part containing the route to Amar Nath and the north-western route leads towards Lidderwat and Kolohai. Pahalgam is the most popular hill station of the Liddar Valley. It is not so wet as Gulmarg or Sonamarg. A short hike takes the tourist to the margs of Baiserran and Khanmoo. An interesting ruin exists at Mamal. Pony rides in Pahalgam form a nice diversion. Evenings are delightfully spent in the Club, situated on the bank of the roaring Liddar stream.

Pahalgam is an excellent base, easily the best in Kashmir, for treks to the wilder scenery of Sona Sar, Tar Sar, Mar Sar, Shisha Nag and other mountain lakes and to Amar Nath Cave, Liddarwat, the Kolohai glaciers etc. From Pahalgam, trekkers can cross over to the small Tral Valley or the smaller Wardwan Valley from over the snow-bridge at Chandanwari.

The Sind Valley is the largest tributary of the Valley of Kashmir, being more than 60 miles long. The diversified scenery of its fertile fields, green pastures, luxuriant herbage, magnificent forests, and snow-capped peaks, constitutes its special attraction. Especially the Upper Part of the Valley, drained by the Sind river, flowing in a torrent, delights the visitor with "one of the finest and most magnificent pieces of scenery in the world". Through it runs the chief trade-route between Kashmir and Central Asia. At its head, Zoji La Pass leads the route to Ladakh, the popular rendezvous of sportsmen.

The starting-place for treks to this Valley is at Ganderbal, situated at the mouth of the Valley and 12 miles by road from Srinagar and also reached either through the Mar Canal and the Anchar Lake or over the Jhelum. From Ganderbal to Baltal, a staging place at the foot of Zoji La Pass, four marches are to be covered. The route posses through the pretty little village of Kangan and the glacier Valley of Sonamarg—the crowded summer camping station. Sonamarg has a bracing climate. It is closely fringed with forests and many crescent meadows lie in beautiful terraces, affording excellent camp sites.

Small glens of the Sind Valley lend themselves to fine photographic and other studies. The Gangabal Lake is reached from here being further off at a distance of 15 miles. Overhead hang the craggy peaks of Haramouk. The tourist is delighted with a close view of the glaciers and of the Matterhorn-like peak of Kolobai.

In fact an interesting though difficult trek can be had from the Sind or Liddar Valley to reach the other through Lidderwat. There are two routes which connect the two valleys. The company of a local guide is absolutely essential. The weather and the passes must be favourable.

At the lower end of the Sind Valley lies the small pretty lake, Manasbal, flanked by well-shaded terraces and noted for the crystal limpidity of its water as well as its lotus blossom during August. The Wular Lake fringes the Valley on the southern side. It is best to camp near the Lake in spring months of April and May. Storms from Haramouk, coming down the Sind Valley, usually sweep over the Lake in the afternoon. Behind the range of mountains that overlook the Wular Lake, there is the Lolab Valley, reputed for its "sylvan charms".

The Lolab Valley is a rich and picturesque expanse of level plain, attaining a length of 11 miles and breadth between 3 and 4 miles. Park-like sheets of meadows, dotted with dense clusters of walnut groves, afford excellent camping sites. The blossom of fruit trees in the orchards is worth seeing. Sportsmen put up in good forest rest-houses and go bear-hunting in the cedar forests nearby. This Valley is situated at a height of 3,000 feet above the Valley level and has, therefore, a very bracing climate.

The are actually many more smaller valleys in Kashmir, but they are not as easily accessible and as picturesque and broad as those mentioned above. Those described already provide the best camping sites and bases for trekkers and other visitors. They are, indeed, so many emeralds set in the pearls of snow-capped shinning peaks of Kashmir.

IV
SRINAGAR, THE VENICE OF THE EAST

"Srinagar owns a large population of sacred cows and bulls that wander vaguely through the streets", says Aldous Huxley in Jesting Pilate. It is an absolute lie, as there are no sacred cows and bulls in Srinagar at all. To remove such misrepresentations from the minds of intending visitors to the Golden Valley of Kashmir, this chapter is dispassionately written on Srinagar, "the City of Sri" the goddess of Fortune which is justifiably merited as the Asiatic Venice.

Srinagar is an ancient city. It has been the political and cultural centre of Kashmir for thirteen centuries and has thus reflected the chequered history of Kashmir. The magestic river of the Valley, the serpentine Jhelum, "born from Olympian heights and cradled in a valley of velvet", flows through it, spanned by seven bridges. It is flanked by two hills, Shankaracharya, bearing a magnificent temple and Hari Parbat, on which stands a fortress. Its population is two lakhs. Trade flourishes in Srinagar. Trade routes lead to Gilgit and ladakh, whose passes open out to Central Asia. Its height from the sea level is 5,192 ft.

To catch a riverside view of the city, with its picturesque balconies, busy ghats, mosques, temples and boats, the visitor goes down the river Jhelum, the central highway of the city, in a Shikara—the gay, swift gondola of the Venice of the East. He sees the Secretariat with its impressive river side facade, built on the site of the palace of the late maharaja. Reaching the heart of the city, he catches glimpses of Pathar Masjid, the stone mosque with the domed roof, built by Noor Jehan, the massive timber mosque in memory of the Muslim saint, Shah Hamdan, the tomb of Zain-ul-Abdin "Badshah", the Emperor, and river-side temples. He observes boats of all sizes and shapes on either side of the Jhelum.

The pointed nose of the Shikara touches the ghat near the third bridge, where the visitor can purchase art products of the city. The Hanji—Kashmiri boatman—sturdy, cheerful and greedy—beckons the Sahib to go up to do his shopping. The Sahib and his family find themselves confronted with shops with catching signboards such as "Sunshine Alley", "Simple, Simon", "Ganymede" and so on. He and his party enter picturesque show-rooms, displaying products of papier-mache, walnut wood-carving, delicate silver work, Kashmir furs, and exotic curios. They forget themselves in the gorgeous setting of the decoration of the show-rooms. Bargaining in the right, oriental style is interestingly carried on for hours. The Hanji groans at the Sahib's delay, but not much. The Sahib has to pay him on an hourly basis. So he complacently takes out his Kangri Kashmiri earthenware firepot and lights his Hookah. he guesses, rightly enough, how his Sahib is lost in fingering a shawl of gossamer fineness or in judging silver work of a gaudy vase and that his lady is excited over stone ornaments, selecting among those of a gate, blood-stone or jade. Perhaps they are watching the stone-cutter, the embroiderer or the papier mache craftsman at his work. After all the Sahib returns to the boat. The party is grotesquely loaded with presents, mementoes and miscellaneous bric-a-brac.

Presently the Sahib directs the hanji to row across to the Carpet Factory. Walking through narrow streets and dirty alleys, the party reach the Factory—wooden barracks, where weavers work sitting in front of hand looms, on which the rug is being made. The visitor is astonished at the sight of the leader-weaver, who quickly dictates, "Two yellow, five white, six blue, ten red, twelve yellow" and so on. The dictation is sonorously delivered, which relieves its monotony to some extent. The weavers, listening intently like so many stenographers, swiftly and skilfully ply the indicated colours.

The visitor is also interested to see the modest compositor in a quiet room, where he translates Persian, Kashmiri and other designs of carpets into directions for the leader-weaver.

Let me give you a glimpse of the well-known Silk Factory of Srinagar. You secure a pass and find yourself within the largest silk filature in India, which is producing a lot of parachute silk these days. Silk worms are bred in villages by peasants on mulberry leaves. Loaded with big bags containing silk cocoons, they come to Srinagar in lorries, cheerfully singing Kashmiri chorus songs. You attentively watch how silken cobwebs are extricated from the cocoons, how silk is carded, spun and woven. The visitor, who stays in Srinagar during delightful autumn, can see a working model of the Silk Factory in the State Exhibition.

The State Exhibition is one of the best autumn attractions of Srinagar, when the visitors come down to Srinagar from popular hill stations like Pahalgam, Gulmarg, Sonamarg, etc. All the famous arts and crafts of Kashmir are exhibited here in a beautiful setting of luxurious green turf and flowers and modern amusements and recreations. It has contributed largely towards the timely revival of arts and crafts of Kashmir, some of which, like shawl-making and Gubba-making, had almost entered a decadent phase. But the discerning eye of the lover of art deplores the fact that arts of Kashmir are getting much too commercialised. Cheap dyes are getting to be current in papier-mache work of an inferior type, whose demand is on an increase. Silver work is more gaudy than lasting. Only the connoisseur's expert eye can appraise good work.

Srinagar offers so many attractions to the visitor. The Museum, one furlong from Amira Kadal, 'the bridge of the nobility', the arched first bridge, is full of interesting specimens of Kashmir art and relics of art and history. In the heart of the city he can visit the recently excavated tomb of Sultan Ala-ud-din, Narpiristan, an archaeological edifice, and Jami Masjid, the greatest mosque of Kashmir. The Weir of the Jhelum below Safa Kadali, 'the last bridge,' attracts many anglers. The Mar and other canals are strongly reminiscent of Venice to the travelled visitor.

The famous Moghul gardens are situated at a couple of miles from Srinagar. The visitor takes a tonga or a bus from the terminus of the lake Boulevardes. Rows upon rows of house-boats, moored among soft, overhanging willows, greet his delighted eyes. Or, better still, he takes a Shikara and a group of Hanjis row it along at a thrilling speed, amdist stretches of lotus, past the so-called Golden and Silvern islands, under the 'camel-arched' bridges, connecting the road across the Dal lake, constructed by the Great Moghuls.

Srinagar is a very dense city. There are at least 30,000 houses in the area of the city proper which does not exceed six square miles. The city proper has been characterised as dirty by many visitors. Their sanitary sense is shocked at the sight of overpopulated slums in many quarters of the city where open, deep gutters run on either side of the alleys. The insanitary living habits of Kashmiris living in Srinagar contribute much to filthiness and disease which is rampant in the city. The sun never reaches many dingy, one-roomed tenements which shelter whole families. In the face of the ill- organised and sporadic efforts of the Municipality, no doctor can hazard a guess when

T.B. and other fell diseases will be extinct in Srinagar. one doctor, however, gave a characteristic reply to me. "I have a plan," he said, "a drastic plan, to exterminate T.B. from the city. A great fire of the city must be organised on the lines of Stalin's scorched earth policy."

Yet the whole of Srinagar is not like that. The civil lines around and beyond first bridge, on either side of the Jhelum, flanked by the Bunds, constitutes a very healthy area. Visitors seasonally hire bungalows or live in hotels or house-boats in this part of Srinagar.

Every visitor climbs the Shankaracharya, the pyramidal hill near the terminus of the Gagribal lake, to secure, the very best introduction to the landscape of Srinagar and its environs : the sheety lakes enclosed in a mountain amphitheatre, majestic and meandering Jhelum flowing through and past it, the distant mountain-ranges, containing the famous peaks of Nanga Parbat, Hara Moukh, Katwa etc., receding farther from the lush rice-fields.

Shankaracharya is about 1,000 ft. high. The climb takes about half an hour. It is capped by a fine, stone temple, of great archaeological and historical interest, built about 200 B. C. and believed to be the oldest temple of Kashmir. No mortar was used in the construction of its lofty plinth, the grand parapet and even the beautiful arch over the broad stone staircase of the temple. It is interesting that the peculiar curve of the winding Jhelum, as observed from the temple, has furnished the popular pattern for embroidery work on Kashmir shawls. In fact the vast gorgeous scene of the valley all around cannot be taken in at a glance. Bright pinnacles of temples and spires of mosques stand out amdist the hazy forest of houses in the city. You see the picturesque galleries and spires of the famous Makdum Sahib shrine, situated at a foot of rival hill, Hari Parbat and spacious almond orchards enclosed within the bastioned stone wall around the hill, built by Akbar. Beyond them, over the beautiful side of the Dal Lake, which roughly measures five miles by two, lie the far-famed, ingenious "floating gardens"—looking like so many carved pieces of green carpet partially covered by pendant willows and tall poplars.

One also snatches a fine view of Ghulab Bhawan, the Maharaja's palace, situated on the southern side of the Gangribal, revealing high aesthetic sense coupled with engineering skill, in the selection of the excellent site, the laying out of lawns and terrace and the grandeur of the huge structure of the Palace that commands a majectic view of the lakes and the distant snow-capped mountains. Beyond the Palace, you see the Peri Mahal, the deserted "Fairy Palace"—a picturesque pile of ruins which served as monastery to Jahangir's son's tutor, Mullah Shah. The Cantonment of Srinagar, one of the most beautiful hill cantonments of the world, presents a dignified look from the top of the hill.

Srinagar, the celebrated centre of the Himalayan Valley, has had glory and greatness in the past. It goes to the credit of the present regime, ably headed by Maharaja Hari Singh, that the historical city has been steadily reviving and adding to its charm, renown and importance.

V
TREKKING IN KASHMIR

The mountain-girt valley of Kashmir is a popular trekking resort of India. Its romantic, upland beauty spots, with the picturesque meadows spangled with wild, alpine flowers, crystalline streams, beautiful tarns, lovely mountain lakes and majestic snow capped peaks, offer abundant opportunities for trekking. Pre-eminent places for sightseeing and camping like the Moghul Gardens, Harwan, Achabal, Kekarnag, Verinag, Pahalgam, Ganderbal, Sonamarg and Gulmarg attract visitors by the thousand. Anglers enjoy their hobby at the trout streams near Sumbal, Gurais, Achabal, Kekarnag, Khrew etc. Big and small game hunters tour the length and breadth of the Valley and the outlying frontier districts of Ladakh, Kargil, Astereetes, which are reached through the picturesque route over Zoji-La pass. Treks are usually based at the camping grounds of Pahalgam, Sonamarg. Kekarnag, Achabal, Gulmarg, Harwan or start also straight from Srinagar.

CAMPING OUTFIT

Camper's kit includes tents, camp furniture-camp beds, easy chairs, small tables, bath tubs, basins and cooking sets, ropes, hiking sticks etc. Smaller tents save transport expenses and are easier to manage at high altitudes. Folding tables are usually preferred. Water proofs to cover the bedding and mackintoshes are indispensable. Sundries of toilet, clothing, bedding and other camping outfit should be minimised as much as possible to reduce trekking luggage.

To guard against extremes of temperature at high altitudes, both warm and thin clothing should be taken. Each member of the trekking party should carry a cotton quilt along with two or three warm blankets. Kashmiri puttoo hats, sold at Srinagar, Pahalgam and Gulmarg prove to be very serviceable. Boots should be well nailed.

All the needed kit is available at Srinagar at well-known agencies like Cockburn's Agency, Matthew's Agency, House Boat Owners' Association, etc., who entertain booking in advance Guide books, published by the Visitors' Bureau, and those written by Dr. Neva, Col. Kinloch, Col. Ward and others are available at many bookshops at Srinagar, and are useful to tourists.

PAHALGAM, SONAMARG AND GULMARG

Pahalgam, the famous hill station in the basin of the Liddar Valley, fifty-nine miles from Srinagar, is the popular camping ground of Indian and European tourists. From Pahalgam treks are based to the holy Amarnath Cave (17,300 ft. high), Chandanwari, Aru, the takes Shisha Nag and Tar Sar and Mount Kolohai, which is close on 18,000 feet in height. Indeed it is Mount Kolohai, the twinpeaked giant of Kashmir, which lures climbers to glacier-topped heights of the Liddar Valley. Seeing the slopy, shining, aweful glaciers, covering an entire mountainside and walking over snow bridges, that ford fierce streams, are delightful experiences.

Sonamarg, situated on a mountain plateau in the Sind Valley, is another beauty spot of the Valley and is a well-known base for treks to the Ganga Bal Lake, at the foot of glacier-surrounded Haramukh, whose craggy top rises to about 17,000 feet. An interesting variant is to trek to the Amarnath Cave or towards Kolohai from Sonamarg in mid-summer. Climbing up towards the Ganga Bal Lake, the so-called Ganges of Kashmir and the destination of annual pilgrimage by Kashmiri Hindus, you see the lakelets, Vishnu Sar and Gad Sar on your route. Vishnu Sar is about three quarters of a mile long and is fenced with awesome, precipitous mountains. Gad Sar sits smooth on an exquisite rocky basin. The Ganga Bal Lake, situated at a level of over 13,000 ft., has a beautiful, blue colour which changes into all shades of green. Redstars, wagtails, and Kashmir skylarks hover over it. Iey patches, broken off from avalanches, float over it, looking formidable under the low, cloudy sky.

Gulmarg is healthfully situated in the Pir Panchal Range at an elevation of 8,500 feet. It is a favourite centre of golf players as most of the grassy plateaux are natural golf links. In winter a well-known ski-ing club has its head-quarters here. From this marg trekking parties set out towards the Tos Maidan plateau, over 14,000 feet, which once formed the summer route from Kashmir to the Punjab and to Khelan and Ailpathar, mountain lake, overcast with clouds even in the middle of summer.

TREKS WITH MY STUDENTS

Last year, with a party of S. P. College students, I had a three-day's trek to Mount Mahadev, about 9,000 ft. high. We started from Harwan, the high water-reservoir, situated at a distance of 11 miles from Srinagar. As we carried most of our luggage ourselves and did the cooking ourselves, the trek cost us only about Rs.10 per head.

The green, meadow-covered top of Mahadev commands an excellent view of the Kashmir Valley which is spread out like a map : Srinagar with its suburban hills of Hari Parbat and Shankaracharya, the smooth, sheety lakes, the green fields dotting the banks of the serpentine Jhelum, the snow-capped mountains of Pir Panchal Range in the background. Upland hamlets by the meandering brooks afforded us camp sites amidst gorgeous scenery of the pine forests, where it is delightful to lie on fragrant carpets of pine-needles.

Another party of the college students was led by me to Ahrabal Waterfalls—the highest falls in Kashmir, falling from a maximum height of 60 feet. Shopian, at a distance of 35 miles from Srinagar, reached by bus, afforded us a very comfortable lodging in the Forest Rest House. The trek that took four days in all cost us only about Rs.15 per head, because again, we economised many of the expenses. Had the weather been better—it was late autumn—we should have trekked on to Konsar Nag, a mountain lake. All along the route from Shopian to Konsar Nag there are excellent Forest Rest Houses, Which can be easily booked in advance at Shopian or at Srinagar.

Initial and final journey expenses to Kashmir being excluded, trekking in Kashmir is cheap. The State Government has controlled the rates of most of the commodities needed by tourists. Indeed trekking in Kashmir is as cheap as it is thoroughly enjoyable.

(1945)

CHAPTER 12

SRINAGAR AND ITS ENVIRONS

By

Samsar Chand Koul

I

The Vale of Kashmir forms an ellipse within the inner mountains of the Himalayan Range, a jewel set in the heart of a rock. These mountains with snow-capped summits and pine-mantled slopes embosom glads and meadows—ideal sites for camping. The high mountain lakes, with turquoise blue waters fed by shimmering glaciers, hold up their mirrors to the azure sky within retreats of reposeful tranquillity, soothing to the fatigued body and mind, and elevating to the soul. The twitter of birds in a region where the deciduous belt meets the coniferous or round the glades is a rare delight. The fragrance from the opal-tinted flora on the torrent banks, or from the flowers peeping through the forest undergrowth, or be-gemming the meadows, is most exhilarating.

The valley runs from north-west to south-east and is about 84 miles long by 25 miles broad. On the east the mountain ranges rear their heads in Gwashibrari (17,779 ft.) and Nun Khun (24,400 ft.). On the north behind the ninth mountain range stands the colossal peak of Nanga Parbat (26,643 ft.) like a crystal cone against the azure-blue sky. On the west and south the Pantsal Range, with peaks rising to over 15,000 ft., separates the valleys from the Panjab. A large number of passes—gateways in the mountain walls—lie in these ranges. Of all the passes the

Zoji La, though comparatively low, is extremely dangerous during ewinter months, when it is a mass of impregnable battlements of snow, and in March when it is the playground of avalanches.

The valley was once the bed of a lake called Sati Sar. The alluvial plateaus (uḍars) are the accumulations of sediment in the lake. It was drained, so goes the mythological account, by Kahyap Reshi whom the gods assisted in killing the demon who haunted it. Only the lower mountain slopes were inhabited then. This alluvial plain is traversed by the Vetasta (Jhelum) which receives affluents right and left, issuing from the high lakes and glaciers.

Shri Ṇagar or, as it is commonly called, Srinagar, is the chief town of the country. 'Shri' means beauty or wealth of knowledge and 'nagar' a city. In ancient times this city was one of the chief seats of learning in Asia. There the students from other countries came to study Sanskrit. There is still a custom in vogue in the plains of Hindustan which requires a boy who is to be invested with the sacred thread, to walk seven steps towards Kashmir. The underlying idea is that the boy is sent to Kashmir to receive his education and returns after completing it. No person in India was in those days recognised as a scholar unless he had a certificate to that effect from the Kashmir University. Kashmir is still called Sharda Piṭ—the seat of learning.

The present site of the town was selected by the pious King Pravarasen II (A.D. 112-172). The old town existed where the present Badami Bagh cantonment stands. The busiest part of the town was the right bank which was also the market place. A bridge of boats connected it with the left bank. the good king is reputed to have flown away to Kailas (in Tibet) through a crack in the ceiling of a temple which had been located near the south-western corner of Hari Parbat where a Mohammedan

Ziarat stands now. He worshipped in the temple and his subjects saw him in the heavens shining like a star and vanishing like a meteor.

Srinagar is gracefully situated on both the banks of the Vetasta which is spanned here by nine bridges. The city is equidistant from Baramulla and Anant Nag (Islamabad) about 34 miles from each. It is more or less in the centre of the valley. Its eastern suburbs extend to the shore of the Dal Lake. It is expanding rapidly in all directions. It is almost equi-distant from Jammu, Rawalpindi, Leh and Gilgit, and is situated at the head of the passes leading into the Indian plains and Central Asia. Hence commercially and strategically it is very important.

Srinagar is encompassed with a large number of gardens which yield various kinds of fruit—almonds, cherries, apricots, plums, pears, apples, grapes and strawberries. They also produce vegetables like peas and beans. Cucumbers, melons and musk-melons are the produce of floating gardens. The Lar area, even now of repute for its grapes, could be turned into the Grape Garden of Kashmir and thus bring considerable wealth to the country. The number of vegetable gardens, too, is considerable, the chief vegetable being knoll kholl (hak).

Spring in Srinagar

About the time when the earth tilts to her position of vernal equinox, vernal breezes begin to vibrate and these are first felt by the kite and the sparrow. We hear mating screams of the former and observe the nuptial dance of the latter. The same vibration, I suppose, rouses an impulse in birds living in other climes which urges them to migrate to rear their young. The first to arrive about the last week of February is the starling, followed by the swallow and the hoopoe.

The oblique rays of the sun begin to assume the vertical position, the earth slowly absorbing the sun's heat gives birth to the pussy-willow, Gagea Kashmiriana, Sternbergia, daffodil and hyacinth, while mountain slopes are graced by the Viburnum, Colchicum luteum and Crown imperialis.

On the morning of their New Year's Day, which falls on the first day of the new moon when she and the sun are both in the Preisces (min), the fit thing which the Kashmiri pandit must see is a dish full of unhusked rice covered with new Viburnum flowers, new orris roots, curds, a bun, an inkpot and a pen, the new calendar, cooked rice, walnuts and a silver coin. Every member of the family takes a walnut and after bathing offers it to the river.

Late in March the almond gardens round the city are in full bloom. An ascent to the Hari Parbat Hill reveals an enchanting panorama to the spectator. The mountain ring round the valley, crested with silvery snow, gleams in the solar rays under the azure-blue sky. The light and deep pink almond flowers stretch for miles, interspersed with golden rape-seed fields. The placidness of the Dal Lake with turfed beach fringed with willow, bearing lemon-yellow catkins redolent with fragrance, presents an entrancing sight. The gardens round the fort are thronged with merry holiday-makers released from the grip of winter—musical parties swaying in ecstasy to the tune of the guitar, picnic groups with their steaming samavars, philosophical gatherings discussing the subtleties of the Supreme Soul, all squatting or lounging on velvety turf sprinkled over with white petals. The poor with affected contentment satisfy themselves by eating roasted water-chestnuts (Trapa bispinosa) mixed with pounded chillis, ginger and salt. The vernal breeze is believed to be at its best when a chinar leaf is of the size of a duck's foot. This is called Yusuf Shahi Hawa (probably after Yusuf Shah Tsak the epicurean king of Kashmir).

Summer

As the earth moves on to the position of summer solstice the vertical rays of the sun diffuse heat over the plain and we have sultry days. The heat occasionally becomes almost intolerable, but it is generally followed by showers of rain. Probably the reason is that the heat creates convectional currents in the valley, which rise high and creates a vaccum. The winds from the surrounding mountains, saturated with moisture, descend into the valleys and when they rise again they expand, their temperature decreases and they fall as rain.

The trees are clothed with dense foliage, especially the chinar (boiñ) which gives a cool, refreshing and animating shade. People hire doongas, especially on Sundays, and spend the day going round the willow-fringed banks of Telbal, turfed islets or roaming about the Moghul Gardens where the fountains play and form hundreds of rainbows; where flower beds of diverse colours meet the eye amidst the well-trimmed turf. Scenes like these cannot but enrapture the onlooker who probably leaning against the shady chinar feels transported to an ethereal world. The cooing of doves, warbling of thrushes, chirping of tits and carolling of orioles heard from numerous trees must aid the overpowering effect of what the wondering eyes behold.

On a festival day or during a fair, hundreds of boats are seen plying on the lake. Some of the passengers give vent to their feelings of joy through song, others play on musical instruments, while others again beat time with rhythmical gesticulations. Early in June the strawberry, cherry, apricot, and the cucumber appear temptingly in fruit shops; while melons, musk-melons, pears, plums and grapes do likewise in July and August. The main valley becomes considerably hot in summer months and visitors find shade and shelter in the side valleys and health resorts situated therein. A drive of a couple of hours would take one to a cool and refreshing atmosphere. Around willow groves and paddy fields the mosquitoes are a pest from late June to mid-August. They are bigger and their sting is more painful round the Wular Lake; but fortunately they are no of a malarial nature. The pomegranate is the last tree to bloom.

The ruby-red flowers in their setting of emerald-green leaves are a charming sight. The fruit when ripe has a cooling effect on the heart and liver. Some of the wild plants which clothe the waste spots round grave-yards and the fort are: Pegasus harmala (isband), iris (white and mauve).

On a summer afternoon the view from some vantage point in the Chashmai Shahi area is wondrously refreshing to the eye. The poplars, chinars and groves of trees in their dark-green liveries, the face of the lake with two islets like glittering eyes smiling in calm repose, fill the heart with a delight too deep for words, while the distant mountains often wearing crowns of silvery clouds, the tin roofs scintillating amidst the green foliage of surrounding trees like constellations, and flowers growing on buildings having birch-bark roofs, present an unforgettable scene. The three hills, Aha Teng on the north, Shankarachar (Takhet-i-Sulaiman) on the south, and Hari Parbat like a crouched lion in the middle, appear three distinct landmarks of the valley. The mountains round the valley become wrapped in haze and the snow begins to thaw leaving a snow-line at Harmoukh and two miniature claciers round Romesh Thong (Sunset Peak) and Tatakoti which can be discerned from Srinagar.

It is believed that the rainfall of the thirteen days of the summer solstice is not beneficial to vegetables. This time is called adör. According to Kashmiris the rainy season begins when the sun enters Cancer. In the past, immemorial custom required every young child to bathe in the river, put on a woollen garment on the naked body and eat cakes prepared from rice-flour and shaped like a coconut cut in half, with Amaranthus (lisa) and plum cooked together. This custom probably owed its origin to hygienic considerations.

Autumn

After the autumnal equinox the leaves of the trees begin to assume various shades of gay colours. Poplars change their leaves to saffron and those of the honeysuckle and peach are a mixture of red, yellow and brown. Willows get greenish-yellow and mulberry takes after his tall brother the poplar. The chinar, the celestial tree, appears in heavenly robes of red emitting as it were flames of fire. The near mountains look brown, but ravines which are filled with witch-hazel are a mine of gold. The Chinar Bagh and Nasim Bagh turn into colonies of white giants with myriads of flaming hands. The reflection of the mountain in the lake in front of the Nasim Bagh turns the water into wine which one drinks aridly through the eyes. The Shalamar and the Nishat flaunt their seasonal flower beds of zinnias and if the footpath along these beds be sprinkled over with red lime under the autumnal tints of chinars the resulting scene is unique.

Every kind of fruit and vegetable is fully ripe for the table. The delicious sappy Kashmir pears, pomegranates and apples are abundant. Swallows, young and old, assemble on electric wires in preparation for migration to warmer latitudes. The adult birds guide their young across the mountain chains, river valleys and seas to their haunts. The river becomes lovely to look at and pond weeds disappear. It is said that the rays from Canopus which appear about the last week of September at 6.0 a.m. on the southern horizon turn all vegetation yellow. It is never seen higher than Orion's belt from the horizon.

THE STARS OF AN OCTOBER DAWN IN KASHMIR

One of the mottoes of the C.M.S. school is:

> Two men looked out of prison bars,
> One saw the mud, the other stars.

What a delight it is to cast a look at the firmament for a minute and transport our thoughts from the turmoil, strife and wars of this planet to the calm immensity of the firmament.

I chose the dawn of October 20th because we can see at this time of the year a star named Canopus, brightest star in the Argo Navis constellation.

It is every year observed about the 29th September at 6.0 a.m., on the southern horizon. It never rises higher than the length of Orion's belt above the horizon, and after tracing a curve disappears behind the mountain. It lies exactly south of Sirius. If a line be drawn joining Betelgeuse and Saiph in the Orion constellation and then produced, it will pass not very far from Canopus which forms the south-western vertex of a rhomboid. It is known by the name of Aghasti Reshi and Suhul. It is said that Aghasti Reshi was the first Aryan migrant to the south (Deccan). There is a myth associated with this star. The Vindayas—the northern mountain range of the Deccan—were rising higher and higher. The gods became uneasy lest the mountain should cut across the sun's path in the sky. They held a meeting and decided to beseech Aghasti Reshi to go to the south. Vindhya was the disciple of Aghasti. If he would behave disrespectfully to his guru (teacher) he would be cursed. They went in a body to Aghasti and apprised him of their distress. Thereupon Aghasti consented and went to the south. When Vindhya Parbat saw his guru, he prostrated himself and fell at his feet. The guru put his right hand on his head and bade him stay in that posture till he returned. But he settled for ever in the south, and the gods rejoiced.

The peasants attribute the drooping of the yellow ears of the rice plant and the falling of the autumnal leaves to the rise of Canopus. In October in the eastern horizon rises Leo in the shape of a scythe and triangle. Near the handle of the scythe shines Regulus and at the apex of the triangle which points southward is Denebola.

At the north-eastern corner in the same month is the Great Bear with the tail touching the horizon. The trapezium of the Little Bear is behind the Lar mountain. On the western horizon

Fomalhaut and Pegasus set. About the 15th of this month at 6.0 a.m. Fomalhaut is on the western horizon and Canopus on the southern.

Some of the constellation towards the interior of the sky are Orion whose belt points north towards Aldeberan and south towards Sirius, Canis major, Canis minor, Aries, Triangulum and Cassiopeia.

About the middle of October the plateaus of Pampor turn into wonderful garden by the purple bloom of saffron (Crocus sativus) called Kong in Kashmiri. The bulb of this plant is believed to be the gift of a serpent-god (Takshak) who was cured of his eye disease by a physician. The stigma of this flower is used in worship and as a spice. It is also used in medicinal preparations. The expanse of this blossom at sunrise and at sunset is most delicious to see.

Winter

The earth now rotating on its axis and revolving round the sun on its orbit occupies the position of Winter Solstice when the Northern Hemisphere is turned away from the sun which brings in the cold weather in this region. Trees become devoid of leaves, mountains look brown, and the Pantsal Range receives the first instalment of snow. The winter migrants leave their summer haunts and appear here. The jungle crow, the Simla streaked laughing-thrush and the wall-creeper and many more of their kind are found around the valley. Almost all swamps and marshes round the valley are full of waterfowl which come down from northern regions where they have their breeding grounds. Some of these waterfowl are the black-winged stilt, the jack snipe, the cormorant, the white-eyed pochard, the peewit, the wood sandpiper, the red shank, the grey lag-goose, the brahmany duck, the mallard, the gadwall, the widgeon, the garganey, the teal, the pintail, the shoveller, the gooseander and the grebe.

We hear the flutter of their wings and their cries at dusk and dawn as they return to their diurnal haunts. The Anchar, the Wular and the Pampor swamps are worth a visit by a sportsman, provided he has a licence, and the reserved areas like Hakor Sar or Hayigam can be visited with the permission of the Controller of the State Rakhs.

The winter conditions in Kashmir are subject to variation. I remember a year when there was no snowfall, and we had sunny days throughout.

Generally the first snow falls during Christmastide. The first fall is an occasion of great merriment. One who receives unawares a sample of the first snow, given or sent to him by a friend or relation, is bound by custom to give a sumptuous feast. Fathers send delicious dishes to their newly-married daughters. It is said that the winters are not so severe now as they used to be. Sometimes it snows off and on for short intervals and the snow which thus gathers on the ground takes no time to thaw. Sometimes it may snow to a depth of two feet and the frost-bound snow may stand for months. According to a local tradition people lived in Kashmir in summer only, but vacated the valley at the advent of winter. An old man unable to walk decided to stay during the winter months. As the snow fell the place was visited by all sorts of nymphs, serphinis, cherubs and other celestial spirits. The old man besought them to let him know how his countrymen would be able to live here in winter. He was taken to Nila Nag their king, who gave him the Nilamath Puran and instructed him to observe all the rites and ceremonies mentioned in that book. When the spring came and the people returned they were surprised to find the man alive. He related to them the whole story. They acted upon his advice and settled in the valley regularly. Most of the food preparations used in these ceremonies—some of which are still observed—are appropriate to the cold weather.

Generally on or after Christmas we see lowering skies and mountains shrouded in clouds. A snowfall is generally preceded by a disturbance in the atmosphere and the Kashmiris, say 'sheen chhu taran (snow is being brought over). Next morning we see everything draped in white. The snow dust resting on the twigs and branches of trees presents a sight which baffles description. Equally indescribable is the scene when, during the day snow flakes fairly big fall from the dark-grey vault above, silence reigns supreme, occasionally broken by the laughing-thrush calling for snow in its note 'sheen-a-pe-pe' (oh snow! fall, fall). Sometimes a branch of tree may give way under the heavy fall, and create a dramatic scene. When it has snowed a good deal and the sun comes out, it is worth while to go for a walk to a hillock. The whole country appears draped in silver. The mountain ranges around with black and white patches look like a piebald dinosaur with the serrated mane of fir trees glimmering in sunlight. The flocks of red-billed choughs, softly cawing, the griffon vultures with extended wings and the black eagles soaring with their brethren the kites, make up an entrancing scene. The Kashmiris allot seventy days to winter, beginning from December 22nd. The first forty days, are called the chilakalan, the next twenty days the chila khorad, and the last ten days the chila bachi.

During this period the sun is absent for days together; the cold wind causes the moisture in the vapour-water to freeze and the cold is intense. This weather is called Kaṭh Kosh. Every drop of water freezes and icicles looking like aquamarine rods embellish the eaves of the roofs. On occasions the water-vapour in the breath freezes on the moustache.

It is said that during Col. Mian Singh's time, about 1833, the Vetasta froze so hard that the boatmen pounded rice on its frozen surface. The Dal Lake has frozen during more than one winter and I know of a time when the Rev. F.E. Lucey took a party of Mission schoolboys to Gagribal for skating. During

Christmastide a skiing party comes regularly to ski aṭ Khellan Marg at the foot of Apharwaṭ, four miles above Gulmarg, under the auspices of the Ski Club of India. They have here a coṣy hut built for the purpose. They visit the place in March, a second time.

Sparrows, tits, jackdaws, house crows, jungle crows, mynas, bulbuls swarm into the houses for food. The little green parakeets which have now taken up their winter quarters in the valleys are seen feeding on the berries of Melia azederick (Persian lilac).

The people heave a sigh of relief when the day called Bomsin Kah arrives. This day falls somewhere in the last week of February. It is said that on this day a cinder falls from the heavens, the idea being that a marked rise in the temperature begins to be felt from this day. Winter is now over and outing to the haunts of pleasure become the order of the day.

II

THE HARI PARBAT AND THE SHANKARACHAR HILLS

The Hari Parbat Hill occupies more or less a central position in the valley, exactly as the Mandalay Hill does in the Irrawaddy Valley. It consists of a type of basaltic rock favourable to the growth of almond trees. The whole of the hill—every stone and every dust particle of it—is sacred to the Hindus. On the southern side is situated the shrine of Maqdom Sahib and the mosque and monastery of Akhun Malla Shah the preceptor of Dara Shikoh, the eldest son of Shahi-Jahan the great Moghul ruler.

There is a myth associated with this hill. Two demons, Tsanḍ and Monḍ occupied the fair valley. Tsanḍ concealed himself in water near the present location of Hari Parbat and Monḍ somewhere above the present Dal Gate. They were a menace to the people of the valley which could not be inhabited owing to their dreaded presence. The gods spent a number of years in meditation and penance invoking the blessing of the Goddess Parvati who assumed the form of a Hor (myna) and flew to Summer from where she got a pebble in her beak and threw it on the demon Tsanḍ to crush him. The pebble grew into a mountain. But as he shook the mountain, she, with her lion and all the gods sat on him and crushed him to death. She is worshipped as Sharika in Shri Tsakra (an emblem of cosmic energy pervading the universe) occupying the middle part of the western slope of the hill facing the city of Prawarsen (Srinagar). The hill is also called Predemna Peeṭ or Kohi Maran.

Ashaḍa Naumi, which falls somewhere in June or July, is a great festival associated with the shrine which is invariably visited by devout Hindus on this day. The outer wall was built by Akbar the Great in A.D. 1590 at a cost of one crore and ten lakhs of rupees. This sum was sent from the Royal Treasury, and along with it also came Indian artisans skilled in masonry work. The inscription in Persian at the Kaṭhi Darwaza commemorating this work can be read even today. He intended to lay the foundation of a new capital inside the fort ad call it Nagar Nagor. The ruins of certain terraces can still be seen on the Pokhiri Bal side.

The fort at the top of the hill was built by Azim Khan, the Pathan governor. It is now an arsenal and permission to visit it has to be obtained from the Director of tourism. The view of the Dal lake and part of the valley from the fort is most charming. Just near the southern side of the outer wall there is a Guru Dwara which commemorates the visit of Guru Hargobind Singh.

SHANKARACHAR OR TAKHET-I-SULAIMAN

Shankarachar is a detached ridge of igneous rock to the south-east of Srinagar, separated from the Shalamar Range by the Aita Gaj Gap. The summit of the hills is crowned with a picturesque edifice. This hill was called Jeṭha Larak and afterwards it was named Gopadari Hill. Some are of opinion that the temple at the top was originally built by King Sandiman (2629-2564 B.C.). There were 300 golden and silver images in it. About 1368 B.C. King Gopadittya founder of Gopkar repaired it and bestowed to the Brahmans of Arya Varta, agrahars which he built on its top. King Sandimati (34 B.C.-A.D. 13) improved and added to the temple. Zain-Ul-Abdin repaired its roof which had tumbled down by an earthquake. Sheikh Ghulam Mohi-Ud-Din, a Sikh Governor (1841-46) also repaired its dome. Recently, the dome was repaired by Swami Shivratnanand Saraswati at the request of a Nepali Sadhu who gave him financial aid.

The present name owes its origin to the great philosopher Shankaracharya who visited the valley about ten centuries ago, and lodged at the top of this hill, where it appears there were small sheds of Brahmanas who looked after the temple. There is a small tank built of slabs of stone just behind the temple. In those days the Archarya or the Chief Preceptor or, in modern parlance, the Chancellor of the University of Srinagar was Swami Abĩnaugupth. A discussion took place between the two sages and according to the local tradition Abinaugupth initiated Shankaracharya into the Shakti cult.

A climb to the hill from the Mission Hospital (now Government Hospital for chest diseases) will take about 40 min. The path is a pony-track. The descent towards the Gagribal spur is gentle. En route is the tomb of Mian Dullo who is said to have squandered away all the money which his father had given him to trade with. He was enamoured of the charms of the Dal Lake which he selected as his favourite haunt for the gratification of his epicurean appetites.

The panoramic view of the valley in early April when the snow is deep on the mountains, or after rains on a summer day from the summit of the hill is one of the best that could ever be witnessed. The mountain ranges on the south, west and north rise one above the other and the peaks, varying in height from 13,000- 15,500 ft., jut out like the teeth of a saw cutting through the sky. On the south lies the Banahal Pass (9,250 ft.) the chief highway to Jummu, and a number of other passes and depressions. Tthe Brahma Shakri peaks, a group of grand cones viewed even from Lahore, the Aliabad Pass (11,440 ft.) leading to Gujrat, the Romesh Thong (Sunset) Peak, Tata Koti (15,540 ft.) guard the Chhoti Gali Pass (14,450 ft.), the highest in the range come one after another. We now turn our eyes to the west where lies the vast plateau of Tosa Maidan, the paradise of sheep, and where the eye meets the depression of Ferozpor leading into Punch (prunts) and Apharwaṭ (13,542 ft.) giving shelter to Gulmarg and affording thrilling sport for the votaries of ski-ing in India.

Beyond the Baramula Pass, towards the north-west, the range is continued in Kaj Nag and Khagan mountain. In between the Tragbal (9,500 ft.) and Zoji La (10,500 ft.) appears the beautiful candy cone of Harmoukh (16,842 ft.) in the north, while the eastern range culminating in Mahadiv (13,013 ft.) and Western peaks completes the enchanting circle.

At the foot of these mountains lie the alluvial plateaus with rich yellow soil yielding maize and rice where water is available. The swamps, marshes and lakes of the valleys stretch as far as the Wular Lake in the extreme north of the valley. The Baramula road bordered with poplars, the sinuous course of the Vetasta (Jhelum), cutting a clean almond called Shivapor Phur, the green house-tops now disappearing with the introduction of galvanised iron sheets for roofs, the minarets of churches and mosques and the shining surface of the temples present a picturesque sight.

Turning now to the Dal Lake we see the Moghul gardens of Nasim, Shalamar and Nishat densely shaded by the deep green foliage of Boiñ (Chinar) trees, the floating gardens and the houses situated on the islands in the lake encompassed by poplars, willows and quince trees. The two expanses of deep blue water separated by the causeway like two great eyes, each with its pupil of an island. The eastern shore is embellished by the magnificent Royal Palace with their crystal sheen, by newly-laid gardens and the boulevard skirting it. A part of the palace has been converted into a hotel with a superb view.

The Government has made the hill a resort and it is hoped that it will one day be clothed with dense herbage and trees providing charming bowers for lovers. A number of paths has been marked out and platforms with suitable seats have been made for visitors. In fact, every effort is made to attract people to the hill.

In olden days a great festival used to be held by the Hindus on the 10th day of the lunar fortnight of Baisak which corresponds to March. Just above the Dal Gate they would come in doongas to bathe. This was called Monḍa daham, probably in memory of the killing of the demon Monḍ by the goddess Sharika. But this festival has now been entirely forgotten as if nothing like it ever existed.

III

THE DAL LAKE

The Dal Lake is one of the chief ornaments of the Kashmir valley. It is situated to the east of Srinagar. (The word 'dal' signifies an expanse of water.) It is 4 miles long and 2½ miles broad and covers an area of about 10 square miles. The western portion is dotted with islets called demb and numerous waterways running inland. The chief canal is called Mar after the high mountain lake Mar Sar which drains the Dachigam Rakh after feeding the Harwan Reservoir and empties itself into the lake towards the north. The islets are covered with willow trees which are of both indigenous and foreign varieties. The former having small lanceolate leaves are distinguished from the larger leaves of the latter. The twigs of the former have a bitter taste and are used as tooth brushes. The immersion of the feet in water in which the leaves of this tree have been soaked for some time results in a soothing effect to the head and eyes. If the water is well strained and pure it is used in some cases for anemia. The twigs divested of bark and pounded into a fine powder and mixed with curds form an effective balm for burns. The wood is highly prized, being used for the manufacture of blades for cricket bats.

The English willow has been introduced and thrives on these islets. It provides an excellent material for basket-making which has grown into an important industry.

Where the land has been cleared of trees, all kinds of vegetables are grown—potatoes, tomatoes, pumpkins, gourds, turnips, radishes and many exotic varieties. The chief manure for these fields is ashes, the silt of shallow canals, and pondweeds, such as Polygonum, water milfoil, Naais major. (The weeds are twisted with a punting pole thrust into water, rooted out and piled in a boat. They are left to rot till they ferment and then are applied to melons, tomatoes, gourds, onions and garlic). Potentilla reptens, Euphorbia and nettle also grow profusely. Here and there cosy huts stand on these islands. The surroundings of the huts are generally insanitary. The aesthetic sense of appreciating beauty is not yet developed. The planting of creepers and rose bushes round these hamlets would improve their look considerably.

The Dal Lake is divided into three parts by two causeways, one of these starts from Nayid Yar Bridge and is about four miles long. This was constructed by a grocer named Mahesh Chowdhery, who miraculously came into possession of a mass of gold. Under the guidance of a nymph, who appeared to him in the form of a serpent, the course of the dam which terminates at Ishibör village was indicated. Should the other course be taken, it leads to Nasīm Bagh and Nigin. The portion towards the east is called Lokut Dal, while the portion in front of Nasīm is called Boḍ Dal. Lately the eastern causeway has been extended from the Nishat side to enable the Government to take the water pipe line through this dam to the city. It is said that the contractors experienced great difficulty in filling up a spring near the Nishat Bridge.

On the south-western corner is an inlet called Sodura Khon which is the deepest part of the lake. ('Sodur' means a sea, and 'khon' a gulf). It is more than 40 feet deep and undoubtedly a spring. It is also said that in olden times there existed two springs near Sodurabal to which people from the city of Baṭapora used to come for pilgrimage when the city was peopled by the Brahmans. The place was called Sodura after the spring which lies at the foot of Bhutsher.

The shores of the gulf are frequented by visitors in house boats. Huge chinars, willows and tall poplars fringe the shore. Apricot and cherry, almond and pear, quince and apple trees decorate the gardens. What a delight it is to keep open the window of a house-boat on a May-dawn, and keep one's ears open to the celestial musical vibrations from a chinar tree under which the boat is moored! If a paradise flycatcher happens to nest here, it is the first feathered friend to break the silence of the dawn. It will be followed by the Tickell's thrush with its incessant melody and next by the golden oriole with its liquid note. Simultaneously the ring-dove will be heard stringing its harp and cooing the crescendo and the dove in repartee filling the morning breeze with melody and concord. As the day advances the other birds join in with their quota till the concert is in full swing. Who that listens to the celestial music would not sing and dance and lose himself in ecstasy! As daylight deepens the chorus begins to subside, but the doves and hoopoes carry on in some shady nook till the Great Orb shows his lustrous face.

Here one comes across bathing boats with catering arrangements. The boats are properly decorated with shoots and arrangements for diving from various heights. The holiday makers swim and dive and make merry in the water. The swimmer stands on a plank which is towed by a motor-launch and holds a rope in his or her hand in an erect position. Very few finish circling round the bathing boat at full speed in an erect posture. This we may call a kind of surf-riding.

There are some fine buildings in the Nigin Bagh which house hotels and a branch of the Srinagar Club. So the visitor does not feel the want of the essential amenities of civilised life. There is also a regular bazar on the road, supplying almost all the needs of the visitors. The wheat and barley fields begemmed with scarlet red Papaver naudecaule present an enchanting spectacle in spring, while the Convulvolus arvensis embraces the tall weeds tightly.

Hazrat Bal ('hazrat' = majesty; 'bal' = place) has grown into a village owing to its being the sanctified repository of the Prophet Mahmad's hair which was brought to Kashmir from Medina in Arabia by Sayid Abdulla in 1111 A.H. The ziarit is beautifully situated on the lake and a good number of chinars stand in its compound which is paved with stones. There is a colony of night herons on these chinars. The carvings on the walls and the latticed windows of the mosque are specimens of exquisite art. This is one of the most sacred spots for the Mussalmans who visit the place from all parts of the valley. Friday is the chief day in a week for congregations to assemble. There are four fairs held annually when the faithful gather in their thousands. It is a great sight to seen hundreds offering their prayers to God facing towards the west. Hundreds of boats are to be seen moored along the beach. Villagers bring here the produce of their fields for sale on these occasions.

Not far from Hazrat Bal is the Garden of Morning Breeze—the Nasīm Bagh. The Great Moghul, Akbar, conquered Kashmir in 1588. This garden was laid by him, and about 1,200 chinars planted in it. So some chinars are 360 years old. There is now a chinar nursery in the garden planted to provide saplings to replace the dead chinars. There is also a small rill passing through the middle of the garden. Also there is a spring of good water in the east of the garden not far from the shore. The remains of some old buildings can be seen on the same side. It is a holiday home for soldiers.

This garden makes an excellent camping ground. It commands an attractive view. In the foreground is a spacious sheet of water surrounding the golden island—Sona Lank, which is like a piece of emerald embossed in aquamarine.

The beautiful peak Mahadiv (13,013 ft.) and the steep slopes of the Shalamar Range are lovely to behold. On the west the Hari Parbat Hill and the Pantsal Range present a more impressive spectacle. The surrounding fields and luscious gardens breathe health and vigour. The cook shake of the chinar resonant with the music of sweet songsters at dawn in May and June transport the visitor to Elysium. In autumn when the chinar turns red and the glowing tints of the setting sun are reflected in the lake, the whole sheet of water is turned into a ruby mine.

One can have quite a number of delightful excursions from this garden.

(a) A Cruise in a Shikara to the Tel-Bal Nala

The water of this nala is drawn from the thawed snows of the Mahadiv and also from the surplus water of the Reservoir.

This stream abounds in fish which is much liked as food. The banks are lined with willows and blue and pied kingfishers find plenty of food in these waters. While going up the stream one comes across a lovely village and from a vantage point a clear view of the valley can be had. In July and August mosquitoes are a pest here.

(b) A Visit to Shalamar Garden

This garden lies to the north-east of the Dal Lake and is a favourite haunt of holiday-makers. The word Shalamar comes from 'shala', a mountain and 'mar', beautiful. It is said that the Saint Nur-ud-din, also called Nunda Reshi, when invited to visit that part of the city refused, saying, 'If I visit this place now, I shall not be allowed to visit Paradise hereafter'. The garden was laid out by Jahangir in 1619. It is beautifully kept and the turf is fairly deep. The seasonal flowers are carefully sown and beds are in perfect order. The fountains playing round the pavillion, shone upon by the sun's rays passing through the chinar leaves, display myriads of rainbow colours. The close proximity of the hills as the background of the garden presents a picturesque contrast to the boldly exposed lay-out of Nishat. After sunset the electric lamps shining in the niches behind the cascades are marvellous.

(c) A Visit to Harvan

Harvan is the corrupt form of Shadirhadvana which means 'grove of six saints'. This place is three miles from Shalamar. Here is an artificial lake in which the water from the Mar Sar Lake is stored. This is the source of the water supply to the city. The reflection in the lake of the dense forest slopes of nearby mountains and the verdant reserved Dachigam defile is a thrilling sight. Formerly the pilgrims to Mahadiv climbed through Dachigam but now they go from Dwara. The excavations of Harvan just above the road are of great historical and artistic interest and hence worth a visit. They have been carried out under the direction of Pt. R.C. Kak and are probably the first of their kind in the world. They belong to A.D. 300 when Kashmir was included in the Kushan Empire and Buddhism prevailed in the country. The fourth Council was held about this time under Kanishka. This was the monastery where the great scholar Nagarjuna lived. It contained a stupa, some chapels and other buildings. The construction work is of three kinds: (1) Rubble, (2) Diaper-rubble, (3) Tile. A vivid account of these excavations is given in the Ancient Monuments of Kashmir pages 105-111.

Just under the shadow of the excavation is the Trout Hatchery. Trout-culture was introduced in Kashmir by Mr. Mitchell in 1900. It was through the hard work and steadfast mind of Pt. Sodama that this fish thrived here. The ova were sent from here to other parts of India such as Kulu, Kangra, Naini Tal and Shillong. Trout fishing is one of the favourite pastimes of visitors to the valley now.

The Dachigam Valley, more commonly known as Döch Gam Rakh or Game Reserve is one of the most charming dales of Kashmir. Its rich variety of flora and fauna, its luxuriant mountain slopes, the wild animals such as the panther, the bear and the deer which haunt its depths, its myriads of songsters make it a rare beauty spot even in Kashmir. A silvery stream emptying the Mar Sar drains this emerald green vale. This lovely spot, which by the way kisses the foot of Mahadiv (13,013 ft.) was deservedly the favourite abode of the Gupth Family, the expounders of Shaivism in Kashmir. There is still a spot in the valley which is called Vasupor, undoutedly the village of Vasuguptha. A little higher up the valley there is a huge rock called Shankar Pal (Shankar's rock). It is said that a Shiva treatise has been transcribed from inscription on a portion of the rock, which is now embedded in the earth. This seems to have been the spot where Shankar Guptha meditated. To this saint's miraculous power is attributed the existence of Gupth Ganga, the famous spring to the north of Nishat Bagh. Now there is a fish pond under this rock. Nagaberan is a meadow situated behind the valley.

About 400 yards to the N.E. of the reservoir under a huge chinar tree is a small spring called Sharadbal. This is dedicated to Sharda, the goddess of learning. The water of this spring is excellent for indigestion.

Nishat Bagh is an excellent pleasance where an afternoon with lunch and tea can be spent with great pleasure. This garden was laid out in 1632 by Asaf Khan, the brother of Nur Jahan, the Queen of Jahangir. It is beautifully terraced and the delicious smell of lilac and the flower beds lying on either side of the two path-ways which run through the garden are most exhilarating. The majestic chinars with their cool shade, the playing of fountains and cooing of doves sent a thrill through every fibre. The view of the Dal Lake is superb. This garden lacks the subdued tone, the deep lawns and the bold background of Shalamar.

The eastern shore of the Dal Lake is full of springs. the Hindus attach some sanctity to almost all these springs and hence in olden days a large number of temples was built and gardens laid out round about them by the kings, their queens and their ministers. The most important of these springs is Gupta Ganga, situated in Ishibör village. Ishibör is the corrupt form of Shri Ishan Bror. Shri Ishan was the spiritual tutor of King Sandimati (34 B.C.-A.D. 13), and 'Bror' is probably drived from 'bairau'—a god. It was here that King Sandimati built a temple in honour of his guru, Shri Ishan, and laid out gardens. Later on his example was followed by Baḍ Shah (A.D. 1420-1470). The spring is sacred to the Hindus who come here to bathe on Baisaki or New Year's Day. It is also visited on Shri Krishna's birthday. There is a peak called Sörshwari just above the spring which some of the pilgrims climb to gain merit.

Gopi Tirth is small spring with clean water just behind the Nishat Bagh. There are two springs just near the road. One of these, called Shri Tsakör, has well-built sides which are covered with maiden-hair ferns. The other, Matsö Bawn, is a miniature representation of the Martand Spring and here people go to remember their dead.

> 'In the village of Thed there is to be seen the junction of seven springs. There are many buildings of stone'.
>
> Ain-i-Akbari.

The Chashma-i-Shahi or the Royal Spring is a bubbling fount of cold, crystal clear water which the visitor in summer would much like to drink. This garden was founded by Ali Mardan Khan, a Moghul Governor in 1632. It is said that in a vision, during one night there, Shiva appeared to him. He composed a poem beginning with the verse :

> 'Huma asle Mahishwar bood, Shab Shahe ki man didam'.
> (He was the real Great God, the king whom I saw during the night.)

It is beautifully preserved and a small garden maintained by the Government is attached to it. The garden has lately been extended. The view from here is one of the most charming and is aptly described in the words of Pt. R.C. Kak : 'In spring, when the fields of the blossoming rape-seed flank the verdant hill slopes with gold; when the snow-capped mountains are being ceaselessly washed by melting snows and frequent showers; when in sunny intervals masses of downy clouds are seen floating majestically in the translucent azure of the sky, their shadow trailing after them as if caught by the sharp mountain peaks; when the lake is free from weeds and reeds—beardless, as the Kashmiri call it; and the two small islets, Rupa Lank and Sona Lank, are like emeralds set in the sapphire shield of the Dal; when vast patches of the slopes of the Chashma-i-Shahi Hill and the Hari Parbat are covered with red and white almond blossom—the fortunate spectator stands entranced as he gazes out of the arch of the baradhari and his feelings are lulled by the gentle murmur of the little fountain that plays in the centre of the hall'.

Just to the left of Chashma-i-Shahi high up in the Bren Nallah, there is the shrine of Baba Ghulum Din, the brother of Sheikh Nur-ud-Din. In early spring the whole place is covered with Colchicum lutem, Crown imperialis and Virburnum nervosum. Here too we see a spring but it is not kept clean. In the rills grow water-cress (Nasturtium officinale) naga babör which is a valuable article of food.

In the same level with Chashma-i-Shahi and to the right of it is the delightful pellucid spring called Chashma-i-Shahibi. In the opinion of some people its water is preferable to that of Chashma-i-Shahi. It lies amid a grove of chinars, mulberry and cherry trees. The wild rose bushes, hyacinth and narcissus are in profusion. Formerly it was looked after by a sadhu who lived there. In summer the pandits of Srinagar spend their week-ends here. It is a pity the spot has been so neglected. With care and attention it will become one of the best health resorts in Kashmir. The view of the lake is most fascinating from here.

Pari Mahal (the Palace of Fairies) or Kuntlun, is a set of ruined terraces on one of the spurs of Zabarwon Hill. These were built by the eldest son of Shah-i-Jahan, Dara Shikoh, the philosopher prince. Here he had philosophic discussions—and what a spot for such exercises—with his tutor, Akhun Malla Shah. It is interesting to examine the structure of the building. It had been founded on the ruins of a Buddhist monastery.

There is another spring in the ravine of Zabarwon. It is dedicated tot he Goddess Zishṭa and is sacred to the Hindus.

People come here for pilgrimage on every Thursday in the month of Zeth (May-June). This furnishes a good outing for the women-folk of Srinagar. Near the spring there is a big chinar and round about it are groves of fruit trees, poplars and willows. A man lives there permanently to look after the spring. Some years back, I remember having seen a rock which had Shiv-lingams carved on it on five sides, partially covered with red lead and a rose bush growing from a crevice in the top. It was enclosed in a baked brick wall in an almond garden. It was called Zeshṭa-Pal.

A spring lies to the north of Ziṭhair in the adjoining wood. This wood is an excellent spot for the study of birds. The whole Gupkar slope is now beautifully turfed and the royal palaces command a charming view of the Dal. The white royal mansions amid the green vegetation appear like a crystal vein in an emerald mine. On a summer day the reflection of the electric lamps of the palace in the lake is a marvellous sight.

There is a ziarat to the Shias on the foot of the eastern slope of Shankarachar under a cluster of stunted pines.

A park has been newly laid out on the eastern slope of the hill. It contains lovely bowers and groves of trees where visitors can enjoy their evening walk. The whole of the Gagribal spur is well covered with rose-bushes, thyme and in early May the whole place is dyed wit pink and replete with fragrance. White iris blends with pink to give another shade of colour.

Just on the opposite side of this spur another island park called Nehru Park has been laid out. It contains a tank where non-swimmers learn how to swim and children bathe. There is also a shed where racing boats of Government schools and colleges are kept. The second storey of this boat-shed is a restaurant where people enjoy delicious dishes amidst the delightful natural surroundings. The park and the opposite

Gagribal spur are artistically decorated with electric bulbs which view with the constellation of the firmament after sunset. The reflection of these lamps in water adds to the charm of the place. In summer the place is thronged with people from the city and visitors. It is a source of income to shikari wala. Occasionally a show is arranged. A fleet of small country-boats demba wari bedecked with lighted candles on the sides and inside the boats, are collected. They move in order. The trees towards the Kotar Khana and opposite it are laden with electric bulbs when thus the whole flotilla moves towards the palace, it shines like a Galaxy. This formation of illumination is called Kongwari (Saffron beds).

A road lined with houses and hotels runs now from the Dal Gate round the lake. It has been built to enable tourists and citizens to have walks along the shore of the Lake and enjoy its superb view.

IV

A CRUISE ON THE DAL LAKE

The water of the Dal Lake is discharged through the Dal Gate into the Tsunṭ Kol (apple stream). The old gate, now known as Pron Khan, was near the temple which stands lower down on this stream. An attractive view of Mahadiv and Kotwal peaks presents itself from the gate where shikaras with spring cushions, clean and beautiful seats are ready to convey the visitor round the lake. There are two canals from the Dal Gate leading on to the lake. The broad canal on the right leads straight on to the southern part of the lake, while the left one winds its way to the busy part of the lake where one can study the life and occupation of the people. We shall take this route.

The boat is propelled by three or four paddlers at a good speed between rows of willows and poplars and amid islets and picturesque buildings. The surface of the water is covered with water milfoil, water-fern and duck-weed. We reach the stately temple which marks the boundary of Rainawari, a suburb of Srinagar. Half a mile from the ghat is the C.M.S. Hospital. The produce of the lake is conveyed to the market in swift small shikaras. At a short distance from the temple thee is a beautiful bridge with an artistic arch under which the boat passes. Set in a pier of this bridge is a stone with an inscription giving the name and date of the builder. It is from this bridge that the causeway across the lake starts. Beyond on the left is seen the Fort and a building which contains the Mourning Hall for Shias. A little further on are three erect stone slabs—two on either side of the canal and the third is in a swamp concealed among the willows. Probably, they used to be the water-gauges in former days, but now they are believed to be petrified human bodies. The one on the right with a pointed top is the banker who charged 36 per cent interest and paid annas fifteen and three pies for every silver rupee (annas sixteen). The other on the left with a flat top is the mat-seller, who had a measuring rod six inches less than the right length and sold mats by this rod. The third concealed among the willows with girded loins and several vessels on his shoulders, is the milk man who mixed water with the milk and sold the adulterated stuff as pure milk. The gods were wrath with these men for their evil deeds, and cursed them and turned them into stones, and they stand thus to this day.

The boat speeding through islets teeming with gourds, pumpkins, brinjals and various vegetables, reaches a point where a magnificent chinar stands on an island with a solitary house which commands a grand view. On the opposite side is an island called Baṭa Mazar, rearing Lombardy poplars on its bosom.

Here the waterway splits into three branches. The one on the right goes to Nishat Bagh, the left one spanned by the Ashai Bagh Bridge to Nigin (Jewel) Bagh and the middle one to

Shalamar. All floating gardens are concentrated in Dal Koṭwal. Punting poles are driven into some of them to keep them steady. These poles afford vantage points for kingfishers and shrikes to pounce upon their prey.

What is a floating garden ?

A long strip of land about twenty yards by one yard is cut off from the side a swamp containing the matted roots of bulrush bed, which is cut off from underneath, allowing a thickness of about two feet and a half, and the whole mass floats up. The floating mass is anchored to a boat and punted to a secure position. In course of time weeds and mud settle down on it and lo ! we have a floating garden. Sometimes it happens that a farmer steals away a garden of his neighbour. The Kashmiri name for a floating garden is rad. These gardens yield tomatoes, cucumbers, musk and other kinds of melons. The manure used is the rotting pond-weeds in coils.

In late July the blossom of the lotus (Nelumbium speciosum)—pomposh—presents a most charming sight. The flower and the cup-like leaf are about a yard above the surface of the water. The fruit is eaten and the roots (nadru) form the chief vegetable used by the townspeople during the winter months. The root-knots pounded and fried in oil are supposed to cure diarrhoea in children. The best lotus blossom can be seen in the southern portion of the Anchar Lake called Khushal Sar.

The bulrushes which grow in the swamps afford a safe shelter to reed-warblers, bitterns, moorhens and dabchicks. The interior of the green stem, called petsi-laḍur, and the pollen above the pappus, called dal masalah, are eaten. The pappurs mixed with fine earth makes an excellent plaster called kalaron. In autumn the plant is mown down and used for mats.

A fragrant white lily (Nymphaea stellata) bomposh, which has great medicinal qualities, is found among the bulrushes. It is used in various forms of concoction with other herbs. The stamin mixed with sugar is said to be good for the blood. The long stem dried an stewed with dried fish is used as a table delicacy. Its fruit kenabob is eaten. The Nymphaea alba is another variety of this flower.

Some islands are covered with quince trees which are of two varieties, the sour and the sweet. The sweet variety is highly beneficial for coughs. Jams are prepared from the fruit as well as the flowers. The leaves of this tree used as tea are said to be good for chest troubles. The seeds of both kinds used in decoctions have a lubricating effect on the digestive organs and make excellent cool drinks.

The narrow channels between islands where the water is still are full of cordate-leafed plant (Limnanthemum nymphoides) called khor, which is the chief fodder for cows in summer and increases their supply of milk.

There is another plant Hydrocharis morsus-ranae (Bhota khor) which is prolific in still waters. One of the most important aquatic herbs is Trapa bispinosa (water chestnut) which is called singhara or gôr. The fruit is eaten raw after peeling, or is roasted. It is found in large quantities in the Wular Lake where it is dried, husked and turned into flour. It is a nerve tonic and forms a specific diet for diabetes.

From Dal Koṭwal the boat enters Boḍ Dal which looks like a sheet of aquamarine embossed with the emerald slab of Sona Lank. The two mountain peaks in the north-east, Mahadiv and Koṭwal, stand like sentinels or as guardian saints to the lake. The pavilion of the Nishat Bagh beckons the wayfarer to come and be refreshed. On the left are conspicuous spots, the hamlet of Hazrat Bal with a chinar grove, the home of night herons and Nasim Bagh.

The Sona Lank (Golden Island) is an artificial island occupying a central position in the lake. It was made as a haven where boats could be anchored during a sudden storm. There are four chinars on the four corners and lately a pavilion has been built, which is surrounded by lilac bushes. Some garden flowers such as pansies, wall flowers and salvias have been planted. The pavilion should have been more artistic and preferably of stone. Possibly, a fisherman may be seen with his long spear furnished with seven barbed points scanning the depth of water for fish. Sometimes when it is dark, he lights a lantern to attract them. The fishes generally found in the Lake are of four kinds :

1. Ali gaḍ.
2. Kashmir gaḍ (it has a flat white body).
3. Chiriv.
4. Theṭa Gurun, the last named variety being generally found near the shore of the lake.

The whiskered terns skim along the surface of the water with their keen eyes in search of fish, and a pair of water-pheasants with white wings and a plume feather n the tail may be seen surveying the lake. Sometimes a crake may be heard in the bulrushes at the entrace to the canal leading to the Shalamar Bagh.

Lunch over, the boat moves beyond the eastern shore of the island over a rather weedy surface. On the way one may come across an aquatic plant, Euryale ferox, with orbicular leaves, densely thorny, green above and purple below. Each fruit of about 20 nuts is enclosed in a prickly pouch. The fruit roasted and eaten with, or stewed in milk, is a powerful nerve tonic. It is called juwar in Kashmiri. The boat passes under a picturesque bridge called Onṭa Kadal (Camel Bridge) with an artistic arch and just in front of the bridge is a spring in the lake where the water is weedless and dark blue. This part has become a miniature lake enclosed by causeways. It is generally full of pondweeds, Myriophyllum spicatum, fringed with willows and bulrushes. On Sundays boats throng the landing place of Nishat Bagh. After having tea on the velvety turf beds, amid flowers of diverse hues with Nature's transcendent glories meeting the eye on every side, one is transported to ethereal realms lost in an ecstasy of indescribable bliss. When the sun sets and sends the reflections of his red light on the fleecy clouds sailing in the sky, the boat leaves the ghaṭ, and under the wooden bridge, Nali Kadal (Pipe Bridge) enters the Lokut Dal—a placid, tranquil sheet of water clasping the lovely Rupa Lank (Silver Island) which looks like a jewel in the head of a coiled serpent. The darting of fishes among the interwoven pondweed can easily be perceived through the transparent water. The bold outline of the Shalamar Range with Twin and Zabarwon peaks and the Shankarachar (Takhet) Hill with its stately temple, cast their shadows into the mirror-like pellucid lake. In early spring the slopes of these mountains, redolent with the fragrance of the almond blossom, the sunset and sunrise on the snow-draped mountain tops, the golden rape-seed fields offer a delicious feast to the senses of sight and smell but paralyse speech.

Kotar Khana (the House of Pigeons) is a delightfully turfed headland with summer houses—an abode of peace and serenity. It is beautifully decked with garden flowers and there is an aquatic bed of imported red, yellow and white water lilies in its foreground. I would suggest the plantation of the giant water lily of tropical South America here. This flower has a diameter of one foot and a round leaf three feet in diameter with upturned edges.

The boat enters through the narrow neck of water into the Gagribal Dal which is he nearest place for bathing. Here are bathing boats and motor launches to give people a surf-ride. Every effort is made to keep the water free from weeds. The water of Gagribal is highly praised for its lightness and purity.

Sometimes a sudden squall overcasts the sky with dark heavy clouds; the surface of the lake turns murky, the raindrops create myriads of bubbles and the pattering of rain on lotus and lily leaves produces a mine of pearls. This in lovers' language is called Siyah Bahar (Dark Delight). Such a scene cannot but send a thrill of ecstatic rapture through the frame of the onlooker.

The lake narrows into a channel from Gagribal. On the left is the boulevard with its grand hotels and graceful houses, while on the right are bulrush beds and islets with willow groves provide ideal harbours for house-boats. Fancy could not picture more lovely retreates for rest and relaxation. What a joy it is to be in a shikara and have lunch or tea under a shady willow grove, surrounded by bulrushes whence issue the strident notes of the reed-warbler, whose hanging nest is seen entwining round the rushes ! Close by a moorhen with red beak and white tail darts of or a dabchick emerges or a little bittern comes out to gaze at you with long neck and pointed beak, while from the trees flow out the soothing notes of a golden oriole, a ring-dove or a thrush. The mountain ranges around with various shades of blues and browns present an unforgettable flash of colour to the wondering eye.

It is a pleasant experience to watch the boys performing aquatic feats on the bosom of Gagribal Dal. These feats were introduced by the late Rev. Canon C.E. Tyndale-Biscoe in 1891 in his school. The sports flat race, hand race, standing race etc., took place every Tuesday at about 5 o'clock in the summer. The schools were divided into houses and the crews wore the colours of their respective houses. The outstanding even in these sports was the sinking of the fleet, when all the boats at a whistle turn turtle, the crews set them right again, baled out the water with their paddles, and were back in their positions in 3 min. The band played 'God save the King' and His Highness salute and all the crews stood up with raised paddles. Now these aquatic feats are performed by the boys of the Government schools and the state band entertains the spectators.

What a fascinating pastime it is to come out at night at the prow or on the flat roof of a house-boat to observe the various constellations ! What a satisfaction it is to recognise some of the glorious luminaries of the firmanent and call them by name ! The angular height of the Pole Star from Srinagar is about 34°N. The two constellations, Urṣa Major (Ursa = a bear, Major = great) and Cassiopeia (Lady's Chair) lie on opposite sides of the Pole Star. The Great Bear is known in Kashmir by the name of Sapta Reshi and the Pole Star by Dhruva. To find out the Pole Star join the two stars of the quadrangle of the Great Bear, called pointers, draw a line in imagination that will pass through the Pole Star. Or trisect the big angle of Cassiopia which is in the form of a W; the trisector will pass through the Polaris. The Pole Star itself forms the tail of Ursa Minor (Little Bear). The Auriga (Chariotccr) with its brighl star Capella (the Goat) with a dim isosceles triangle called, 'Kids', close to it, perseus (the King) with their opposite on the other side Draco (The Dragon) are some of the circumpolar constellations. The point of the trapezium of the Little Bear if produced will pass through Vega the brightest star of Lyre (the harp) and the tail of the Great Bear if lengthened will pass through Arcturus the brightest star of Bootes (the Eagle). There is a small star close to the middle one of the tail of the Great Bear. It is called Arandati by the Kashmiris. There is a local superstition that anybody who cannot see this star, is likely to die within six months.

V

EXCURSIONS FROM SRINAGAR

1. Trips by Boats

The journey by boat down the river is a very interesting experience. Starting from the Dal Gate we fist see on the left the C.M.S. Hospital (now a Government Hospital) standing out boldly on a ridge and on the right the Golf Course. At the other extremity of the canal near the flood-gate there is on the left the All Saints Church and on the right at its confluence with the river Vetasta (Jhelum) are the Srinagar Club and Government Arts Emporium. A new bridge at this place is under construction. Further down on the left are the Convent College and Museum, and on the right there are the Post Office, the Judicial Court buildings and shops. The boat passes under Amira Kadal, the first bridge. Closeby another bridge is being built. On the left is the white mansion with the golden temple which used to be the residence of H.H. the late Maharaja Pratap Singh. Now it houses the Secretariat, almost all the Government offiçes being accommodated in it. The water from the Dal Gate flowing through the Tsunt Kol canal which skirts Chinar Bagh falls into the river on the right. On the left is an overflow canal, Köṭa Kol, which draws water from the river to avert floods, and re-enters the river below the sixth bridge. On its left bank is the Government Hospital.

The Haba Kadal, the second bridge, is the busiest part of the city ad its medley of old and new buildings is well worth seeing. On the left is the biggest temple in Kashmir, Rugh Nath Mandir, and below it is the famous C.M.S. High School (now Central High School run by the old staff and old boys of Canon Tyndale-Biscoe) where boys receive physical, mental and moral education and which has character building as its principal aim. The principal was the Rev. Canon C.E. Tyndale-Biscoe, the reformer of Kashmir. Visitors are welcomed every Thursday morning.

The Fateh Kadal, the third bridge, is the market for curios and articles of wood-carving, papier mache, embroidery, silver work and many other objects of interest. On the right bank is the mosque of Shah-i-Hamdan beautifully and artistically made of wooden slabs and small bricks. It is one of the most important mosques in Kashmir. In it there is a spring dedicated to the goddess Kali (Nature) sacred to Hindus.

On the left bank is the Pathar Masjid built by Nur Jahan. The Government handed it over to the Mohammedans and it is at present the headquarters of the National Conference.

Zaina Kadal is the fourth bridge. On the right bank are the ruins of Baḍ Shah—comprising a mosque made of bricks and some tombs of interest belonging to the fifteenth century. These are enclosed by an old stone wall. There was a belief current among the Kashmiris that the sores caused by small-pox would get cured by the application of a brick of the Baḍ Shah mosque rubbed in water. Closeby is the Maharaj Rambir Ganj Bazar, the chief centre of trade but this is now shifting to the first bridge. Many stonecutters' shops can be seen here. A temple built by a Kashmiri, Pandit Rama Koul, stands out as a landmark in this part of the city.

Ali Kadal, the fifth bridge, has been lately rebuilt. It is not designed for wheeled traffic. Below it on the right bank is the mosque of Bulbul Shah, the first Mohammedan fakir who converted Raintan, the Buddhist prince, to Islam as the Brahmans of the valley had refused to admit him into their fold.

Nawa Kadal is the sixth bridge. On the right ban is the temple built by Pandit Ram Joo Dhar. It is here that the Köṭa Kol enters the river from the left.

Saffa Kadal is the seventh bridge. Closeby is the Yarkand Sarai where traders from Yarkand stay with their merchandise. Just below the bridge is the weir built to raise the level of the water in the river. The fall of water here with the fish jumping high is an interesting sight. The background of mountain ranges is fascinating.

If the water is high it is better to take the boat by the Köṭa Kol canal. On its left bank we first see the granaries of the Kashmir Valley Food Control Department. Past Tanki Kadal the boat enters the river from the left, crosses into the Tsunt Kol canal, and passing under a flood-gate, finishing the circuit at the Dal Gate.

2. The Dal Lake

A number of trips can be arranged to the Moghul Gardens and to the secluded retreats of the lake. There are some charming picnic nooks between the Leper Asylum and Pokheri Bal. At this point a canal drains the water of the Dal Lake into the Anchar Lake. In July the lake is carpeted with lotus flowers.

3. A trip to the Anchar Lake

The Anchar Lake is a lovely and often forgotten lake, seven miles to the north of Srinagar. It is about 3½ miles long 2¼ miles broad and covers an area of about 7½ squire miles. A bus runs daily at about 8-30 a.m., to the Sowura village which is one of the ghats of Anchar Lake. There are boats without roofs which would carry a person to the various parts of the lake, or a boat may be engaged from Srinagar for a day and enter the Khushal Sar through the Mar Canal. There are a number of villages situated on the shores of the lake.

A trip to this place will occupy a whole day. Tea and lunch should not be forgotten. A boat can be hired for Rs. 5 to Rs. 6 with three men paddling. There are islets with poplars and willows of stunted growth. There are also a number of floating gardens. They yield vegetables and fodder for cows, which the boatmen bring to the city in their boats every morning. Moving in a boat round these islets one comes across lovely patches of water in between these islets. On the northern side of the lake enters one of the branches of the Sind with its glacial water which changes more or less the colour of the water towards that side. The northern portions of the lake are being silted up by the branch of the Sind which empties itself into the lake and deposites hundreds of tons of sediment and there are a number of deltas which are covered with the Kashmiri and the English willows. Some islets are covered with milfoils, pink flowered thistle-plant, yellow buttercups and Lythrum salicaria (Sman thör) and nettle.

Moving the boat towards the southern side one would enter into an expanse of lotus blossom in July. The graceful orbicular leaf of the plant and the gorgeous flower, a couple of feet above water is most attractive. It appears as if it is a corner of Eden. Amidst this romantic place the pheasant-tailed Jacana builds its nest on a floating mass of weeds. the paddy-bird with its white wings flies from one place to another, the moorhen, the grebe, the tern and wagtails are seen here and there after their prey.

Surveying the lake, one would now find time to land on an island towards the west under the shade of a chinar tree. Spreading one's table cloth on the velvety turf laden with victuals. A look on the mountain ranges round the place will reveal in the east the Mahadiv, in the North the Harmoukh and in the west the peaks of the Pantsal Range It is said that the poison of the serpent bite gets ineffective wherever the peak of Harmoukh is perceived. There is a glacier running from the top of this peak. The reflection of these attractive ranges into the pellucid water of the lake is charming and a movement into the water cause them to dance and jump round the spectator.

It will be now time to land at the Ghat and retrace your steps towards the bus which would deposit you near First Bridge.

In winter the lake is full of mallards, pochards, gadwalls, snipes, teals, dabchicks and many more varieties.

4. Ganderbal

Across the Anchar Lake and up the Sind river, or, along the Jhelum via Shadipor.

It is the spot where the Sind, rising from the Harmoukh and the Amar Nath glaciers, enters the plain stage. The turfy banks and shady chinars afford excellent camping plots and mooring sites for boats. A branch of this river enters into the Anchar Lake where several trips can be arranged for bird observation and lotus blossom. There are some charming picnic recesses. The eastern shore abounds in floating gardens (Rad). It will take about three hours by the Mar Canal and about six hours by the Jhelum. It is about 12 miles by land from Srinagar.

There is a power house built lately to generate electricity for the city lighting. The flume has been dug from Prang and there are two tanks wherein water is reserved. One of them is fairly large and appears like a mountain tarn graceful to look at. The view of the valley and mountain ranges round, looks magnificent from the road going along the flume.

5. Khirbhawani

The spring of Khirbhawani is 2½ miles from Ganderbal. This spring is sacred to the Hindus. It is situated in the village of Tullamulla which is surrounded by islets densely covered with poplars, willows and walnut trees. The spring is on an island. In the centre of the spring is a small marble temple. People generally go there on the ashṭami shuklapak (eight day of the bright fortnight) and a great fair is held on the Jeshta Ashṭami about May. The water of the spring changes its colour. It has been observed to turn rosy, various shades of green, diluted milky and light blue. It is a phenomenon worthy for the research of a scientist. When people go there they wash their clothes and abstain from eating meat. They offer, milk, candy sugar, raisins clarified butter candles and chant vedic and tantaraic hymns. The place is well paved with dressed stones and improvement is going on. The road from Ganderbal to Tullamulla passes through paddy fields and in summer it appears like a green-sea for miles around. The chief plant of fragrance is Mentha sylvestris which has a great medicinal value. In this connection reference is invited to the booklet 'The Mysterious Spring of Khirbhawani'.

At Ganderbal, there is a dispensary, and a post and telegraph office.

6. The Manasbal Lake

en route to the Wular Lake.

7. The Wular Lake

The doonga (house boat) takes a day to reach Banayari the point where the river enters the lake. The lake should be negotiated before noon, as it is often windy in the afternoon. The wind is dangerous when it blows from Naga Marg, and it is then called Naga Kôn. The deepest part of the lake is towards Baba Shukar Din side. It is called Möta Khon, (the Gulf of Corpses) because the current carries all dead bodies into it.

A good mooring spot is Sodur Koṭ, where the boat can be punted up through canals. A delightful view can be had from the green spur of Sodur Koṭ where there are the remains of an old fort.

Not very far from the road is a sulphur spring and about a mile and a half from Sodurkot, there is a spring with an old temple in the Garur Village. The spring is dedicated to goddess Gauri. Pandits of the villages come here to bathe on Sundays. It cures some diseases. Bandipor is an important town at the foot of Tragabal pass. It is a trading centre, and commands the route to Gurais, Gilgit and Central Asia. In early spring the shore of the Wular lake is beautifully carpeted with golden blossom of rape-seed fields which stretch for miles round. Skylarks are seen here soaring and singing. A lorry runs daily from Srinagar to Bandipor.

Trips on Cycles

(a) Starting from the Dal Gate along the Boulevard, we leave on our right the Distillery and the Royal Palace and on our left a transparent sheet of water, where the holiday-makers bathe, dive, swim ad bask in the sun on the flat planked roofs of bathing boats. The greenness of the vegetation, especially after a rainy day, presents one of the most unique sights in the world. Between the fourth and fifth miles the road branches off towards Chashma-i-shahi. Moving between apple, pear, cherry and apricot gardens and newly-built houses we come to Nishat. Leaving Nishat we come to Ishibör, where there is a spring under a grove of walnut and Boin (chinar) trees. The stretch of land on the left is swampy and is covered with Veronica, water cress and Mentha Sylvestris. Closeby is the State farm where experiments for the cultivation of various kinds of crops are carried on. Have your lunch in Shalamar Garden. You are eight miles from the Dal Gate. It is now three miles from Harwan, where there is the great reservoir which supplies water to the city. There is a bungalow on the slope of the hill where Lord Minto II stayed when he visited Kashmir. Near the garden are the trout-culture farm and the excavations of a monastery dating back to A.D. 300.

Return by the causeway which starts from the Nishat Bagh. The water to the city is conveyed in pipes laid on this dam. Land when you come to a bridge, lean on its railing and drink deep of the natural beauty around you. You emerge at Nayid Yar (Rainawari). The road will lead you to the C.M.S. Hospital, Rainawari and from here direct to the Dal Gate.

(b) Start from the Dal Gate along the Nasim Bagh road for Nasim which is five miles away. Thence make for Shalamar through gardens, fields and villages. On the way is a picturesque bridge (Onta Kadal) on the way to Nayid Yar then to the Mission Hospital, and on to the Dal Gate. (Part of the road is unmetalled, hence not fit for bad weather.)

(c) The Manasbal Lake is about 18 miles from Srinagar. The main road branches off at about the fifth mile into what is called the Gilgit Road. We come to Shadipor and cross the river at Sumbal. Here we get a glimpse of the lake. About ten miles from here is Sodur Koṭ and from its grassy spur a perfect view of the Wular Lake can be had. Return by the Ganderbal Road.

Wayil Bridge, 18 miles via Ganderbal—view of the Sind Valley.

In summer, bus takes visitor to the Wular Lake for an excursion. At Naga Boni Miss A.E. Wishart has established a dispensary for villagers.

Near Kangan Shrimati Mira Ben has founded an ashram for looking after cows, etc.

(d) The Banihal cartroad branches off on this side of Pampor, towards Zewan. This spur contains fossils worth studying. Here is a spring dedicated to the serpent god Takshak from which it is believed the bulb of saffron came out. 'The spring at Reyvun (Zewan) is considered holy. Saffron came out of the spring. When people commence planting saffron they first pour cow's milk in it, if it sinks it is a good omen, if it floats it is considered bad'. Ain-i-Akbari. Further on at Woin there are sulphur springs. Near Khonamoh village on the mountain ridge there is a natural cave dedicated to Shiva called Harshishwar. The mouth of the cave is believed to close every year the length of a barley grain and a rock outside the cave growing so much bigger. There is a natural lingam inside the cave and a quartz vein on the ceiling which drips water is called Vasak Nag (the Lord of Serpents). It is visited by Hindus on New Moon and Full Moon.

(e) Minor trips can be taken to :

The Museum, the Silk Factory, and the Böd Masjid (Jama Masjid). The Museum is housed in an exquisite building. It contains a natural history section where wild ducks and other birds and stuffed animals are arranged. Types of men found in the State, old paintings, stones and minerals, shawls of different designs, ancient writings on birch bark and Kashmiri paper are some of its other features. The office of the Meteorological Observatory and the Public Library are also housed in the same building.

The Government Arts Emporium. The Government has opened centres throughout the city and in large towns where craftsmen are employed to manufacture goods which they sell under their own supervision at the Emporium which is located in the old Residency in a beautiful garden. There are articles of exquisite beauty for sale.

All-India Khadi and Village Industries Board has opened centres in the towns of he valley where villages are employed in spinning and manufacturing woollen goods thus encouraging cottage industry. There are all hand made goods. There is a sales shop in the Hari Singh High Street. The Head Office is at Nawab Bazar Road.

Tourist Reception Centre. Just near the Srinagar Club the Tourist Reception Centre contains a number of fine buildings which gives every possible convenience to visitors. All offices concerned with the visitors' welfare are located there. There is also catering arrangement for those who require such facilities. It is under Director of Tourism who looks after the comforts of visitors in every possible way. There is also Government of India Tourists' Officer to help visitors.

The following cycle trips are also suggested :

(a) Dal Gate via Rainawari along the causeway to the Moghul Gardens and back to Dal Gate, via boulevard.

(b) Dal Gate to Nasim Bagh then to Shalamar and Nishat and back by the causeway or boulevard are recommended. The cyclist is reminded not to forget to carry lunch and tea.

(c) Dal Gate via Gagribal to Chashma-i-Shahi.

(d) About two miles from the Dal Gate on the Ganderbal Road is a small building called Roza Bal near Dastagir Sahib's Mosque. Local tradition calls it the tomb of a prophet named Yusa Asaf who was of unusually tall stature. When he died and was buried, this tomb was erected on the navel of his body. A stone which is about 20 yards away from the place, marks the extent of his feet. Some people call it the tomb of Jesus Christ.

Trips by Motor Car

1. To the Moghul Gardens along the boulevard, not missing the Harwan Reservoir and excavations.

2. To the Manasbal Lake about 18 miles from Srinagar. At the fifth mile on the Jhelum Valley Road turn to the right and cross the river by the Sumbal Bridge.

A view of the Wular can be had from Sodur Kot about ten miles from Manasbal. Motor along the shore of the lake and return by the Ganderbal Road.

3. To Gulmarg. Gulmarg is 25 miles from Srinagar via Magam. From Tang Marg to Gulmarg is an ascent of three miles, which can be done on ponies. There are hotels. Khellanmarg takes an hour from Gulmarg. There is a spring and a seasonal tea-stall for summer. There is a regular bus service between Srinagar and Gulmarg. For detailed information please refer to 'Gulmarg and Its Environs'.

4. To Sonamarg. It is about 51 miles from Srinagar. A charming view of certain glaciers can be had from here.

5. To Pahalgam. It is 61 miles from Srinagar. The drive is through rice-fields and the scenery is grand. On the way, the ruins of the Pandrenthan temple near the cantonment, Awantipor temples of Shiva built in the ninth century A.D., the spring at Anant Nag (Islamabad), the sulphur spring of Malak Nag (rather neglected), the spring at Bawan, the Martand temple built by Lalitaditya (A.D. 693-720) are all interesting. The cave temple at Bumzov is worth seeing. Returning from Pahalgam one can visit the Achhabal Garden.

Anant Nag is one of the famous springs of Kashmir. It is situated in the Tehsil of the same name in the southern division of Kashmir. Anant which means endless, is another name of Shish the vehicle of Vishnu. The water of the spring comes from the base of hillock with a great rush somewhat like the spring of Achhabal. It enters into another spring in the middle of which is a lingam. Lately a garden has been made and another spring built with a cascade which lends grace to the garden.

A tradition is connected with the spring. When Indra was cursed by Gotam Reshi, his whole body became sore with one thousand scars which iritated his physical frame very much. Thereupon he worshipped Vishnu, who became pleased and told him to wash himself first in the Malak Nag. Through the dirt of his body, it became a sulphur spring which lies in the middle of the Anant Nag town. He was then asked to wash himself in the Anant Nag Spring. All his scars turned into eyes. Hence Indra's another name is Sahasra kosh (one thousand eyed), and the spring also is called Acchha Nag (eye spring).

A fair is held on the fourteenth day of bright fortnight in Assuj (September-October) when some people observe a fast, and eat only one meal without salt. They pour khir (a preparation of milk, sugar and rice) into the spring. The spring contains fish and one of which was seen of a golden colour.

The Martand Spring. The word Martand means sun. The following tradition is connected with these springs. It is said that Shri Vyas Manishwar when roving about in higher planes felt thirsty. He saw a boy and asked him for water. The boy forgot. Thereupon the sage cursed the boy and imprecated him that he will take his birth in the lower plane.

Kashyap Reshi had two wives, Kodru and Venata. Venata gave birth to 13 eggs, one of which was addled which was thrown out lest it would harm others. This fell into the Sati Sar (Kashmir) Lake. When Kashyap Reshi reclaimed Sati Sar, he found something shining like the brilliance of hundreds of suns at the place where the present Martand Spring lie. He did not venture to go near. He entreated Brahma who requested Vishnu to solve the difficulty. They both went to the Kailas Mountain, the abode of Shiva whom they entreated to come the spot and see what it was. Shiva appeared and saw the egg in super-effulgence shining like several hundred suns. He, with His trident split the egg into two, the one part became the upper spring called Wemal and the other part became the lower spring called Kamal the energy like a flame went out of it and turned into a goddess called Burga Shakha which is worshipped on the mountain just above the springs. The water from the egg turned into stream, called the Tsaka on the left bank of which Shradas in the memory of the dead are performed.

This is how the boy who disobeyed Shri Vyas Reshi was incarnated on the lower plane.

Shiva blessed the springs thus : He who dies unnatural death shall have peace if a shrada is performed in his name at this tirtha. There are special stellar dispositions when shradas are performed here. One is Vija Saptami, and the other is on all Sundays of the intercalery month which comes after 2 and a half years when the solar and lunar calendars according to Hindu calculation are adjusted. Dwadeshi is another ceremony for the peace and Nirvan of the dead which is performed here.

There is a specified area where shradas are performed. The sun is believed the chief agent through whom good wishes and belessings are conveyed to the dead.

The springs are situated at the foot of a plateau. They abound in fish. There is a spacious camping ground outside the springs. It is shaded with glorious chinars. These elegant trees entertain, thrushes, flycatchers, kingcrows and ringdoves. The willow groves also grow-nearby, they invite mosquitoes, but they are not malarial. The popular name of the village is Bawan.

The great kings Ramdeva and Lalitaditya (A.D. 693-720) built temples in honour of this tirtha on the plateau. There is a canal from the Lidder to irrigate this plateau which yields thousands of maunds of paddy.

Achhabal Garden

Returning from Pahalgam one can visit Achhabal garden. Here is a fountain of water gushing out of a mountain side. It is believed to come out of the Brangi which disappears at Dewalgam. The water of Achhabal Nag flows out at three different places from under a densely covered mountain with deodar trees. The water is highly digestive and refreshing. According to Pt. Anand Kaul the old name of Achhabal was Akshāvala, founded by King Aksha who reigned over Kashmir from 486-426 B.C. It has been remodelled by the Moghul rulers and a garden laid out in A.D. 1640 by Shah-i- Jahan's daughter.

There are ruins of an old Hamam on the western side of the garden from which warm water used to flow. There was no outward sign which would give people an idea of the mechanism of warm bath. Some investigators opened the Hamdam and found inside a candle burning under a big iron pan—so people say which warmed water. What kind of oil was used and what kind of wick, no one knew. The candle got extinguished and it was found impossible to light it again. It had been burning for several centuries. Today we see only walls and building of the Hamam but no warm water.

The water of the spring is turned into three canals which flow over three terraces. The main canal has several fountains. The greater number of fountains is in the main tank. There are three cascades over which water flows. It is lovely to see fountains playing when the rays of the sun fall on them.

The garden is shaded by graceful chinar trees. There are three pavilions on the upper terrace, where visitors sit to have their meals. A pair of plumbeous-redstart may be seen skimming along the water, or a hoopoe working hard on the lawn with its beak, also a turtle-dove peacefully cooing on chinars, might be heard.

The well-decorated lawn and garden flower beds, the cool shade of chinars, the breeze blowing from the wao-mal, resting on the Banahal ridge, sieved through the pine leaves; the natural beauty of the place, produce their effect to the full, on the beholder who, forgetting his physical aspect, enters into the mental plane of All Consciousness. Will he evermore abide in this Realm of Bliss. Shri Utpal Dev Achariya has said:

> Bavat devshatan pashyn
> Bavam bavam bavan mayem
> Vetiseeyam nera Kañkhya
> Preharsha paripurita.

Possessed by Thee, I see Thee prevade through everything in the Universe, May I rove about desireless, filled with ecstasy.

The Government has improved and extended the garden a great deal. There is also a post office, a hospital and regular bazar. Buses run daily from Srinagar to Pahalgam. A bus from here goes to Kokernag a collection of delicious water springs. Here is a restaurant also. There is a trout hatchery attached to the garden. Brown and Rainbow trouts are reared.

When water flows out of the garden it turns into a river, just outside the garden the banks are covered with watercress and willow groves. It irrigates a large tract of land which yields thousands of maunds of paddy.

There is an annual fair held in the month of Ashad (Sept.-Oct.) which lasts for a week. People come from all villages round, to make merry. Dances take place, singing parties recite songs. It may be called a kind of May-day.

Koṭhair Nag

Koṭhair Nag is about 6 miles from Achhabal garden. The road is partly metalled and partly kacha. Past Naga Dandi Ashram, it passes through a dense pine-forest along the southern boundary of the Khundroo Military area. It then goes over the Karewa (udar) and enters into the Kothair village. The spring lies on a raised spot of the village above the habitation. It was through the courtesy of one of my relatives that I visited the spring on the 3rd day of August 1955 with my daughter and grandson.

When we sat on the edge of the spring my thoughts ran in imagination to the tenth century A.D. The whole valley was then densely covered with elm and pine trees with thick undergrowth of hazel. The circular (kond) spring was then glittering with blue water from the reflection of the surrounding coniferous trees, just as we see today Nila Nag of Ver district (Shahbad).

The village must have been lower down. The medicinal quality of the water of the spring must have attracted the people from the various parts of the country just as today people go to bathe in the hot spring of Meru Wardwon. At annual fair people brought diseased persons to be cleansed. Hence the name of the spring is Papashudan Nag (Sin cleansing spring). The whole area was called Koṭhair Wan (forest).

The present position. The Koṭhair Nag is a circular spring. Its radius is about 5 yards. It is covered with pond weeds. We saw a clear blue line from one side to another and we told by the villagers that those who know swimming, swim in it. It appears fairly deep. The edge of the kond (spring) is walled with stones. It seems that there are steps of stones round it. The water of the spring flows from the north. There is a small place for bathing, from where the water flows down, just on the edge of this side, there is a baderapeth without any lingam. Close to the baderapeth (pedistal) is an image of a bull (Nandikishwar) in a sitting posture. The head of this image is damaged. There are some stones rubbed with Siondur (red lead). There are 3 old elm trees.

The spring is enclosed by a wall. The plinth of the wall and its northern side is partly intact. On the same side there are the remains of five temples. One temple has a staircase of 5 steps, the other has a mono-stone ceiling in the centre of which is a beautiful carved lotus. There are ruins of the other temples in the north eastern corner. The middle temple which is also in ruins, rests on the wall and on its left and right are nine inches of man's height where one can easily sit or stand. It would be interesting to excavate the whole place for the sake of historical research.

There are no pine trees in the village which is now near the spring. People depend for water on the spring. The pine trees densely cover the mountain slopes. The whole valley is dotted with walnut trees. There are maize fields on the submontone side, while the area which is drained by the spring water, yields rice (Shali). Ashad, Shuklapak, thritisi (Sept.-Oct.) is said to be the annual fair.

On enquiry from a peasant about the tradition of the place, he said 'You people know well' and recited:

> Mökan Rajas moñshi hend kam
> Yudvai gatsihe Koṭhair wan
> Tati tas tsalahan moñshi hend kan

> Mokan Raja has the ears of a buffalo,
> Would that he would go to Koṭhair forest,
> There he would become free from buffaloe's ears.

It is said that one Raja Matsakund of the Deccan had the ears of a buffalo. No one knew it, except the royal barbar. When the barbar died, his son entered the palace to shave the hair of the Raja, who admonished the new barbar not to expose the ears of the Raja to the public. He restrained it for some time. When he no longer could suppress his thoughts, he went to a forest and shouted at the top of his voice, the above couplet and ran away. The Raja searched for Koṭhair wan and he got rid of buffalo's ears by bathing in the spring. According to Pt. Anand Koul, the enclosure round the spring was erected by King Bhoja of Malva during King Anant's time (A.D. 1028-63). The tank of the spring was constructed by a Raja of the Deccan name Matsakund.

Kulgam Valley. Fishing plentiful. View charming. A road branches off from Khanabal (surface good in fair weather).

Nila Nag (of Gogjipatheri)

Nila Nag is a beautiful spring, 23 miles from Srinagar on the aerodrome route. The wheeled traffic is as far as Nagam 11 miles from Srinagar, and pony-track 12 miles from Nagam to Nila Nag. It can be made base camp for climbing some peaks in the Pantsal Range.

V

MOUNTAIN CLIMBS

1. *Shankarachar Hill or Takhet.* A pony-track.

2. *The Zaberwan Peak.*

Start early from Aita Gaji Gap outside the fence through almond gardens. The footpath is good. The ascent is gradual. Higher up, the path enters a belt of pines which ends on the summit. The path along the ridge to the twin peaks has several steep descents and ascents. The ravines are thickly covered with witch-hazel trees where occasionally a black bear may be encountered. Antelopes sometimes may be seen. To avoid the thorn bushes, the path which leads down the twin peak spur should be followed right up to Chashma-i-Shahi.

3. *Twin Peaks*

Start at 7 a.m. from Chashma-i-Shahi. Go along the path to the foot of the hill. Avoid thorns on the right. Follow the path.

As you ascend higher and higher the valley opens, you see the mountain range and the plain below bathed in sunlight. Have you lunch at the summit and return to have tea at Chashma-i-Shahi. The whole range is a Reserve.

4. *Mahadiv*

It is possible to do the climb in one day. Drive to Harwan. Start at 6 a.m. Dwara is the last village. There is a hut at Dwara Won where a bridge crosses the stream. It is possible to get milk here. Another hut is at Nila Pantsal. Bobjan is five miles from Dwara and Ledwas (10,500 ft,) is five miles from Bobjan. Ledwas is a meadow. Here are five or six temporary sheds of Gujars in the middle valley ascent to the col. From here go along the lower slope of the ridge over the boulders and you will reach the summit (13,013 ft.) in six or seven hours. The view of the mountain ranges stretching in front is magnificent. Among the boulders in the grassy spots rich floral vegetation grows. The Macrotomia Benthami, the wild rhubarb, the Allim, Hedysarum cachemirianum, the Jurnea macrocelphela and many other varieties are common. Gariffon vultures may be seen hovering round the peaks. The peaks may be attempted by the southern side also. The descent may take three to four hours, depending on the speed of the trekker.

There are some other peaks which can be attempted but they will take seven to ten days.

1. Romesh Thong (The Sunset Peak)		(15,000 ft.)
2. Tata Koti	... ...	(15,645 ft.)
3. Harmoukh	... ...	(16,842 ft.)
4. Kolahoi	... ...	(17,779 ft.)

Consult the Beautiful Valleys of Kashmir.

A Mahadiv Climb

Mahadiv (13,013 ft.) is a conspicuous peak to the north-east of Srinagar overlooking the Dal Lake. An isolated spur towards the south about 12,000 ft. high is the sacred spot which is visited by Hindu pilgrims on the full moon day in August, which is also the day when pilgrims worship in the Amar Nath Cave. A grand view can be obtained from the summit of all the higher peaks of the mountain ranges which encompass the valley—on the east Kolahoi and Nun Khun; on the south and west the Brahma Shakri, Romesh Thong and Tatakoti; on the north, Nanga and Harmoukh; while the valley is set among the surrounding mountain ranges like an emerald slab fretted with silvery sheets and streaks of lakes and rivers and embossed with the amber of arid portions. Alluvial plateaus are spread beneath these ranges.

The climb of Mahadiv can be performed in one day, two days or three days. The main secret of reducing the difficulties of the climb to a minimum is to start early—about 6 a.m. from Dwara. Arrangements for coolies should be made beforehand from Harwan village and they should be told to meet either at Farm Bagh or at Shalamar. He who aims at climbing to the summit in one day should take a coolie carrying all his foodstuff with him, while he who attempts it in two or three days must carry a light tent and pitch it at Ledwas. He should also carry all necessaries except firewood.

Dwara is about 800 ft. higher than Srinagar and is 14 miles away. One can drive up the Farm Bagh which is full of Spanish chestnuts, apples, pseudo-acacia, cherry and other fruit trees and is a good camping ground outside the New Thid. It would be a pleasant trip by boat to Shalamar, where coolies, to be arranged beforehand, should be told to meet. On both sides of the road from Shalamar to Dwara there are paddy-fields which in some places are in terrace-formation. Orioles, thrushes, ring doves and shrikes are heard warbling on the trees while the bulbul with its grey crest and yellow vent is seen flitting along the roadside.

The path from Dwara passes through a close defile, by the right bank of the stream, carving cascades and pools round which whistling thrushes, redstarts and occasionally forktails catch their prey above the spray. From the bush-covered slopes of the mountains are heard the notes of thę bush chat and pale bush warblers. The guelder (Kulim) whose lovely blossoms adorn the early spring, the hazel (virin), the ash, the maple, the wild walnut and the chestnut are some of the trees which shade the path. About three miles from Dwara is Darawon where the path passes a bridge and there is a Gujar hut. It is pleasant to breakfast here. At Nila Pantsal there is another hut. Some ravines retain snow throughout the whole year and this is taken by coolies to various hotels for the preparation of cool drinks in summer months. There is a hamlet of four temporary huts at Bobjen (7,500 ft.) on the left bank of the stream. There we see a large variety of Alpine flowers. Cynoglossum and Mentha Selvestris are in profusion. This place is about six miles from Dwara. The ascent from here is moderately steep and pines clothe the mountain side till we reach Ledwas which is the corrupt form of Rudrawas (11,000 ft.) which is ten miles from Dwara and takes about five or six hours to reach. It is from here that the birch and Rhododendron campanulatum show their heads. The flowers of the latter are dried and used as snuff for bad colds.

Here we come across five or six temporary sheds of Gujars who migrate here for summer months. Sites for pitching tents under pines are clearly marked.

Ledwas

Ledwas is a meadow where Alpine flowers rear their heads. As soon as the snow thaws the primulas burst into blossom. The buttercups and pedicularis are met with in plenty.

Sometimes even in early June the valleys are covered with snow. There are three valleys leading to the highest peak. To gain the summit the usual way is to go up the middle valley leading up to the middle pass—Wover Gol (Weaver's Pass) being flanked by a ridge and being marked by many ascents and descents dotted with boulders. Among these boulders, the wild rhubarb, the Allium (wan pran) the borage, Macrotomia Benthami, Fritillery Royleana, Androsia and Sedum may be found. It is possible to attempt the peak from the south. The glorious view which unrols before the conqueror of the peak is an ample reward for his strenuous climb. If time is of no importance in descending one may spend a night at Ledwas, or if he is in a hurry, it will take him five or six hours to reach Shalamar.

VII
MANASBAL

Manasbal is a delightful lake situated on the Jhelum Valley at a distance of 18 miles from Srinagar via Shadipor, and 17 miles via Nasim and Ganderbal road. The word Manasbal is derived from Manusarwar, the sacred lake which skirts the Kailas Mountain along with Gauri-Sar and Rakhas Talav. As it was very difficult for Kashmir Hindus to go on such a far-off pilgrimage, they satisfied their religious craving by naming the secluded sheet of green water Manasbal.

This is not the only instance of the derivation of geographical names in this manner. The shrine of Sharada up in the Northern mountains is several marches from Srinagar. In order to avoid the difficult journey to the shrine without losing the merit of a visit to it, the Brahmans or Srinagar have named a small spring to the north-east of the reservoir, Sharad Bal. The water of this spring contains medical properties and is highly digestive. It is under a huge chinar outside New Thid. Vitsar

Nag which is five miles from Srinagar is called Ailapator after the lake to the west of Gulmarg.

A journey by a doonga house-boat occupies about six hours. The boat leaves the Chattabal Weir and glides downward propelled by two or more paddles. The passengers lounge leisurely in the boat, their eyes open to the sights which meet them from various directions. White vultures, crows and kites are seen feeding on floating carcasses, while kingfishers blue and pied are busy hovering over their prey. The holes in the river bank are made by these birds and deserted nesta are used by sparrows and hoopoes. In April the river banks are gracefully carpeted with yellow- blossomed rape-seed fields and blue iris beds. It behoves lovers of colours to attire themselves in yellow, eat yellow-coloured rice and sit and observe the play of colours under a peach- blossomed tree and compassed by rape-seed fields. I do not recommend this for a person afflicted with jaundice. Any distracting noise will be the hum of bees gathering nectar. The call of a fish-eagle, with white head and white bars in the tail, may sometimes be heard.

As the boat moves down, the mountain peaks in the east—Mahadiv, Koṭwal and Harmoukh stand out conspicuously. There are lovely, shady, chinar groves where the boat can be moored for some time. One of these is Naran Bagh opposite Shadipur where the Sind enters the Vetasta (Jhelum) from the Gangabal lakes. In the middle of the river is an islet shaded by a dwarf chinar. This is a holy spot called Prayag and is a miniature representation of the Prayag (Allahabad) of the plains. Thousands of pilgrims gather here in boats when there are ten stellar combinations. There is a waterway from here to the Khirbhawani spring which is worth a visit. The occasional changes in the colour of the water of the spring invest the Hindu shrine with mystic sanctity in the eyes of its votaries.

About two miles from Shadipor on the alluvial plateaus of Paraspor and Divar are the remains of old temples and other shrines dedicated to Vishnu, Buddha and Shiva and built by the renowned king Lalitaditya, his queens and ministers in the heyday of their glory, about A.D. 700. They contained gold, silver and copper images of enormous value. A stone minaret 54 ft. high with the bird Garuḍa resting on its top served as a flang. The enormous size of the stones in these ruins and the exquisiteness of their dressing and finish, strike the onlooker with wonder. A graphic account of these buildings is given in Ancient Monuments of Kashmir on pages 146-149. The course of the Vetasta then lay along the side of the plateau. It was afterwards diverted by the great engineer Suya in Avantivarman's reign (A.D. 855-883). Shadipor, which was founded by Sultan Shab-ud-Din (1337-1354), is one of the important fishing centres. Fishermen in small boats sweep the river with various kinds of nets. The fish belong to the following varieties: (1) Chhriw has a dark spotted back, white belley and a large pointed mouth. Some of these weigh more than 12 lb. (2) Sattar Gad has also spots of various colours and white sides. (3) Ail Gad is black in colour. (5) Rama Gurun is a small fish with black bars on its back. (6) Anyur. (7) Rupit Gad.

The fish of the Sind are prized more than those of the Jhelum. It is said that the best fish are found at the time of the rape-seed blossom and near those fields. Probably the reason is that the reflection of the yellow blossom falling in the river attracts the fish.

Sumbal is the next important village. Just outside the village on the river bank are some huge chinars and an elm, enclosed by a wall. This spot is sacred to the Hindus and dedicated to Nanda- ki-shuwar. A temple has been lately built there. The Gilgit Road passes through the village. A little lower down the water from the Manasbal Lake flows through the canal which is its only outlet into the Jhelum. There is a small village over this canal. A close examination of the masonry walls supporting the bridge on either side leaves little doubt as to the existence of temples in the ancient time on the shores of the lake. In these walls are seen stone images which must undoubtedly have adorned some Buddhist temples.

The boat is towed or punted up the canal shaded with willow to the mouth of the lake. Herons, starlings and frogs are seen in the fields. When the water of the river is high, the peasants dam the water at the bridge, to save their fields from inundation.

There are two camping sites on the shore of the lake. One is near the ruined Moghul Garden built by Nur Jahan, as the local peasants say. This is called Garoka or Joroga, which means a bay window. It signifies a royal mansion with a highly ornamented and artistically built pavilion, with a seat on the window for the Moghul queen, from which she could survey the charming lake. It is possible that Aha Teng (6,256 ft.) the hillock bordering the lake in the south was in those days clothed with groves of cypress, the most favourite garden tree of the Moghul monarchs. There are four terraces at the foot of the ruined wall. One is practically silted up. The Government might with profit restore this site, lay out a garden or build a rest-house in it. Here can be seen a big chinar tree and a slab of stone belonging to some old temple. When the water of the lake is very low a submerged temple can be seen, roofed like a quadrangular prism. The other encampment site stands at the farther end of the lake under chinars known as Padshah Boni (Royal Chinars). This is one of the best camping sites in Kashmir. This spot is also called (QozBagh having probably been planted by the Moghul judge. A canal taken from Sind by the great king of Kashmir popularly known as Baḍ Shah (A.D. 1421-1472) irrigates the alluvial plateau of Safapor. Closeby is a cave, dug by a fakir whose grave lies just outside it, near a small shrine. He came from India and married a Kashmiri girl.

The soil is sandy and this may lead to the cave being closed one day.

The northern and eastern shores of the lake are riddled with springs and covered with watercress. On the south-eastern side a stream from the Sind enters into the lake. There appears a fissure right in the middle of the lake running east to west.

On the north-east of the lake there is a village called Konda-Bal (Kiln Place). This village owes its existence to a quarry from which stones are sent to Srinagar. The stones are burnt for lime. The pebbles are preferred for macadamised roads and are known as mansabal rod. It is an excellent site for founding a cement factory.

What a pleasure is a cruise on the lake! The land shelf (submerged bank) is covered with various kinds of pond-weed, Naais Major and water milfoil in which fish are seen darting about. As the boat moves outwards the colour becomes turf green, perfectly weedless and refreshing to the vision. The high mountain wall which surrounds the lake renders tranquillity impregnable to all external disturbing forces. The air breathes peace and the care-worn heart is soothed. The delight of diving and bathing as experienced here beggar description.

Fishermen are often seen standing on the prows of their light boats, their eyes scanning the depths of the lake for fish and their hands holding a spear with which to strike and catch the fish. Sometimes one may see a hook and line used for this purpose. The line is about 1,000 yards long a hook with a weight is placed after every yard, a small fish being used as a bait. After two days the line is taken out and the fishes are captured. We took soundings at five places and the depth was between 30 and 40 feet, but in some places it must be much more.

It is worth while to attempt a climb, if not to the top of Krosh Peak, which is used as a station by the survey party of

India and stands at a height of 10,300 ft. above sea level, at least to lower heights from where the finest sights in the world burst into view.

The ascent begins from the Manasbal Gap. The spur is devoid of trees but the gems of Nature raise their heads among the rocks and on gravelly paths. The conspicuous flower is the Eremurus with radical leaves and white flowers on a stout raceme. Beds of iris and Kashmir tulips decorate the path. The higher one climbs the more attractive becomes the panorama. The valley unrolls, like a cinema reel, scene after scene of the rarest beauty before the spectator.

In front of him rises the Pantsal Barrier with its flat top covered with dazzling snow, the peaks of the range, Tatakoti, Romesh-Thong (Sunset Peak) Brahma Shakar, all over 15,000 ft., project like crystal cones draped in silver sheets. The forest-clad slopes are seen steeped in sombre light and the dark shades of blue which play on them are beyond the power of pen to describe. On the far east we see Nun-Khun over 23,000 ft., and Gwashi-Brari, above 18,000 ft., towering giants which appear to stand sentinel on the valley. The whole place spreads out like a chequered carpet of patches of green and yellow, standing against the silver expanse of the Wular, the Anchar and the other lakes, while the Harwan Reservoir twinkles like a star in the Eastern corner. The majestic sinuous flow of the Vetasta (Jhelum) emptying itself into the Wular and flowing out towards Sopor adds greatly to the beauty of the valley. The greater part of the valley appears covered with water which lends support to the view that Kashmir was once a lake.

Higher up the climbing is over rocks and one has to be rather sure-footed to reach the top of the peak. It is possible to have snow near the summit—which is crowned with a cluster of fir trees—as late as early May. Patches of Saxifraga ligulata and Corydalis rutaefolia variegate the landscape here. This climb should always be tried in the early part of the day. The essential equipment should include water, carried in bags or bottles. On one occasion we assembled with the boys and we offered a prayer for the peace of the world.

Close to Krosh Peak is another peak called Halder where there is a rock underneath which water is flowing every year on Nirjala Ekadashi day a fair is held here. According to Pt. Anand Koul, the pilgrims sing in one chorus.

Balbhadro Haldaro Palah talah poni trav

O Balabhadra Haldara (Lord Krishna's elder brother) allow water to flow out from under this rock.

Then suddenly water flows out in a large volume from underneath this rock which suffices for bathing of the pilgrims assembled.

A tourist who has not much time to spare can pay a flying visit to the lake in a car. I suggest the route, Srinagar via Shadipor, crossing the bridge of Sumbal and leaving the car on the eastern shore of the lake under the Padshah chinar; where he can have his breakfast. He can then hire a boat from a fisherman and have his lunch under the chinar at Jaroga Moghul garden. Next he can drive his car through the fields, and the cherry and apple gardens and have his tea at Nasim Bagh on the Dal Lake watching the whiskered terns skimming along the surface of the water and return for supper to his hotel or camp.

With his base camp at Manasbal a tourist may make excursions as follows:

1. Khirbhawani about six miles. The famous spring changes colour occasionally and is sacred to Hindus.
2. Manasbal to Kangan, 16 miles; Kangan to Gund, 13 miles; Gund to Sonamarg, 14 miles. A car now runs direct to Sonamarg.

3. Manasbal to Rama Radan, via Vusan (not a good camping ground); Rama Radan to Malish, climb to Bharat Bal, about six hours (start early); Malish to Gangàbal, about three hours along the meadow; Gangabal to Wañgath, 12 miles; Wañgath to Ganderbal, 13 miles. (Consult The Beautiful Valleys of Kashmir pages 114-122).
4. To the sulphur spring near the road, not far from Ajus.
5. Manasbal to Erin Valley.

Manasbal to Nod-hal; Nod-hal or Kiud-or; Kiu-dor to Sarbal lakes.

VIII
SONAMARG

Sonamarg is a charming valley, 51 miles to the north-east of Srinagar. It is about 9,000 ft. above sea level. There is a legend that somewhere in the valley lies a well, the water of which has the property of turning anything into gold; this is the origin of the name Sonamarg (golden meadow).

The road to Sonamarg runs through the rich Sind valley drained by the Sind River, flanked on one side by the densely forested mountain slopes and on the other by a bank covered for the most part by the bush, Indigoferra hereantha. Often the passerby hears the note of the pale bush-warbler which cannot be mistaken. The road is now open to wheeled traffic and in the near future Sonamarg will be a rival summer resort to Gulmarg and Pahalgam. There are two rest houses on the road, one is at Kangan and the other at Gund, where there are catering arrangements. The tourists' committee is doing its best to open up the country extensively, making it easy for visitors to reach every delightful nook of the valley.

There is a short-cut to the marg which saves at least 15 miles, via Shalamar and Dwara across the Hayan Pass. It starts from Dwara and is a pony track. The Sind slope is well forested and there are many varieties of Alpine flowers on either side of the road. The view of the Dal Lake, the city and the peaks of Pantsal Barrier from the top of the pass is charming. Some of the flowers are Lillium Polyphyllum, large yellow Potentillas, Strobilanthes alatus (Acantheacea family) and asters. There is a forest hut on the other side of the pass in the Sind valley commanding a fine view. The path meets the general road exactly at the Ganiwan Bridge. The river abounds in fish and trout, a joy to the angler.

A neighbour of mine told me an interesting story pertaining to a time when he happened to be at Akahal, which is the corrupt form of Mahakak (Great Time), the Angel of Death, who is the guardian saint of the spring found there. The village is on the left bank of the Sind, four miles from Hayan. He saw a party of five men panting and running, and falling down unconscious when they entered the house where he was.

Presently, he brought some sugar and water and opening their mouths poured it into them one by one. When they came to their senses they related to him the following story. They had taken then contract of felling the trees in the forest. When they crossed the Hayan Pass they sat under a pine to rest. While sitting, one of them absent-mindedly scratching the ground with a piece of twig found the top of a plant. This aroused his curiosity and he dug deeper and deeper, till he routed the plant out. He took it in his hand to look at it. Presently, he saw in front of him a completely nude 'nymph' demanding the plant. The man with downcast looks addressed the lady : 'Are you not ashamed of standing quite naked in front of men !' She smiled. Then more nude 'nymphs' joined her. The man got frightened and handed over the plant to them. They all disappeared. The men ran away in terror. They heard behind them the beating of thousand of drums and the blowing of trumpets till they entered the house where they fell senseless.

The valley is encompassed by mountains ranging from 14,000 to 16,000 ft. above sea-level. A well forested hillock, the spur of Thajiwas Range, divides the valley into two parts, Sonamarg and Thajiwas.

Sonamarg is drained by the Sind River which rises from the glaciers and springs of the Amar Nath Range It is an extensive meadow. Clover is very common all over it. Alderbery is also abundant. It is a valley in which avalanches work havoc. The mountain slopes are obviously responsible for this.

As one enters the valley, the eye falls on a village of about a dozen huts, called Shita Kör. Their light in winter when their huts are buried under snow must be similar to that of the Lapps. The produce of their fields is very scanty. In summer, of course, they are in Paradise, provided they have enough to eat. On the extreme end of the valley are the Police Chowki and the Telegraph Office. The telegraph master is also postmaster and meteorological observer. The servants of these officers have built houses on the right bank of the river. In winter they find it difficult to cross over owing to heavy snowfalls.

Thajiwas is an excellent camping site. It contains miniature plateuas naturally separated into distinct compartments. It is also well shaded with pines. It is watered by a lovely spring, and a torrent which is fed from the adjoining snowfield and glacier on the mountain range. The banks and islets are not devoid of floral beauty. Corydalis and Pedicularis grace the shady nooks.

Thajiwas has a rest house nestling among pines. It was the favorite camping site of Dr. Neve who used to carry on medical work for the benefit of the people living in this part of the country.

It is worth while to pay a visit to one of the glaciers. I specially recommend the one which lies on the extreme end of the valley beyond the snowfield. Outside the camping are, there is a level spot containing a sheepfold and further on there is a grove of birch trees. The path to the fourth glacier leads along the right bank of the stream on to the snowfiled which is littered over with pieces of ice broken from the avalanches which sweep down the glaciers from time to time. Great care should be taken that the snow over the stream is not loose or else a watery grave with a yawing mouth awaits the traveller. Climbing over the sandy and shaley ridge profusely covered with Allardia tomentosa (a kind of pin daisy with ashy leaves) one may be able to reach the glaciers. The snowfield continues right on to the col called Hapat Gaṇḍ (Bear's Knot) which possibly leads to one of the peaks of the mountain system. If the traveller walks through the valley with a watchful eye he may be rewarded with pieces of crystal sometimes seen among the pebbles dislodged from the mountain slope.

In contra-distinction to the geological theory about the formation of crystals, there is a belief among the people here that crystal is formed from the ice imbedded in the earth for a considerable period through chemical changes. A snowflake being hexagonal, the crystals also have the same shape.

A delightful diversion for an afternoon is a climb over the ridge which separates Sonamarg from Thajiwas. The Sonamarg slope of the ridge is steep and densely covered with firs and birch trees. The ascent on the Thajiwas side is gradual and the path begins just opposite the first glacier. It passes through the alder-berry plants, then under the sycamore trees, the leaves of which bear a striking resemblance to those of the chinar tree. Higher up the path continues under trees, turns a little to the left, and leads to a settlement of Bakörbans. As we climb higher and higher we seem every now and then to see peaks which are not real peaks. As we leave the tree belt, we find ourselves on the grassy slopes of the mountains. The slope is really a lovely flower garden. A stretch of Marino coulteriana with its lemon-yellow flowers and prickly leaves gracefully decorates the margin of the slope. Every variety of Alpine flowers is there; of course edelweiss not excluded. From the highest point of the ridge on a clear day the view is superb. The sight of glaciers which cover the Thajiwas Range and the water flowing from them in silvery streaks, as if falling through sieves form these slippery rocks above, is highly pleasing. The ring of conical ashy-coloured peaks appears like a flock of herons pecking the sky. A snow peak peeping through a hole in the clouds is a thrilling sight. The soil on the slope is yellow, hence during rain it is muddy and sticky.

While descending we saw an animal larger than a jackal, with a long tail, brown colour a white band over the back and tail, running over the ridge with a tilt of the hind legs. We were told that it must have been a wolf.

There are a few places round about which are worthvisiting.

Nilagrad (not a Russian village) is a settlement of Baltis, about four miles from Sonamarg. This village will give an idea of life in Baltistan. Some of these people in times past built a few huts on the area between Sonamarg and Thajiwas. A woman died there. Every winter this woman would appear to them wrapped in a sheet and shroud. The people got frightened and deserved the village. The foundations of the huts are still there.

A small stream falls into the Sind near Sonamarg. The sediment of the stream is red. Every Sunday morning Baltis come here to bathe. They believe bathing here cures some diseases.

Baltal (Under-mountain) is nine miles from Sonamarg. A route goes from here to Amar Nath cave. It is passable only during June when the snow pavement over the torrent is still hard. Later on the snow becomes loose and going over the ice is dangerous. It is not a pony track.

Another route from here goes to Har Nag and thence to Arau and Pahalgam. The third route runs over the important Zoji La Pass to Baltistan. The path, though comparatively low, is supposed to be the most perilous of all the Himalayan passes. In winter heavy snowfall and avalanches block it for some time. In summer the floral vegetation is magnificent. How refreshing to a traveler from Baltistan is the sight of the green valley drained by the serpentine, silvery Sind ! There is a rest-house under the trees on a raised piece of ground. The Sweet music of the goldfinches, cinnamonheaded finches and bullfinches is most thrilling.

The Rudrawas side is infested with snakes. One of us went in search of a shepherd with a guide who killed six small and two biggish snakes. While we were having a camp-fire with big dried trees trunks, an adder came out of a hole in a tree. It was dark grey with chequered back and thin tail. It was about two feet long and two inches thick in the middle.

There are some charming lakes, Vishna Sar, etc., about two marches from Sonamarg across the Zöj Marg which are worth seeing. There is a metalled road to Sonamarg now and extended to Baltal, engineering skill will surely finish it at the Amar Nath Cave, and it will then be irresistibly alluring to the hiker to go by Sonamarg and return by Pahalgam.

IX

NILA NAG

Nila Nag is erroneously called Ver Nag. Ver is the name of the district, as the Nag (Spring) happened to be in this district hence this mistake. It lies at the foot of a mountain densely covered with blue-pines. According to the Puranic story, after Kashyap Reshi reclaimed the valley of Kashmir, he made his son Nila Nag, the king of Kashmir Nags. This is one of the largest springs not only in Kashmir, but in India too. It is said that the Nilamat Purana came out of the spring. It mentions the rites and ceremonies which were performed by the people of Kashmir, and which enabled them to live in the valley.

The original shape of this spring must have been circular (kund). When Kashmir became part of the Mughal Empire, Jahangir in 1620 A.D. changed the shape of the spring into an octagonal basin. Its circumference is about 240 ft. It is surrounded by a brick-wall with a number of vaults. Just near the entrance there are some murties inside a vault where a Brahman performs puja. The water of the spring is clear as crystal. The reflection of green pines in the lake and the serenity of the surroundings presents a calm and peaceful scene to look at. The flow of water through the channel is rapid. One finds it difficult to stand erect in the shoulder deep cool water. It abounds in fish. Just outside the enclosure there is a temple which is dedicated to Shiva whose satellite is Nila Nag. People come here to bathe on the New Year's Day according to the Lunar calendar. Near the eastern wall there is another spring the water of which bubbles up like an artesian well. There are flower beds of Zinnias, Petunia, Marigold etc., hoopoes, redstarts, bulbuls and thrushes may be seen on the lawn. The Government has improved the garden considerably. There is a rest-house under construction with catering arrangements. The new road from Jammu will pass through Verinag village. This place is worth a visit.

About one mile and a half from this spring is Vethavuthur the original source of the Vetasta (Jhelum). There are a number of springs closely called Sapta Reshi (Great Bear). These run dry from October to March as these are probably intermittent springs. The waters of springs mingle at Sangam (confluence) where people bathe on sacred days. There is a fair held on Bahadron thriyudeshi of the bright fortnight (about September) which probably must be the birth day of the Vetasta. There is a sadhu living here. It is a natural hermitage, a place of meditation.

X

WILD FLOWERS

Some of the wild flowers which grow round Srinagar and their indigenous use.

Pegasus hermala

Kashmiri name	...	Isband
English name	...	Rue
Family	...	Malvaceae
Locality	...	Malla Khah

Uses—It has a white flower. The ashes of this plant are used in washing the hair and the leaves are fatal to bugs. The seeds are burnt on wedding days to avert the evil eye.

Malva sylvestris

Kashmiri name	...	Sotsal
English name	...	
Family	...	Malvaceae
Locality	...	Waste lands. Also cultivated.

Uses—It is a pot-herb. The seeds are used in decoction (sherbatt). The root has a lubricating value and is used in anaemia.

Cannabis sativa

Kashmiri name	...	Bhanga
English name	...	Hemp
Family	...	Labiatae
Locality	...	River banks

Uses—It grows mostly above Pampor on both the banks of the Vetasta. Its fibre is used for making ropes and for sankering boats. The cheras, an intoxicating drug, is made from this plant in three ways:

1. The live plant is rubbed by hands and sticky substance is collected.

2. The pollen dust.

3. The dry plant is pounded and sifted. The material is placed in the maize-cob sheath, or paper or birch bark and well-wrapped in rush and baked in hot ashes. It is then smoked mixed with tobacco.

Lanatuma marrubrium

Kashmiri name	...	Tropör
English name	...	
Family	...	Labiatae
Locality	...	Waste lands

Uses—It bears a white flower. It is boiled in kanja and applied to a rheumatic limb.

Melilotus alba

Kashmiri name	...	
English name	...	
Family	...	Labiatae
Locality	...	Shankarachar

Uses—The flowers which are on a raceme are white. The flowering season is August, September. The leaves have delicious fragrance.

Salvia Moorcroftiana

Kashmiri name	...	Sholur
English name	...	

Family	...	Labiatae
Locality	...	Hari Parbat and Shankarachar

Uses—It has bluish white flowers.

Mentha sylvestus

Kashmiri name	...	Wena
English name	...	Horse-mint
Family	...	Labiatae

Uses—The leaves have an acute fragrance, and are used as fløwers in worship by the Hindus. Mixed with salt and chilli, it is eaten as chetni, and is considered very stimulating.

Plectranthus rugosus

Kashmiri name	...	Madal
English name	...	
Family	...	Labiatae
Locality	...	Shankarachar and sandy soil

Uses—It has grey-white flowers and sweet fragrance. The leaves are used in worship by Hindus.

A decoction of leaves is given to a person fallen from some height.

Thymus serphyllum

Kashmiri name	...	Jawen
English name	...	Thyme
Family	...	Labiatae
Locality	...	Hari Parbat, Shankarachar and sandy soil

Uses—The plant bears pink flowers in clusters. Their jam is an excellent stomach tonic. It is also put in Kanja (sadurkonz). It is good for weak sight, stomach and liver troubles. It can be used to flavour vegetable or fish.

Artemisa Moorcroftiana

Kashmiri name	...	Teṭhawen
English name	...	
Family	...	Compositae
Locality	...	Malla Khah

Uses—The leaves are made into a pill as a medicine for worms. It is also used to protect clothes and paper against fish insects.

Carduus nutans

Kashmiri name	...	Konḍ posh
English name	...	Thistle
Family	...	Compositae
Locality	...	Gardens and waste lands

Uses—It is a thistle with a crimson flower. Its root dug in autumn mixed with cane-sugar, half and half, is taken as a medicine for neural diseases.

Taraxacum officinale

Kashmiri name	...	Maidan hand
English name	...	Dandelion
Family	...	Compositae
Locality	...	Outside Srinagar

Uses—It has a yellow flower. it is a potherb. When dried, it is well cooked and applied to a sprained limb.

Cichorium intybus

Kashmiri name	...	Won hand
English name	...	Chicory
Family	...	

Uses—It has a beautiful blue flower. It is used as a vegetable and is given to women after child-birth.

Datura stramonium

Kashmiri name	...	Datur
English name	...	
Family	...	Solanaceae
Locality	...	Waste lands

Uses—It bears a white trumpet-like flower which is highly prized for uses in worship. The seeds which have a narcotic effect; are found in a thorny capsule. The leaf, lubricated with warm rape-seed oil, is applied to a diseased eye.

Daphne oleodes

Kashmiri name	...	Gaṇḍalun
English name	...	Daphne
Family	...	Thymelaceae
Locality	...	Shankarachar

Uses—It is a shrub bearing creamy white flowers. The leaves are used for some neural disease and nausea.

Caucalis leptophylla

Kashmiri name	...	Mohora Kach
English name	...	
Family	...	Umbelliferae
Locality	...	Waste lands

Uses—It has white flowers. The seeds are used as medicine.

Achillia millifollium

Kashmiri name	...	Phal gasa
English name	...	Milfoil
Family	...	Umbelliferae
Locality	...	Round fields

Uses—It has white flowers. The leaves are used in preparing medicine for stomach affections and the root for toothache.

Feniculum valgare

Kashmiri name	...	Phakazur
English name	...	Fennel
Family	...	Umbelliferae
Locality	...	In fields (rare).

Uses—It is a beautiful plant. In some European countries it is used as a spice. 'As much as eight and a half pounds of fennel was brought for King Edward I's household for one month's supply'.

Rumex

Kashmiri name	...	Oboj
English name	...	Dock
Family	...	Polygonaceae
Locality	...	In fields and gardens

Uses—It is a potherb. It has a little sour taste. It is cooked with or without fishes. The root pounded and mixed with oil or ghee is used for boils.

Rubus niveus

Kashmiri name	...	Chanch
English name	...	Raspberry
Family	...	Rosaceae
Locality	...	Shakarachar, Zaberwan

Uses—It is a shrub. The fruit is edible. It is good for blood.

Altnea officenalis

Kashmiri name	...	Saza posh
English name	...	Holly hock
Family	...	Malvaceae
Locality	...	Gardens

Uses—The flower, along with the wheat bran, is used is washing the feet of a sick person. The seeds form the chief ingredient in decoction of sherbat. The root has a lubricating effect used for anima.

Urtica dioica

Kashmiri name	...	Soai
English name	...	Stinging nettle
Family	...	Urticeae
Locality	...	Waste lands

Uses—The leaves are pounded and applied to wounds. The root boiled in tea and sugar is believed to cure malaria. In old schools (maktabs) this plant was thrashed on the naked boys as a punishment for bad behaviours.

Amaranthus Rumentacus

Kashmiri name	...	Ganhar, lisa
English name	...	
Family	...	
Locality	...	Fields, also cultivated

Uses—The seeds are eaten mixed with sugar. The ashes of this plant are used as saz, in soap preparation.

Analysis of the plant

Moisture	...	19.43 per cent

Ash	...	3.19
Protein	...	11.50
Carbohydrates	...	66.62
Fat	...	4.45
Fibre	...	2.1
		Dr Joachim

Oxalis corniculuta

Kashmiri name	...	Sebargi
English name	...	sorrel
Family	...	Geraminaceae
Locality	...	Fields

Uses—It has a yellow flower. The leaves are used in chetni. It is good for eye-sight. A medicine for eyes prepared from the juice of the plant.

Gagea-kashmiriana

Kashmiri name	...	
English name	...	
Family	...	Liliaceae
Locality	...	Malla khah

Uses—It has a yellow flower like a star. It is one of the first flowers to bloom.

Acorus calamus

Kashmiri name	...	Vai
English name	...	Sweet flag
Family	...	Araideae
Locality	...	In swampy places outside Srinagar

Uses—It is used on New Year's day. It is good for memory. Jam is prepared from it.

Solanum nigrum, dulcamara?

Kashmiri name	...	Kambai
English name	...	
Family	...	Solanceae
Locality	...	In waste lands

Uses—It has a white flower. The seeds are used in decoction. The juice of the plant mixed with butter is applied to a swollen limb.

Capsella bursa-pastoris

Kashmiri name	...	Kralamonḍ
English name	...	Shephered's purse
Family	...	Cruciferae
Locality	...	In all places

Uses—It has a white flower. The plant is eaten raw.

Verbacum thapsus

Kashmiri name	...	Bolar kon
English name	...	Mullein
Family	...	Scrophularineae
Locality	...	In waste lands

Uses—It has a light yellow flower. The leaves mixed with oil or butter are used for itches.

Chenopodium blitum

Kashmiri name	...	Wan palak
English name	...	Goose foot
Family	...	Chenopondiaçeae
Locality	...	Shankarachar

Uses—The fruit and leaves are eaten.

Berbebis lycium

Kashmiri name	...	Kava dach
English name	...	
Family	...	Berberideae
Locality	...	Shankarachar, Zaberwan

Uses—It is a shrub. The fruit is eaten and is a blood purifier. The root is used in preparing medicine for eyes. It is said to be a remedy for cholera.

Fumaria paviflora

Kashmiri name	...	Shahtar
English name	...	
Family	...	Fumariacea
Locality	...	In fields

Uses—The juice of the plant is taken internally along with whey to give a cooling effect.

Dioscorea deltoidea

Kashmiri name	...	Krats
English name	...	
Family	...	
Locality	...	In fields

Uses—In spring the leaves are eaten as a vegetable and are supposed good for eye-sight.

CHAPTER 13

OFF TO KASHMIR

By

C.G. Bruce

There are many travellers at the present time who are fortunate enough to journey East and West. The North and South poles even have their visitors. But there are still a great majority who cannot, for various reasons, even hope to cross the Channel. For their sake those of their countrymen who have the privilege of foreign travel try to describe by pen, brush, and camera the interests and charms with which either professional duty or leisurely trips have made them familiar.

In the old fairy stories we all love, who does not remember the travelling carpet, and how it transported its owner thousands of miles in a few minutes to whatever place he wished to visit?

There is always some moral or symbol underlying fairy stories, and the travelling carpet was intended to represent a keen imagination, for we can transport ourselves, by the help of this wonderful department of our minds, to places which we may perhaps never be able to see with any other but our minds' eyes.

These eyes, however, work very well, when trained, so long as correct pictures are drawn for them. So I ask you to step on to the magic carpet and fly with me to Kashmir.

The name of Kashmir is familiar to every educated person, and so it is hardly necessary to add that we must fly to the north of India.

There are some advantages for the carpet traveller —he misses all the miseries of a rough voyage ; all the heat and dust and fatigue ; all the badly cooked food of the wayside inns ;— so he has some compensations for remaining at home.

I can imagine nothing more delightful than to travel through the air, provided there were no danger of disaster, and to swoop down upon Srinagar, the capital of Kashmir. But I think we shall get a more distinct idea of its whereabouts if we imagine ourselves to have journeyed to India by steamer, to have landed at Bombay, and, after two days and nights in the hot and dusty train, to have left the railway at Rawal Pindi, military station in the north-west of the Panjab, and to have packed ourselves with our baggage into a tonga and an ekka for the forty-mile drive to Murree, a hill station 7000 feet above sea-level.

A tonga is a rough two-wheeled cart, on anything but cee-springs. It is open, but has a curved roof, and four people can be seated in it back to back, that is to say, three Europeans and a native driver ; but a tonga usually expands if natives engage it, and I have seen a family of eight apparently packed in quite happily. The ponies probably disagreed, and preferred an English load. Two ponies of a nondescript appearance and grooming are harnessed to the tonga, and a clanking steel bar heralds the approach of the vehicle. The ponies are changed every five miles, so is the syce of groom, who perches anywhere he can find room—sometimes on the roof. The driver, in very antique garments, blows a battered horn, from which he produced dismal sounds to warn bullock carts or other obstacles to our progress.

Our bedding, without which one cannot travel in the East, small boxes, and baskets, are tied on with rope. So behold yourself in dust-coat and sola topee (pith hat) arriving at Murree. And now give a sigh of relief as you breathe in the fresh hill air. How delicious it is after all the aroma of Indian railway travel and the hot drive! The ekka is following more slowly, the man servant, a native bearer, in charge, and will bring our heavier baggage.

An ekka is also a two-wheeled cart, chiefly framework and rope- netting, with a tattered red curtain, not for the sake of shelter to our boxes, but for the protection of native women from curious eyes when they travel.

The chief thing which strikes one about both these carts is that they always look very old—almost at the last gasp. I have never met either a new tonga or a new or even second-hand ekka. How amusing it would be if we drove down piccadilly, or even through our own village or town, in a tonga, an ekka bringing up the rear! A fine crowd would soon collect.

But we can only spend one night in Murree, as there are still 150 miles of tonga-driving before we arrive in Kashmir by the modern route, which is quite different from that followed by the old Mogul emperors when they travelled from Delhi to Kashmir. There were two routes from the Panjab before the Murree road was engineered. Both of them pass through picturesque country, through fir woods and meadows bright with flowers, and from the high passes magnificent views are caught of the snow mountains.

The Pir Pangal range is especially fine. At various points along the road ruined towers speak eloquently of days when travellers had to be protected from sudden surprises, and the large caravanserais were the halting-places and rest-houses of the old Delhi Emperors. They travelled on horseback and in palanquins with large retinues of retainers, and a travelling bazaar, or provision booths, and they took considerably longer than we have since we passed Delhi at midnight three days ago.

Is it to be wondered at that kashmir, with its snowy heights, deep rivers, and gushing streams, calm lakes and dense forests, flowers and fruits, should, even from so great a distance, have acted as a magnet to eyes which smarted from the dust and ached with the glare of the fierce sun beating on white marble and red sandstone? Kashmir has attracted outsiders for many centuries—are we not here ourselves?—and it will continue to draw visitors for as many more, as far as we can foretell anything. One of the ancient routes was through the city of Jammu, now the winter capital of the Maharajah of Kashmir, and led over the Banihal Pass some 9000 feet high, but passable even in March, though it is hard going then on account of snow. The other road from the plains of India started from Gujrat and led over the Pir Pangal Pass 11,000 feet. Some travellers even now vary their journeys to Kashmir by following one or other of these routes, though we are bumping along that most commonly used. The road winds down by zigzag till we get to Kohala, and we pay one rupee toll as we cross the bridge into Kashmir territory and frank our ekka too.

The next halting-stage is Domel, where we sleep a night. Here the two rivers, the Jhelum and the Kishenganga, flow side by side, much in the fashion of the Saone and the Rhone, for a short distance. You can easily distinguish the Jhelum, brown and muddy with the deposit it has gathered in its long course through the Kashmir valley, from the Kishenganga, light green and cold from the snows.

Barnier, the French traveller who wrote about Kashmir in 1665, declared that he was reminded of his own mountains of Auvergne as he gradually mounted from the heat of the plain, finding temperature and vagetation changing as he went.

Travelling from the Panjab to Kashmir in April, we leave ripening wheat behind us, passing on to fields of wheat only in the ear. Higher still we find a few blades just beginning to show, while the trees are only now uncurling their leaves ; and yet higher it is still winter, the fields are bare, and snow lies about in shady patches.

The scenery between Domel and Chakoti is wilder and bolder, and the river is narrow, and spanned by only a rope bridge. It seems incredible that such a slight structure can bear the weight of Laden men. Twisted rope of branches, with a central one as footway, are connected with stays of bark. The natives think nothing of crossing these bridges, but they are terrors to people who have not very strong nerves.

Chakoti dak bungalow (wayside inn) is perched on the hillside, and has a very pretty view down the valley ; but even as dak bungalows go it is a poor one. Very different from country inns at home are these Indian makeshifts, and yet one is glad enough of them. They consist usually of four austerely furnished rooms, with the bare necessities for bed and board, and more dust than is necessary. You bring your own bedding, and, on arrival, call for the Khansamab, the man in charge. He rolls off a fine menu in answer to your question : "What is there for dinner ?" It is not so grand on the table as in mere words, but you are hungry after your tonga-drive, and watery soup, tough chicken, anchovied eggs, and custard pudding are helped down with Worcester sauce and extras from your own tiffin (lunch) basket. Besides, Kashmir lies before us, and we shall soon be able to cater for ourselves and give orders to our own cook.

On the way to Uri the road winds along under steep precipices, for it has been cut out of the sheer hillside. In the rainy seasons heavy slips often occur, and the road may be blocked for days. As a rule, one spends two nights on the way from Murree into Kashmir, and the third day we pass Rampur with its great cliffs of limestone rock. Fine deodars grow on these steep cliffs, and farther on one passes the ruins of an old HIndu temple, dating back to A.D. 100.

The tonga route now takes us along a pretty road, often under branching trees, beside the rive, which has now broadened out into a placid stream. Here and there the water dashes up in spray as it rounds rocky edges, then it flows in a clear, brown current reflecting pebbles, or darkening into silent pools under the willow trees.

Fine trees are now plentiful—walnuts, chestnuts, and firs of several kinds. Picturesque wooden huts, with gabled and thatched or wooden roofs, look much more civilised than the flat-roofed mud huts of the plains which we so lately passed.

At last we come to Baramulla, the first large village in Kashmir proper, and the approach to it is almost like a Surrey village on a wide common, the river shining through the trees. Fine plane trees are planted along the banks, and a rough wooden bridge conducts you to the main town across the river. The domed roof of a temple and the background of mountains soon show that it is neither English nor Dutch, as the avenues of poplars might suggest. The houses are very like Swiss chalets in rather a tumble-down condition. Closer acquaintance still further betrays their inferiority, for they are very dirty. "Patch up for to- day, let to-morrow patch for itself," might be an honoured Indian proverb, so closely is it observed.

There are plenty of river craft about. Houseboats awaiting tenants ; Doongas, which are like wide punts with roof and side blinds of rush-mats, also used by travellers. We are reminded of a broad reach of the Thames with bits of Switzer-land thrown in.

There is a fine view of Mount Haramouk, which is 16,000 feet high, and the ranges of the Pir Pangal and Kaj-i-Nag form a beautiful background.

Our next move, after a rest in the bungalow on the river, is down the poplar avenues which stretch from Baramulla to Srinagar. They were planted by Nur Mahal, the great Mogul Emperor Jehangir's wife, and are lovely at all times of the year : in the spring when their delicate leaves are a glitter of tender green and silver, through the sober green of summer, till they turn to gold in the autumn's crisp nights, still keeping their silver at the back of their leaves. Even in winter they form avenues of delicate tracery, their straight, slender branches penetrating the landscape as if with notes of admiration at its beauty of form and colour.

And so we come in sight of Srinagar, the City of the Sun, which must have a chapter all to itself, and if you were bona fide travellers by this time you would be quite ready for a rest and another meal, having driven twenty miles more.

(1915)

CHAPTER 14

GULMARG

By
Dermont Norris

As the summer advances Srinagar becomes too warm to be comfortable. The days are oppressive and the nights no longer refreshing, and Society begins to consider moving to Gulmarg, which fills up towards the end of May, though a few hardy visitors go there much earlier, when the snow has hardly left the golf course and an occasional belated ski-runner may still be discovered lurking or Killanmarg. Gulmarg is situated in an undulating basin about three thousand feet above the valley and and two thousand feet above Tangmarg, which is the village where the motor road from Srinagar ends, and is surrounded by extensive forests of pine. Above, the main range of the Pir Panjal rises to height of over fourteen thousand feet and below the wooded hills fall steeply to the level of the plain.

The distance to Tangmarg from Srinagar is twenty-four miles along a good road, and motors and lorries for heavy luggage can easily be hired for the journey. From Tangmarg a well graded pony-track leads up to Gulmarg, and tats or dandies can be obtained to carry those who are not sufficiently young or energetic enough to make the ascent on foot. The road branches off from the main Baramulla road about eight miles out of Srinagar, close to the famous Hokra Jheel, and for the last few miles rises steadily, until Tangmarg is reached, whence the remainder of the journey must be completed either on foot or by pony. There are two routes up from Tangmarg, the main bridle path, which zig-zags and has an easy gradient throughout, and the collie track, which runs straight up the face of the khud, and, though considerably shorter, is very steep.

At Gulmarg there are all the usual amenities of a hill station, and most of the hotels, shops and boarding houses of Srinagar open branches there during the short summer season, which lasts from June until about the end of September. The Maharajah has a house there, and there is the Residency, church and club, with two golf courses and several hard tennis courts, so altogether life is Gulmarg need never be dull. The climate is delightfully cool even in the middle of the summer, but the one great drawback is the heavy rainfall, which far exceeds that of the valley.

Most of the visitors live in wooden huts dotted about the low hill-sides bordering on the marg. These huts are really bungalows with several rooms. They are usually fairly well furnished, and can be made very comfortable at small expense. One of moderate size can be rented for about eight hundred rupees for the season, and sometimes less. There is also Nedou's hotel and several boarding houses for those who prefer to avoid the worries of house-keeping. Living is slightly more expensive than in Srinagar as all supplies have to be carried up the hill.

Golf is the chief form of amusement and competitions are held almost daily. There are two first-class courses, which are certainly the best in India, and golf in Gulmarg is played in surroundings that are almost English, even to the frequent rain. A big tennis tournament is held each year and dances take place at Nedou's hotel several times a week.

For people who prefer the simple life there are innumerable delightful walks through the forest, which extends for miles on either hand, or over the open uplands between the tree-line and the snows. Through the clearings in the forest and from the lower slopes of Apharwat there are incomparable views of the valley, Sunset Peak and the stupendous mass of Nanga Parbat, rising to a height of 26,620 feet, nearly ninety miles away to the north.

Nanga Parbat is the ninth highest mountain in Asia and one of the very few really great mountains that are easily visible from a centre of civilisation. It is also one of the few great peaks that is a peak in the literal sense. This, coupled with its isolated position, makes it one of the most imposing mountains in the world, for it towers more than nine thousand feet above every summit within a radius of sixty miles. Wonderful though it appears from Gulmarg, it is even more impressive when viewed from the north, where the Indus flows along the bed of a stupendous gorge, and an observer on the further side can see towering above him no less than twenty-three thousand feet of cliff and crag and glacier, culminating at a distance of a few miles in this glorious summit ; at view, perhaps, that is not equalled, and certainly is not excelled, by any in the world, but which, owing to its remoteness, can be seen only by a fortunate few.

There are several longer expeditions which can be made in the course of a single day : down the steep sides of the Ferozepore nullah, to picnic beside its icy waters, in which there are numbers of small snow trout : or up the further side to the ruined tower at Damdama : or to Killanmarg and over the top of Apharwat to the Frozen Lakes on the further side. It is a long expedition to the top of Apharwat and entails a climb of over five thousand fee, but the masses of flowers in the woods and on the lower slopes above the tree-line, and the magnificent views from the summit well repay the effort.

Further afield a number of delightful trips can be made in the direction of the Tosh Maidan, the Chor Panjal pass and Tutakuti. Coolies for transport are sometimes difficult to obtain and those taken from Gulmarg will probably have to be kept throughout the trip, as places where others can be obtained are few. Applications for coolies should be addressed to the Tehsildar at Gulmarg. The usual rate is from eight annas to a rupee for each march, according to its length and difficulty.

The Pir Panjal range has been much neglected, but, when the rainy mid-summer months are over and the air is crisp with the promise of autumn, a short trip along its northern side is a delightful experience. The marches are short and easy, in the woods and upland meadows, deserted for nine months of every year, there are masses of glorious flowers, and, rising above, are friendly snow peaks, interspersed with rocky crags and lovely mountain tarns, and there is none of the overwhelming size and desolation of the further Himalayas.

CHAPTER 15

KASHMIR—THE SWITZERLAND OF INDIA

By
Dermont Norris

I

The natural beauties, the glorious climate and other attractions of the Kashmir valley have received such extravagant praise in the past that the new-comer is apt to picture to himself a Paradise on earth. Too much should not be expected : the country has an immense amount to offer in charm and interest and amusements, but, as in other countries, cold and rainy days occur, and there are places within its confines that have little natural beauty and no charm at all.

The climate of Kashmir is as unlike that of the plains of India as possible, and is excellently suited to Europeans, either in health, when there is an enormous variety of out-door attractions, or during convalescence. Spring and autumn are entirely delightful, but during July and August the valley itself is too hot to be pleasant, while January and February are usually cold and damp.

Arriving at the New Year, the visitor will very probably find the whole valley covered with a few inches of snow. Days of sleet and storm will alternate with longer periods of fair weather. On most nights the thermometer will drop below freezing point and a good deal of skating on ponds, or the remains of summer floods, will be obtainable, while in really cold spells the Dal lake is sometimes safe. The weather in February is much the same as in the preceding month, but by the middle the same as in the preceding month, but by the middle of March the spring sets in with a suddenness and determination that is quite unlike the hesitating approach which it makes in the British Isles, and in the space of a few days the willow trees begin to show a tinge of delicate green and some of the hardiest wild flowers burst into blossom. In the gardens of the European residents snowdrops, yellow crocuses and daffodils make a first splash of colour, and are a reminder of the glories of the past summer and of the beauty that is to come.

April, which lives up to its showery reputation, and during which the days are still quite cool, sees the valley perhaps at its best. The spring is fully established ; every tree and shrub has covered itself with new green leaves, and almond, apricot, peach and early apple blossom cover large areas on the outskrits of Srinagar with clouds of white and pale-pink loveliness.

May is distinctly warmer, but, even in the middle of the day, the heat is by no means oppressive and the chenar trees, which are one of the chief glories of Kashmir, are a magnificent sight in all their fresh new foliage.

Along the river banks drooping willows and graceful slender poplars make a cool and shady setting for the rows of moored house-boats, which by this time are rapidly filling with visitors, and the Golden Oriole, with its brilliant colouring, the friendly, cheeky Bulbuls, busy with domestic cares, and the slender, sinuous grace of the Paradise Fly-catcher all combine to tell us that summer has arrived. During this month roses and sweet peas, both of which grow to perfection, are among the chief glories of the garden, and on the outskirts of every village masses of mauve iris add to the beauty of the country-side.

With the advent of June the weather gets rather too hot to be pleasant during the middle of the day and the majority of the visitors move up to Gulmarg, or take a camp to the cooler uplands of Gurais, the Lolab, or the Sind valley. Apart from the increased temperature the valley loses some of its attraction, as the foliage has lost its first freshness and hangs in heavy masses of a darker green. Fruits come into season now ; strawberries arrive first, followed soon after by mulberries, cherries, apricots, raspberries, and later by pears and apples.

In July and August the valley is definitely hot and oppressive and few Europeans remain voluntarily in Srinagar. But visits should be made to the Dal and Manasbal lakes to see the famous Lotus Lily, which is then blossoming in all its glory.

September marks the beginning of the autumn, and, as the month wears on, the evenings grow chill and the days cool. The weather from now until Xmas is almost invariably fine and clear, and autumn, with its russet tints and the rich colouring of the chenars, framed against the distant mountains of the Pir Panjal, which once again have been capped with white by the first falls of snow, closely rivals, if it does not exceed, the glories of the springtime.

These are the seasons of the year in the valley. But its confines are so small that a day's journey, even in the height of summer, is sufficient to effect a change to the climate of early spring, and allows the traveller to pitch his camp on some upland marg, where the wind blows cold and pure from the snow-fields and Alpine flowers star the scanty turf. The mildest winters are severe in the valleys a thousand feet above Srinagar.

The Europeans visitor will find Kashmir delightful, not only because of its pleasant climate, but also for the variety of amusements that it has to offer. If he is an artist, there is work for his brush at every turn. There is no day in the year on which the sportsman will not be able to amuse himself. The botanist has ranges of upland hill-sides, which are studded with scores of varieties of wild-flowers for five months of every year. For the ordinary individual there are excellent golf courses and tennis courts in Srinagar and Gulmarg, there is the Dal lake in which to bathe and on the bosom of which to flirt, and there is the Club and Nedou's Hotel in which to dance and entertain. But all these things are summer joys, and,. when the wind blows cold from the mountains and the leaves begin to fall, the visitors depart, the butterflies disappear, and only a handful of residents remain.

In the winter life in Srinagar is much like that of a small English village, and there is little in the way of amusement other than the individual can supply for himself. But during these quiet winter months the valley exercises an indefinable charm, and it is with not unmixed relief that the residents, who live there throughout the year, watch the lengthening of the days and the mark the arrival of the first of the visitors, whose numbers during the height of the season reduce Srinagar and its immediate surroundings to something closely approaching the vulgar.

II

Kashmir, including the outlying provinces, covers a very considerable area and the inhabitants of the various districts differ enormously from each other. The sturdy, primitive hill-men of Baltistan and Ladakh are described in a later chapter, the martial Dogras of Jammu are rarely encountered by the visitor, and it is with the inhabitants of the valley itself, with whom he will first come into contact, that we now have to deal.

The temperate climate and fertile soil of the valley have not proved to its occupants the unmixed blessing that they should at first sight appear to be. For the inhabitants of the mountainous districts to the north and of the hot infertile plains that lie to the south have constantly turned envious eyes upon this lazy, pleasant land, and much of the history of Kashmir is a record of the exploits of adventurers, who have subjected the inhabitants to the tyranny of a foreign and oppressive rule.

When, therefore, we hear contemptuous remarks regarding the character of the Kashmiris and their lack of physical courage, about which there are a score of proverbs current among the more martial neighbouring races, we must remember the centuries of misrule, oppressive taxation and official bullying to which they have been subjected without any hope of redress, and without any authority to which they could appeal with the smallest hope of success.

The little that is known regarding the remote past is, perhaps, not of great interest except to the historian, and forms no fair basis for comparison with modern conditions. But, even if we confine ourselves within the limits of the past hundred years, we find that it was not until some years after the late Maharaja began to reign that the kashmiris have had any other than fleeting and infrequent opportunities of developing manly virtues, or any independence of outlook.

From remote until quite recent times the peasantry were systematically treated worse than the inhabitants of the capital. They were taught by long and bitter experience to consider themselves as serfs, and to regards themselves as having no rights whatever. They were left for their own use so small an allowance of the produce of their land, that they never, even in prosperous years, had more than barely sufficient with which to tide over until the following harvest. And in Srinagar itself the lower orders of society were better off only by comparison with the inhabitants of the villages.

In his interesting book, "The Valley of Kashmir", Lawrence has much to say regarding the wretched condition of the country when he began his famous work of land settlement in

1889, a mere forty-odd years ago. In it he draws as apt comparison between the condition of the Kashmir peasantry then and that of the French peasants just before the Revolution, and greatly to the advantage of the latter, who, however bad their plight, had never sunk to the same depths of hopeless degradation. In these circumstances it was not perhaps surprising that Lawrence found the people auspicious, sullen, and furtive, with every man's hand turned against his neighbour, thrift and honest labour to be almost unknown, and bands of hungry peasants roaming the valley, anxious only to avoid the ubiquitous tax-gatherer and to find the where-withal for a hand-to-mouth existence.

Forty years have not been sufficient to wipe out the imprint of these past centuries, and the children of the present generation have inborn in their character many of the traits that were necessary to ensure survival up to the time of their grandfathers, but which to-day are superfluous and form a perpetual source of irritated wonder to the Westerner, more fortunate in his ancestry. Dr. Arthur Neve, who knew them as well as any man, sums them up effectively when he says "They are as treacherous as the Pathan, without his valour ; more false than the Bengali, but equally intelligent ; cringing when in subjection, they are impudent when free."

Nor does nature, who present so fair and smiling a face to the summer visitor, always treat the inhabitants kindly. From time to time disastrous fires have swept the city, which, with its wood- built houses and narrow alley-ways, presents similar opportunities for the easy spreading of an outbreak of fire to that afforded by the London of the seventeenth century. Earthquakes occasionally occur, floods, with famine in their train, have caused serious havoc and much loss of life more than once, while cholera and smallpox have decimated the people upon several occasions. These visitations, together with the grandeur of the scenery in which they live, have kept the might of natural forces before the eyes of Kashmiris and have fostered their apathetic and fatalistic attitude of mind.

Of these disasters, floods are by far the most feared to -day. Modern medical science, aided by improvements in sanitation and a gradual awakening on the part of the people to some of the more elementary principles of hygiene, is able to keep cholera and smallpox from assuming serious epidemic form, in spite of the over-crowding that still prevails in the towns. And, now that communications are better, serious famine is a thing of the past. But all the efforts of the State engineers, aided from time to time by the advice of experts brought in from abroad, have so far failed to prevent serious floods being of almost annual occurrence. At enormous expense the gorge below Baramulla has been dredged to a greater depth to allow of the quicker outlet of flood water, spill channels have been cut above the capital, and the Bund, which is the embankment protecting Srinagar, has been raised and strengthened. Yet, is spite of all these efforts, the city and the low-lying portions of the valley are still threatened with inundation, whenever prolonged and heavy rain causes the Jhelum to rise much above its normal summer level.

We must bear these facts in mind before we begin to criticize the present-day Kashmiri, and temper the harshness of our conclusions accordingly. The inhabitants of the villages, who form the vast majority of the people, are strong physically and can carry enormous weights on their backs for long distances, merely pausing occasionally to rest their loads on the short T-shaped sticks, which they carry with them. But, according to our standards, they are arrant cowards ; their instinct, to which they give free rein, is to fawn objectively upon anyone with any vestige of authority, and they are dirty and slovenly in their habits. On the credit side, they live exemplary domestic lives and crime among them is rare ; they have a considerable, if crude, sense of humour, and, once they are convinced that profit will accrue to them, they are capable of exerting themselves considerably.

Their whole outlook on life, however, is warped by official oppression, which still continues on a large scale at any rate among the petty officials, and there is no worse tyrant than one of their own people vested with a little authority over them.

In the city, the Mussalman, who forms a large majority of the population, is, as a rule, a poor imitation of his village brethren, but the Hindu Pundits are quite a different type, for they are very intelligent and quick-witted and are renowned throughout Northern India for these characteristics. As they have almost a complete monopoly of all State employment, their power in the past has been enormous and still is very considerable. According to Western standards they are unscrupulous and dishonest in their dealings and only too frequently make unjust and rapacious officials. In the past they were extremely bigotted and the social evils, which the Hindu religion so carefully fosters, were rampant in their society. But to-day, largely due to the efforts of a few devoted Englishmen, who have worked among them for many years, there are signs that some of them are becoming more modern in their ideas, and are Prepared to cast aside the more harmful of the conventions which guided their forefathers in every action of their daily lives.

The Kashmiri's fashions in dress are not attractive, and at first sight this may seem odd, for they have well developed artistic tastes and there are among them talented workmen in wood and metal. It is probably originally due, like so many other things in this curious country, to the oppression under which they lived in the past. God clothes, or even a neat appearance, would then have been construed to indicate that the wearer was in easy circumstances and would have attracted tax-gatherers as surely as honey-scented flowers attract the bee.

The single loose-sleeved garment, worn by men and women alike, which hangs in heavy folds from their shoulders, is nondescript in colour and formless in shape, and the greasy woollen skull- cap, which is worn on all but gala occasions, when it is replaced by the infinitely superior white puggarree, are both indescribably mean and effeminate in appearance. But so long as the Kashmiri is wooded to the use of the kangra. so long will these garments remain in general use.

During the warm summer months the men wear short tight-fitting cotton drawers, but, as soon as the weather turns at all cold, the heavy loose cloaks reappear and the kangra is brought into use. This consists of a small wicker basket lined with earthenware and filled with glowing charcoal. The kashmiri carries it with him wherever he goes and would no more be without it than would a modern lady be without her vanity bag. When he sits, or rather squats, he places this charcoal stove beneath his cloak, which he then frills out round him on every side, and basks in its warmth amid the acrid fumes of burning charcoal. Sometimes he falls asleep unexpectedly and serious burns are frequently caused in this way, while cancer, which is believe to be induced by the hot kangra being always pressed against the same part of the body, is not uncommon.

The earlier visitors to kashmir were full of praises for the beauty of the women, and many of them would indeed be comely enough, were they but clean, even if they do not merit the extravagant praises that have been bestowed upon them in the past. They are markedly Jewish in appearance and no more swarthy than many of the inhabitants of southern Europe, and in consequence the Kahsmiris have inevitably been accused of being descendants of the lost tribes of Israel. Hard work and privation soon cause whatever beauty the women of the village may naturally be endowed with to face, and it is rare to see a woman of this class of more than a moderate age without the signs of care, hard work and child-bearing deeply imprinted upon her worn features. The purdah system prevents the ladies of the country from showing themselves to the vulgar gaze.

The visitor will gain a fair idea of the hard manual work that is the lot of the women, if he will pause beside one of the numerous boats that are moored along the banks of the Jhelum, to watch the manji's wife husking the rice, which forms the chief article of their food. The daily ration is placed in a massive stone, or wooden mortar, and the pestle consists of the trunk of a sturdy young tree cut away sufficiently in the middle to allow it to be easily gripped by one hand. This is lifted to a full arm stretch above the head and is brought down with the whole weight of the body behind it. Husking rice is a daily task that takes a considerable time, and the biceps of the kashmiri peasant woman so developed command the respect of her husband and are a powerful factor for order in the home.

CHAPTER 16

PAHALGAM AND ITS ENVIRONS

By

Samsar Chand Koul

THE LIDDER VALLEY

The Lidder valley forms the north-eastern corner of the Kashmir vale. It has a pleasant and mild look and a calm and peaceful atmosphere is radiated from sober forest-covered slopes and woodlands which border this valley.

The word 'Lidder' is a corruption of lambo-dari which means a goddess 'long-bellied'. The main stream receives a number of tributaries from both banks. The first mountain torrent rises from Shisheram Nag and carving a deep gorge round the Pisu Hill, flows past Thanin or Tsandanwari on to Pahalgam. At Tsandanwari another tributary rising from Astan Marg—a stream of pure water mainly from springs—joins it on the right. Near Pahalgam a torrent rising from the snout of Kolahoi glacier, receives a tributary from the Sona Sar lake near the Kolahoi valley, the water from the Tar Sar lake joins it on the right at Lidderwaṭ, and a stream from Katri Nag near Aṛau, enters it, the whole volume of water, swelling and flowing with rapidity to join another stream at Pahalgam. It is this stream rising from the Kolahoi glacier, which is called Lambodari. It passes through Lidderwaṭ which means Lambodarwaṭ (Lambodar's stone) where in olden days the god Ganish must have been worshipped, and it is also here that the tributary from the sacred lake of Tar Sar joins the Lambodari.

The Lidder irrigates a large rich tract of alluvial soil and for miles from either of its banks one can see a green sea of rice-fields during the summer. Occasionally, the white wings of terns in the fields throw the greens of the fields into bold relief. The aqueducts full of glacial water infuse life everywhere and we hear the rush and flow of water all along.

A canal has been opened from the Lambodari at Ganishpor to water the Mattan Uḍer (plateau). This canal is called Shah Kol.

Picturesque villages are scattered all over the landscape. They are nestled among huge shady chinar, mulberry, poplar and willow trees. The walnut, apple and pear trees with drooping branches laden with fruits intercept the rays of the sun. Sometimes hay is stacked on trees for the winter fodder of animals.

The houses are generally two storeys high, the ground storey consisting of cattle-shed. A portion of the room is covered with a ceiling on which the children of the family and guests sleep in winter, the room being made comfortably warm by the breath of animals. Only a very small widow opens from this part of the ground floor which is called 'Dangij'.

The second storey consists of a verandah and two or three rooms. In summer they sit and cook in the verandah and in winter in the rooms inside. Some have handlooms for weaving blankets or coarse cotton cloth. Here are also large earthenware cauldrons in which they store various kinds of seeds for their farms. In winter women are at work on the spinning wheel.

The roof is generally covered with rice grass. It is very steep so that rain and snow easily slip down. The loft is a store-room where grass from rice, ropes of dried turnips, with beans, knol khol and wild vegetables such as wopal hak (Dipsacus inermis) and hand chicory are kept hanging.

A barn and a fowl-pen are generally found in the compound. The rich farmers have several barns wherein they store rape-seed, maize, linseed and other produce of their farms till their price rises to the maximum when they dispose off their stocks. Thus they accumulate wealth which should not be the sole aim of man in this world. He has been taught from time to time by higher souls who have appeared on the world's stage in different epochs to be unselfish, and mitigate the sorrows of the destitutes. Unless we raise ourselves to that level, we are not true men and can only be a burden to society. Glimpses of the Great illumine our path here and there and this keeps the world from being engulfed in total darkness.

Trees round the village vibrate with the celestial music of their feathery denizens in the months of May and June. Out in the rice-fields on a solitary tree or on telegraph wires a roller (nila krosh) flunting its blue green plumage may be seen watching its prey. The paradise fly-catcher (phambaseer) in his angelic white and black garb opens the orchestra long before the break of dawn. It is followed by Tickell's thrush with its yellow beak grey body incessantly singing at the top of its voice untiringly right on to sunrise. The golden oriole in his royal bright yellow breast and pink beak sends forth his liquid note. Now the ringdoves from various quarters join the concert. The song is now in full swing. Later on the bulbul, the starling, the myna, the sparrow and occasionally the jackdaw chirp and contribute to the concordance of the chorus. Some other birds too in their own way make a display of their musical talent. The rufous-backed shrike which is a mimic does not withhold its harsh note. The wryneck clinging to the willow harps on its fine six-note chirp. The tree creeper with its long curved beak and striped back scours the tree from stem to top for its food. The tits with their white cheeks and white bars in their wing strike a creaking note. If the village happens to be near a mountain the gregarious black bulbuls make their appearance with their red beaks and legs and adds a sweet whistle to the harsh noise and the streaked-laughing thrush joins in with its delicious whistle like note. The cockoe and the hoopoe also string their harps. The kite screams from the top of a mulberry or chinar tree. The song gradually subsides as the orb or the day begins to flood our planet with his brilliance. What a blissful hour it is for him who keeps his ears open to receive this heavenly music and thereby merges his spirit with the universal soul that pervades the universe!

Attached to every house is a small croft where the farmers cultivate their vegetables—knol khol, egg plant, gourd, cucumbers, beans and pumpkins. A small rill diverted from the main canal passes through the croft and ever enters their compound where they clean their utensils. The water rills wash the roots of the willows leaving them red and these are sometimes used by thrushes to build their nests on.

In the village there is always a mosque and a bathing house and sometimes a temple on a spring dedicated to some god or goddess. A village may also contain a ziarat or shrine sacred to some saint which sometimes has artistic lattice-windows and of which the roof is always covered with either red tulips, crown imperialis or iris. The village grave-yard is generally covered with white and mauvie iris. At Aker there is a shiv-emblem bearing one thousand marks representing so many Shivic images, probably a remnant of those emblems which were made by the pious king Sandemati, (34 B.C.- A.D. 13) who renounced his throne and dedicated his later life to the service of the spiritual seminary at Sodura, in Wangat valley . The remains of this institution are still to be seen at the foot of Butsher at the head of the Wangat valley. There is also at this place a spring called Naran Nag where pilgrims on their return from Gangabal give away staves and grass shoes to Brahmans.

Interesting sites en route from Srinagar to Pahalgam:

Pandrenthan

This place is about 4 miles from Srinagar. Here was the old capital of Kashmir, which was founded by king Ashoka of Buddhist fame. The word is a corrupt form of Purana—old, adhishthan—capital. There is now a cantonment at this place. Not very far from the road there is a very low spring in the middle of which stands a beautiful stone temple. The roof of the temple consists of one stone artistically carved. This was erected by Meru the minister of king Partha who ruled Kashmir from 921-931 A.C. It was dedicated to Vishnu and was called Meru Vardhana Swami. It must have been a place of pilgrimage in the olden times. Mention of it has been made in the Amar Nath Mahatmya, but the place now lost its sacred associations.

Pantachok

About six miles from Srinagar there is a stone quarry where towards the road side stands a stone image of Ganesh which is besmeared with red-lead. It is said that just opposite this image is a spring in the middle of the river. There is a myth that when the Vetasta flowed down the valley for the first time the whole of it was drunk by god Ganesh and for sometime the river disappeared till the god was appeased and the river flowed again.

On the other side of the road there is a mosque which was built by Haba Khotan the queen of the Epicurian king Yusuf Chak (1578-1584 A.D.). The mosque was exclusively made of wooden slabs, but now it has been rebuilt with stone in the modern style. Closeby, another mountain spur also a quarry, a little out of the way towards Zewan village, contains fossils of marine animals and plants which testifies to the fact that the land was once under the sea. Last year when on an excursion with my boys I found a piece of rock on one side of which was a shell fossil and on the other the form of a trilobite.

Pampor

This is a small town about nine miles from Srinagar. Its alluvial plateau has saffron beds which impart a glorious beauty colour to the place in late autumn. From the plateau we see a dharmasala (an inn) and a temple on a mountain spur in the north-east built by Dr. Balkrishen Koul in memory of his mother. This spot is dedicated to goddess Jwala which points to the probability of the existence here in olden times of a volcanic strata or the occurrence of a slight volcanic eruption. Hence the place is considered sacred like Kangra. An annual fair is held here on Ashaḍa Choturdashi when people offer the lungs of sheep and cooked rice coloured yellow as a sacrifice to the goddess. Near the temple are sloping smooth slabs of stone down which children love to slide. At the foot of the hill is a spring round which a festival is held on the day. The spring is sacred to the Hindus, and is one of the guardian goddess of the pandits. The place is a fine resort for outing for the city people.

On the plateau there is a cedar round which there are stone images which are dedicated to goddess Bala. H.H. the late Maharaja Partap Singh used often to visit the place as a pilgrim.

The depression in the village is called Lalla-trag. This place was the birth place of Lalla the saint. It was also the favourite haunt of the Razdan family, the famous votaries of the Shaiva cult. Here is also a beautiful Ziarat of Mir Mohammad Hamadani.

Awantipora

This is the site of the ancient city of that name founded by king Avantivarman who ruled Kashmir from A.D. 855 to 883. The ruins of two temples which lie here about show that he dedicated one to Shiva and the other to Vishnu. The impressing architecture, the artistic carvings on the pillars, the magnificence of the design bewilder the on-looker. This was a place of pilgrimage in olden times. When there was no wheeled traffic and people used to travel on foot from Srinagar to Anantnag, there were professional masseurs who used to massage people to remove their fatigue. This was done without using any kings of oil. They were called Moṭshah. People gathered round a huge hubble-bubble and smoked tobacco till sunset. This was called Wontpor Jajir (the hubble-bubble of Awantipor).

Bijbihara

The place is called Kashi of Kashmir. There existed a very grand and large temple just in the middle of the present town where a small temple has been lately erected by the people. It is said that the temple was so high that its shade at sunset rested on the Martand plateau. This temple had a strong wall round it. This spot has been the target of numerous attacks by herds of hillmen during the Middle Ages.

Sikander Butshekan (A.D. 1394-1416) demolished the great temple and on one of its stones found in inscription which runs thus: 'Bismullehi mantrena nashanti vijayishwara' (by the incantation of Bismullah the temple of Vajishwara will be demolished). He is said to have been struck with remorse in later life for destroying those temples and incurring everlasting stigma for this vandalisim. Sikander died in A.D. 1416. It is possible that the raised part of the town was built on the debris of this huge temple when in course of centuries earth covered and concealed the debris.

There is a stone temple built by Maharaja Ranbir Singh (1857- 1885) outside the town on the bank of the Vetasta. There is a small ghat to the south-east of the temple. Here is a big Shivaling and the walls contain stone images. It is called Raja Hari Chandra's ghat and much sanctity is attached to it. Tradition says that every day two souls who end their earthly sojourn here go to Nirwana. Just outside the temple there are huge chinars on both the banks of the river which were once joined by a bridge. There is a chinar on the left bank the trunk of which has a circumference of 56 feet the largest in Kashmir. This garden was planted by Mughal rulers.

In the town there is a mosque which has a stone in which there is imbedded an iron axe supposed to have been driven into wall of the mosque by a Hindu saint Shankar to give stability to the mosque. Hence it is now called 'Shankaran Mokōts' (Shankar's axe).

On the right bank there is a plateau called Tsakadar (Tsakara dhar a name given to Vishnu). In olden times this was a place of great importance, but no trace of any temple is to be found here now. The religiously minded people go round (prakram) it to again merit.

On the plateau towards the town there are two spots where godesses Jaya and Vijaya are worshipped. This was one of the stages on the old route to the Cave of Amar Nathji which led across the bridge to Pahalgam. Lately a new bridge has been constructed which will shorten the road to Pahalgam. Bijbihara is famous for wood carving and artistic lattice work.

Anantnag

This town is thirty-four miles from Srinagar. The road branches off to the right to a lovely place called Achhabal (Achha—peace, Bal—place). It is said that the garden at the place was laid out by a Hindu king and remodelled by Mughal rulers. Water gushes forth from the mountain slope which is covered with coniferous trees. The water is directed into canals and waterfalls to create an exquisite scenic effect. Here is also a trout-culture farm.

Closeby not more than two miles away in Naga Dandi ashram founded by Swamiji (popularly known as Sumbaluk Babaji). It is an excellent pace for meditation. Refreshing breezes from the pines laden with fragrance, the cooing of turtle doves, the singing of orioles and thrushes the murmuring of the stream, add to the loveliness of the hermitage. An artificial lake with graceful water plants, the flowers such as Forget-me-nots, Cranesbills, Strawberry and various alpine flowers beautify the surroundings.

In this part of the valley there are many charming springs. Anantnag (Islamabad) is a great commercial town. Here is a large spring dedicated to Anant a satellite of Shiv. A fair is held on Anant Choterdashi when some Hindus keep a fast and particularly abstain from salt. Another fair is held when pilgrims to the Amar Nath Cave camp here. Close to the spring a beautiful garden has been laid out by the people. There is a Guru Dwara which commemorates the visit of Guru Nanak Dev. There are two important sulphur springs in the town, but they are not kept clean. The water supply of the town is plentiful. The Municipality should improve the drainage system.

The town is famous for wooden articles, toys and beautifully designed gabba work. The road turns towards left among rice-fields. From Chinars, mulberries and poplars we hear the incessant song of Tickell's Thrush, orioles and doves. The aqueducts are fringed with Balsum, Milfoil and Senecio.

Bawan

This is a famous spring on the way to Pahalgam. It is full of fish. In the intercallery months and on the occasion of particular stellar dispositions in the heavens (Vejay Sapthami) the people from India and Kashmir come here to remember their dead. The spring is called the Martand spring dedicated to the sun who is believed to be the intermediary through whom good wishes are passed on to the departed relatives.

The Martand temple is situated on the plateau. This temple was built by the famous Lalitaditya who ruled Kashmir from A.D. 601-738.

'Of all the ruins in Kashmir the Martand ruins are both the most remarkable and the most characteristic. No temple was ever built on a finer site. It stands on an open plain, where it can be seen to full advantage. Behind it rises a range of snowy mountains. And away in the distance before it, first lies the smiling Kashmir valley, and then the whole length of the Pantsal Range, their snowy summits mingling softly with the azure of the sky. It is one of the most heavenly spots on earth, not too grand to be overpowering, nor too paltry to be lacking in strength, and it is easy to understand the impulse which led a people to raise here a temple to heaven'.

Younghusband

Bumazuv

Near the road is an interesting cave-temple with artistic carvings on the door pillars. There lived Boma Reshi (sage).

Aishimukham

The Ziarat of Zain Shah Sahib

Perched high up on a mountain spur is the shrine of Zain Shab Sahib known among Hindus as Zanak Reshi. He is the guardian saint of the Lidder valley and is reputed to be one of the followers of Shiekh Noor-Ud-Din the chief saint of the Kashmir valley.

The road now passes along the Shah Kul canal which has been taken out from the Lidder river from Ganishpor to irrigate the Maṭṭan plateau. Here gradually the deciduous trees give place to coniferous ones. Bird-life here presents an interesting variety and laughing thrushes, black bulbuls, warblers, tits and wood-peckers and many more species cross one's path every now and then. Before we enter Pahalgam we see a rock in the stream on the right bank. It is dedicated to god Ganesh the supposed divine gate-keeper of the defile which contains Pahalgam.

Pahalgam

The hinterland of Pahalgam is in mythological parlance called Shiva Bhumi (the realm of peace). There is no lake, no meadow, no mountain peak which has not been named after a deity. In ancient times probably there existed in this place the hermitage of Bhrigu Reshi (sage). A spring believed to be sacred to this sage can be seen here and the pilgrims to Amar Nath Ji are expected to visit it. In course of time a number of hamlets sprang at the site near the bridge. To serve the dwellers in the hamlets a shop-keeper found his way here. These people began to live as shepherds. As this small village stands at the head of the Lidder valley the inhabitants of the lower village sent their flocks and cattle to be looked after by these shepherds who took them to various meadows for grazing. The place occupies a central position in relation to the side valleys crowned by high meadows which the shepherds distributed among themselves. Hence this village came to be named Pahalgam, the village of shepherds.

Recently this place has grown into a famous sanatorium where the people came to escape the sultry heat of the plains and enjoy the blissful breeze of the mountains. The Government has effected considerable improvements in the town. It has a Revenue Officer, a police station, a post and a telegraph office, a dispensary and a Health Officer. There are beautiful bungalows nestling among pines and hotels giving perfect comfort and satisfaction to the visitors. A church, a mosque and a temple are also there for people who seek to steep their souls in peace by communion with God. It is thus that they develop a love for unselfish service to humanity which is true worship.

The Lidder drains Pahalgam and a torrent from the Kolahoi glacier enters it just near Mamal. Flowing majestically among the pines like a fritted sheet of silver murmuring the sonorous song 'Men may come and men may go, but I go on for ever', the stream rushes in a hurry to irrigate the valley below. This is the only charm—a silvery stream—in which Gulmarg lacks.

Modern conditions have turned the place into an active health resort. Rows of shops provide all kinds of amenities for the visitor. There is no dearth of hotels but any one wishing to enjoy tent-life can hire tent equipment from shop-keepers or contractors. Rajwas (place of Rajas) is a plateau on the right bank of the stream covered with pines and this is an ideal camping ground. A bungalow can also be hired by previous arrangement through the Director of Tourism or such arrangements can be made through some hotel-keepers. In fact there is nothing wanting to a person who wishes to enjoy his holidays according to his own choice. The writer places a table and a chair under the shady and fragrance emanating leaves of the pines and fills the pages of the book as his brain is refreshed by breezes from the mountains and flowery meadows. The artist works at his brush and board to draw life-like sketch of natural scenes, of pine groves, old temples, cataracts, cliffs, hamlets of people. The philosopher absorbed in thought on the various aspects of human life might reflect here on the ways and means of the betterment and unification of humanity. The naturalist finds before him a wide field for research to keep himself busy. He can collect and examine wild flowers round about him, he can watch the movements of birds and discover their haunts. Men of all kinds of intellecutal and artistic pursuits can find ample material for their purposes. The beauty of his surroundings overwhelms the beholder with wonder at this magnificent handiwork of Nature.

While we see Nature in perfect harmony, all peace and perfection, we cannot fail to observe Her at Her work of destruction which goes on unceasingly. We see wood-peckers beating hard against the bark of trees to take out grubs or insects which feed upon trees. We see tree creepers going from trunk to top to eat insects. We see pine needles falling on the earth and huge pines resting flat on the soil rotting and to enable saplings to incarnate. We see huge rocks reduced to sand and soil by the external agents of change on the surface of the earth. We see rushing torrents rolling boulders and stones and engaged in destruction and construction side by side. We watch the trout going after the small fish and dippers diving deep in the rushing flow of the torrent to feast on water-insects, the redstarts keeping a sharp look-out for stay gnats and darting after them in the air and the sandpipers dashing with open mouth to catch an unfortunate insect. Vultures and kestrals hover about in the air to prey upon rodents, voles and other creatures which they can carry. This aspect of Nature is inseparable from her role as the creative energy for destruction and construction are interchangable terms. If, in our imagination, we stand in the ether outside our solar system we can watch procession in which the stars, planets, star-cities, the earth and the sun rush ceaselessly to complete their circuits, of course, in perfect order and in strict obedience to cosmic law.

Such are Nature's ways, as has been said by Utpala Deva Acharya :

'Pana shana prasadhana
Sambhukta samasta Vishwaya Shivaya
Pralayotsawa sarabhasaya
Dridham upagōdham Shivam vanda'.

Translation

'I merge myself in Shiv (peace) whom Shiva (Cosmic energy—Nature) embraces in all her haste, after creating, beautifying, protecting and destroying the universe'.

The Government has appointed energetic officers to improve this famous health resort and year after year new improvements are carried out for the comfort of visitors. As artificiality encroaches on this charming haunt of Nature, its Arcadian simplicity beats a retreat towards Arau, Astan Marg and other far away place where solitude reigns supreme and Nature stands alone in her virgin purity an serene grandeur.

Pahalgam is the nearest health resort to New Delhi from where it can be reached within two or three days. It is an ideal spot where to recoup ones health and to engage one's self in various healthy pastimes. Equipped with a staff and a nailed shoe or chappani, one can go for a mountain climb or to a glade right in the centre of a mountain slope surrounded by pines and fringed by ferns or maiden-hair plants such as, Baisaran. Tulin or Shikargah. It. is necessary to carry a good quantity of victuals. Walking sharpens appetite which calls for substantial nourishment. Water proofs are indispensable. There are lovely pools formed by streams in which one can bathe, but the stones at bottom of the pools ar slipery and care should be taken that one is not carried away towards the deeper parts of the stream where the water flows with irresistible force. Trout fishing is another interesting occupation. Permission should be obtained from Chief Game Warden. Muddy water is harmful to the trout. When the river rises in rains and gets filled with yellow mud many a trout died because of the turbid water.

The islets in the stream are beautifully fitted up with seats. Gay tea parties and lunch dishes are seen everywhere under the shady pine trees. Some seats project over the waterside to enable the holiday-makers enjoy the refreshing sight of water. There are badminton courts here and there and matches are played between parties previously arranged. Persons interested in bridge are seen busily carrying on the game. The islets are connected with each other by means of bridges and one can cross over from one to the other with ease. The glacial-water like a milky stream circumambulates the islets with its eddying currents. Roads are well kept and cars can easily reach the interior parts of the Rajawas plateau.

The Pahalgam club

The Pahalgam club is run by the Government. The secretary of the club is the Executive officer of the place. It maintains an office which is in the charge of a clerk of the department of Tourism. All enquiries regarding membership should be made from the office.

The club has a superb location. It is situated on an island surrounded by the branches of the lidder. The rapid torrent with its milky glacial-water forming pools and whirls, encompasses the place with its cool breezes. The cluster of pines and firs which covers the premises casts a refreshing shade and fills the atmosphere with fragrance which enlivens the body and the mind. The island stretches from south to north. There are a number of tanks built for women, children and non-swimmers for bathing purposes. It is dangerous to go out into the torrent, because the flow is rapid and the rocks of the beds are slippery. When once caught in the rapids, one cannot easily get back to the safety of dry land. For children there are trapezes to ride on. There is a lovely stretch of land attached to the club, but the pity is that round about the place acacia is being planted instead of pines. The place should have trees which harmonise with plant life on the surrounding mountains.

There is a few Sunflowers, Zinnias, Crysanthemum and other garden varieties planted round the building. But there is a rich variety of wild flowers for a botanist to study. An expanse of Mentha sylvestris, with sweet scent, deep blue Delphinium and Erysimum altaicum. The club is the centre of activity. The Visitors' Association performs various games to entertain the public. One of their chief functions is the show which is given on the Independence Day (15th August).

In the morning at 9 a.m., the Indian Union Flag is hoisted, lectures and talks are delivered, the purpose of which is to cultivate one's own character, to follow Gandhiji's footsteps, to serve humanity, be unselfish and let India lead world in world peace.

Sweets are distributed among children and then sports are held between the ages from five to under sixty. After 9 p.m., a bon-fire is lit by a group in the disguise of forest dwellers and cosmic dramas are performed on the stage, songs are sung and buffoons create in audience an unbounded jubilation. The sparks from the fire rise higher to kiss the stars in the heaven. While, they in their turn shed luster and effulgence from various quarters. In the east a little above the eastern horizon is the Altair the first magnitude star of the Aquila, in the west near the horizon is the Acturus the brightest star of Bootes, in the north lies the Poloris in the middle of Cassopeia and Ursa major, in the south is the twisted tail of Scorpio with two horizontal stars, while on its neck shines the red star Antares. In the centre of the firmament, the Cygnus Lyre, the Corona, and Cepheus are the principal constellations. The Glaxy spans the heaven from north to south.

In the dark forest covered mountains slopes, with red and white electric bulbs shedding light in tents, buildings and hotels, the whole place appears like a star-city.

RAMBLES FROM PAHALGAM

Ganesh Bal

This place is on the right bank of the Lidder and is about a mile from Pahalgam and is dedicated to god Ganesh who is believed to remove all obstacles in one's way when he is worshipped before any undertaking is taken in hand. There is a rock besmeared with red-lead (sindhur) in the stream. The people from the lower villages come here on some occasion to offer sacrifices. There is a tradition that Sikander the Iconoclast intended to go to the cave of Amar Nath to desecrate it. When he arrived there, he smote with his hammer on the Ganesh rock. Out flowed blood. Thereupon he did not venture to proceed to Amar Nath. There is a dharmasala at this place. It is a delightful experience to sit under a tree and watch the foamy flow of the torrent.

Mamal

This spot is also about a mile from Pahalgam. It stands across the Kolahoi stream up towards the mountain side. There is an old temple there the pinnacle of which was adorned with gold during the reign of one of the early kings. There is also a spring beautifully banked with long dressed stones of about 8th century. This was dedicated to Shiva and was called Mamalishwara. It is said that Ganesh was placed as doorkeeper not to allow any one to enter the temple without his permission. So it was called Mam Mal—Don't go. There is a priest to look after the temple. In summer the place is regularly visited by the populac of Pahalgam.

Baisaran and Tulian

These are two glades in the mountain side surrounded by pines. The going is a bit steep and involves some exertion. Hence sufficient quantities of eatables should be carried to satisfy hunger which acquires a keen edge as a result of the march.

Baisaran (Vaisaran—breeze blowing)

It is about three miles from Pahalgam along the Hospital road. It is a quiet camping ground right in the heart of the coniferous region vibrant with fragrant breezes on all sides. Thee is also a spring and a small rill passing through the glade. There is a big rock in the centre of the glade. It is said that saint Zain Shah (Zanak Reshi) meditated 12 years on that stone. There was then living a Gujar with his family. He had a cow from which he gave milk continuously to Zain Shah for 12 years. Once the wife of the Gujar murmured that during 12 years they would have obtained 12 calves from the cow. The saint heard this and called for the Gujar and told him to go to the cowshed and call calves by their names from the door. Thereby 12 calves came out from the shed. When the Gujar was busy with calling the saint left the place. The Gujar searched all sides and found him on the bank of the Lidder at Langan Bal where he crossed it and finally settled at Aishimuqam where his Ziarat is existing.

Tulin

Likewise is a peaceful camping site. It is twelve miles from Pahalgam. There is a mountain tarn.

Shikargah is another interesting glade to visit.

Tsandanwör or Thanin

Tsandanwari or Chhandanwari (Tsandan—pleasure giving coolness, Wari—a farm) is the second stage from Pahalgam on the Amar Nath pilgrimage route. It is eight miles from Pahalgam. There are sheds for pilgrims on the way. It has a nice bridle path and will make a good days ride for an excursion to enjoy the glories of Nature. The path goes along the bank of the torrent with pools and cataracts under the cool coniferous trees refresh the eye and enliven the brain. Here a stream of pure water joins the Sheshi Nag torrent from Astan Marg. Under the trees some of the alpine flowers, the Cran's bill, forget-me-nots, Myiosotis, Asters and various kinds of flowers are to be found in the vegetation.

The old name of the place is Thanin which is a corruption of Thaninshwar an aspect of Mahadiv. Here are a few Gujar sheds and now and then one comes across a snow bridge spanning the torrent.

Here is a tourist hut.

Astanmarg

Pahalgam to Tsandanwari—seven miles, Tsandanwari to Astanmarg—four miles. The word Astan is the corrupt form of styan which means frozen-marg, a meadow. In times gone by when the slopes of mountains were covered with glaciers their gradual and slow movement scooped out this valley and the avalanches cleared trees from the place leaving a plain altogether bereft of trees. Here shepherds find green pasturage for their cattle and flocks.

This is the valley where Arcadian simplicity unveils herself in her primeval bloom. The trees, mountains, streams and the feathered world deepens the all pervasive solitude. Stealthily flows the slow, smooth stream as if taking care not to disturb the tranquillity of Nature. It rises from various springs and contains no glacial water carrying sand-particles flowing from mountain flanks. The valley is bounded on the west by Rabi Marg which is a watershed between Astan Marg and Harbagwan Nag on the east by Göb Dalan which is the watershed between Astan Marg and Sheshi Nag. Wood is available and birch trees are in plenty. The folds in mountains are very conspicuous and summits are like serrated edges forming fantastic shapes to beguile the imaginative on-looker.

The Sasököṭ, slope, over which a path goes to the Amar Nath Cave is covered with gravel, sand and scree, hence during bad weather this pass is very difficult. Consequently the Kashmir Government has banned this route for pilgrims. At the foot of the pass there are flower beds of Edellwesis, Dandelion and Geranium growing among stones. A little higher Corydalis falconeri grows side by side with these flowers while Euphorbia and Iris cover the higher slopes. Still higher Rhododendron and creeping willow cover the slope below the naked peak. The Oxallis digyna, yellow and pink Corydalis and Saxifage show themselves near the top where the pack ponies can make their way with difficulty. All peaks round about have been reduced to pebbles and sand owing to insolation and weathering and heaps of small stones are seen everywhere.

This is an excellent camping ground where fatigue, boredom and mental worry vanish effortlessly. It is a spot for philosophers, writers and saints. All nature is astir during the day and at night the moon and star constellations send their ray through pines needles to embrace the beauty of the place. The reflection of the full moon in the clear depths of the stream creates the illuision of a shining pearl glowing in the abysmal deep. Such is Astan Marg, the home of peace, serenity and sublimity, the restorer of health and vitality.

Arau

Arau is seven miles from Pahalgam. The path is a pony-track. On either side of the path Balsam and Stacys grow in abundance. The maiden-hair and ferns hide themselves in shady nooks behind the rocks. Viburnum nervosum and witch hazel grow under pines. Dodder, a parasite grows on the former and feeds on it. Mentha sylvestris a fragrant herb is also common.

The path sometimes leaves the steam and sometimes follows it. Watching its flow will yield ample recompense in the sigh of the beautiful torrent. Birds such as redstart, whistling thrushes, grosbeaks and yellow-headed wagtails are also observed.

Arau is a hamlet of about a dozen huts exclusively made of unhewn planks with very little iron used in them. They are huddled together as a safeguard against the severity of winter. a few willows grow round the huts and a few maize and potato fields surround the village. The fields are encircled by fences made of the branches of trees on which meadow huntings sit to watch their prey.

The word Arau means a sound, the mountain torrent which flows down out of the Katri Nag over the Danawat mountains produces noises which probably gave the place its name. It is a rolling meadow of velvety green turf, fringed with fir and pines on which in summer tits, wood-peckers, turtle-dove and nut-thach find their food, and emit melodious song. It is worth-while to explore the surroundings of this place and for that may lead to the discovery of the remains of a an ancient temple hereabout. It is a quiet camping ground enveloped in solitude.

Here is a hut for tourists.

Tar Sar and Kolahoi Glacier

The most suitable site for camping in Lidderwaṭ 8,952 ft. above sea level. It is seven miles from Arau and lies at the junction of several routes. Here is also a tourist hut. The stream from Tar Sar joins here. The path at times skirts the stream and at times leave it to go up a few hundred feet above over the densely forested plateau. Slowly the coniferous belt change into the birch and meadow region. The shade of trees gets more and more scarce and hence it is better to start early.

Arrangements for this trek should be made from Pahalgam. All camp equipment can be hired from certain agencies and warm bedding and clothing should be necessarily brought over. Pack ponies and riding ponies can be obtained from contractors. It is necessary to have an axe for cutting wood and a spade for digging a trench round the tent as soon as it is pitched. A staff, several grass sandsals and boots with nails are essential. Grass sandals are best to walk over rocks and snow. Lighting arrangements should be carefully attended to. Cinnamon should be freely used in tea and some good stimulants kept at hand. The camping site should not become a pool when it rains, the slope should keep it always dry.

The path passes through the boulders round which dock grows in profusion. On some islets in the torrent there are a very many specimen of alpine flowers. A couple of logs or a bridge over the stream and when it is in flood it always sweeps away this bridge. Care should be taken when loaded pack ponies cross the bridge. the scenery is wild precipitous mountain slopes rise on both sides of the valley which is strewn over with boulders among which alpine flowers peep out most magnificently. Occassionally a grove of birch trees may be seen growing in some shady places or in the joints where two stratas meet. Before we enter the Kolahoi valley a torrent from the Sona Sar lake which lies at the foot of Basmai Galli 13,885 ft. flows over a precipice and is divided into a number of distributaries before it falls into the Lidder. These are called Satalnjan (seven branches) which also means streams or koloha and this might be the origin of the name of Kolahoi.

The valley spreads out bounded by the high mountains devoid of coniferous trees but covered more or less with birch and Juniper bushes. A number of Gujar sheds can be seen here. These are occupied for two summer months by the Gujars who come with cattle to live here. There are also shepherds with their flock. The valley is well covered with Senecio chrysanthemoides an dock which is a potherb when it is young. There are a number of islets which contain clusters of Corydalis thrysiflora and Erysimum altaicum and caltha palistris. On the east of the valley over the precipice a torrent flows in silvery sheets to join the main stream in the valley. It rises from the Dudh Nag (milk spring) which is fed by glaciers and lies on a plateau. It is circular in shape. The whole slope is beautifully covered with alpine flowers. From here one can have a charming view of the Kolahoi glacier with its crevasses and boulders and glistening surface. The rumbling noise of water rushing underneath the glacier can be heard from here. A walk to the snout of the glacier is a delightful experience. The lower part of this icy valley is covered with debris and moraines so much so that no trace of ice can be seen. The thickness of the ice is at least 200 ft. and its flow must be 4 to 6 inches in 24 hours. The glacier scratches rocks and scoops lakes while at the same time it is constantly receding. It is possible that it will in course of time retain its mountain flank only.

It is very interesting to walk over the glacier for some yards. Care should be taken that there are no crevasses. If the snow at any point looks yellow or loose a crevasse must be underneath. An ice-axe is an important item of equipment. In going over a glacier covered with crevasses it is necessary that the party should tie a long rope round their loins so that if by chance some one falls into a crevasse, he will not sink deep into the fissure. Sometimes planks are used to cross a crevasse and sometimes one has to take a zigzag course or to jump over the crevasse where it is narrow.

The other extremity of this glacier is towards the Harbhagwan valley, where it has a frowning aspect and is full of dangerous crevasses. It must be about six miles long. These fields of ice are perennial sources of water supply on which the prosperity of our country depends. The Himalayas are skirted by many glorious glaciers which are extended to very low levels, but now owing to changed climatic conditions are retreating to their mountain origins. It is possible to find here a stone with fossil impression of the fenestella type. For there is a strata of fenestella in the western mountain system which we discovered in 1925.

The bold peak of Gwashi Brör (Kolahoi) 17,779, ft. rises 6,000 ft. above the surrounding mighty peaks of the valley. It can be observed from Gulmarg and other high plateaus of the Kashmir valley like cone of crystal kissing the sapphire cheek of the heavens. These magnificent peaks wrapped in haze and lending perpetual glory to Kashmir are symbols of peace, disinterested service and firmness.

'A look at the mountain peaks is a perpetual delight. They are an emblem of purity, dignity and repose. They strike one as a vision of soft pure white in a gaze-like haze of delicate blue, too light and too ethereal for earth, but seemingly a part of heaven; a vision which is a religion in itself, which diffuses its beauty throughout one's being, and evokes from it all that is most pure and lovely'.

Selecting a suitable spot for lunch right in Nature's blossom, catching a breath of everlasting happiness, one would observe a white-breasted dipper sitting on the rock in the stream, moving its body up and down or diving in the steam, a yellow-headed wagtail or a whiter-capped redstart searching after its food near the stream, or a pair of snow-pigeons or swifts coming out of rocks and flying past the ledge. On the mountain slope a brick- red kestril would be balancing on its wings to scan the ground for a vole or mice for its meal, or a swarm of kites, vultures, lammergiers may be found feasting themselves over a dead sheep.

It is always advisable to arrive at the camp early, because late arrivals causes anxiety in the camp and walking over stones and boulders without a light is not a pleasant experience. A march to the camp at Lidderwaṭ covers 13 miles. A good dinner would remove all fatigue and ensure sound sleep for the night. The dawn would greet you with the melodious symphony of whistling thrushes and grey-head thrushes from the adjoining area round the tent. The cooing of the turtle-dove and the croaking of the jungle crow would assail the ears again and again. Even occasional hoots of the wood-owl would be heard. If time is not consideration, it is worth-while staying for the day and survey the bird-life or plant-life round the place.

Tar Sar

Lidderwaṭ Tar Sar—ten miles. Leaving Lidderwaṭ we pass slopes covered with rose bushes, Geums, Potentiallas. Sometimes it is possible to cross a snow-bridge near Hamwas. There are few Gujar Chalets here. A clear view of Kolahoi peak can be had from here. A little higher up a stream from Sekiwas (sandy place) joins the stream from Tar Sar. Skiwas is an open valley. It is strewn over with boulders. The vegetation is luxuriant. The Phlomis, the Salvia hians, blue Corydalis and many different varieties of alpine flowers are found here. This is also a junction of several routes. One on the right, passes over Yemher pass 13,400 ft. staircase of the Angel of Death—via Zaiwan on to Kulan on the Zojila road. The middle path passes along the shallow lake of Tsanda Sar over Sonamus on to Sumbal on the Zojila road. While the left one winds along TAr SAr via Dachigam valley to Shalamar (Srinagar). The last route is not opened to public.

Going along the Tar Sar stream we enter Dandabari where stones smoothered by weather are scattered all over the valley. In between them grows floral vegetation. The birch trees are not in a presperous condition. The stream flows over boulders and to avoid these it is necessary to leave the stream and walk high up over the grassy spur till we reach Tar Sar Lake (12,500 ft.).

Tar Sar lies among mountains open from one side. It is shaped like an almond. It is not awe-inspiring like Koñsar Nag. The shores are low and form an excellent camping ground. The mountains are not high but are devoid of trees. They are covered with herbal vegetation and water is transparent and very sweet. This is a calm and quiet place. The appetite is apt to acquire a sharp edge here. There is no fuel available. To prepare tea one should bring some fuel along with him. It is worthwhile to bathe in the lake, but one should not venture into its deeper parts unless one is a strong swimmer and an resist cold. One is enveloped by Nature and She permeates the whole of his being—physical as well as mental. when the wind ruffles the surface of water a little, the crests of wavelets catching the suns rays turn the water into a sheet of sparkling diamonds. In such sublime moments man's little self merges into the Universal Soul which pervades the universe and is the life of all things.

Near the western shore of the lake there are two islets and a deep inlet where sometimes icebergs can be seen floating. Many legends and folk-tales are associated with this lake. The southern slope is more or less precipitous. On the eastern shore Potentillas are in profusion. A climb up the Tar Sar pass which is the demarcation line of Dachigam Rakh reveals another beautiful Lake Mar Sar (cupid Lake) the waters of which drain the Rukh skirting the base of mount Mahadiv empties itself into the Srinagar Reservoir.

The meadow round about the lake is an excellent pasturage. Where shepherds bring their flocks. They have a great veneration for the lake and offer a sacrifice on their first arrival and departure. In 1925 when we visited this lake, the following conversation took place between the shepherd who lived here and myself.

Shepherd : 'You should not bathe in this sacred lake, saints only can do so'.

Myself : 'How long have you been coming here ?'

Shepherd : 'My grandfather and my father also used to come here and I have been coming with my flocks for forty years'.

Myself : 'Have you ever felt the presence of the Great Power in this sacred place ?'

Shepherd : 'Whata simpleton you are ! Listen, sir, people entrust their flocks to me and sometimes I sell a lamb for Rs. 2 or Re 1- 8-0 and insist on my customers returning to me the skin and the head of the animal so that I can show them to the owners and can tell them that the lamb was eaten by a panther or a wild beast. Do you think that with such a sinful mind I shall ever be able to feel the presence of the Supreme Power ?'

Ten years later we launched a rubber canoe in the lake and surveyed every nook and corner of it. Bird-life in this region is not plentiful. Several flocks of red-billed choughs and some griffon vultures sailing round about the craggy peaks may be observed. Return by the same route to the camp at Lidderwaṭ, one can have some rest and, if possible, stay a day longer if one be not in a hurry to move down to Pahalgam or Srinagar.

Har Bhagwan Lake

This is one of the most exciting treks which could last at least for a week. One should be equipped with tents and every essential for ones comfort etc.—warm clothing, grass sandals, thermos, binoculars (if possible) and a camera. There are three stages :

Pahalgam to Arau	...	7 miles
Arau to Armin	...	7 miles
Armin to Har Bahgwan Nag	...	5 miles

The whole path is a pony track. The path from Pahalgam to Arau is a lovely walk along a river among conifers which nurse small bird-life and the undergrowth consists of beautiful Geranium, Gentians and Forget-me-nots.

The path from Arau runs under huge shady fir trees. Here one can find edible mushrooms under the trees. Arisaema tortuosum (the top of this plant is like the head of a snake) and

Podyphyllum emodi, with its red fruit, Oxyria digyna, a potherb grow round the rocks. Several varieties of them are found and after one crosses the bridge near Girwad clusters of blue poppies are found growing among the rocks.

Gagri Pather is a flat spot where the morning meal should be prepared or a lunch served. Among the vegetables found here, mushrooms and Oxyria digyna cooked together make a good dish. In the centre of this spot is a big rock on the top of which various alpine flowers grow. I do not like to burden the mind of the trekker with their names. Let him observe and see for himself and consult The Beautiful Valleys of Kashmir, page 55. Towards the right bank of the stream is a small fall. Slaty-blue fly-catchers, pied-woodpeckers and jungle crows can be observed here.

Further away the slopes are covered with wild dock, Jacob's ladder, Senecio, Cynoglossom, Swertia and Verbasium thapsus. White-capped redstarts and plumbeous redstarts might be seen on some rock in the torrent.

Armin (Armini—beauty all round) is a flat spot and good camping ground. It is covered with Senecio chrysanthemoides which along with dock is generally found between 9,000 ft. to 10,000 ft. above the sea level. A stream flows from the north-east by the side of the valley. The northern aspect of the mountains is covered with fir and birch while the southern aspect owing to insolation and weathering is rocky and precipitous. Here one finds some Gujar families from whom milk, butter and milk-cakes can be purchased. There are also a few springs here. Spring water is clearer than glacial water and should be used preferably for drinking purposes. Grey wagtails and whistling thrushes can be observed. Brown dippers are to be seen sitting on boulders raising and lowering their bodies. It is interesting to see how they dive after an insect in a rushing torrent. There flight is straight, almost touching the water, while wagtail, fly in curves. Flocks of yellow-billed choughs may be observed flying over the slope.

An ascent of 300 ft. leads to a flat spot called Arm Pathri. The Floral vegetation on all sides is magnificent. Near the lower Nafaran there is a beautiful fall. There are also some Gujar Sheds. The upper Nafaran is a fairly large valley where no fuel is obtainable. The mountain flanks and some snow-beds give rise to the Armin stream, which joins the Lidder at Arau.

The Har Bhagwan Ghatti (12,729 ft.) leads to the Har Bhagwan valley. The slope of the pass is covered with slate, shale and scree. Among the slate we found Corydalis govaniana and Corydalis crossifolia with three fan-shaped thick leaves and purple flowers. The last lap of the pass is a series of steps where pack ponies have to be unloaded. The view from the pass is superb. Right at the foot of the pass is the turquoise-green Har Nag (the lake of peace) shining like a glittering eye at the head of an emerald green body. A part of the lake is silted up. Towards the N.N.E. are the snowy peaks of Baltal with glaciers interspersed among them. On the right is the Har Bhagwan peak 16,041 ft. and on the left is Kolahoi surrounded by glaciers. On the top of the pass Potentilla plants are to be found.

The slopes of Har Nag (12,269 ft.) are steep, covered with Geum and Red Potentilla. There is a pony track up these slopes, but in bad weather it becomes very slippery and dangerous.

There is a legend connected with the spring. Har Nag sent his son and daughter-in-law to find a spot where he could live near Kolahoi (Gwashi-brör). They went back and told him that there was room for them but none for him. He then sent his son-in-law, who returned with the news that there was room for his father-in-law but not for himself. So he cursed and petrified his son and daughter-in-law and made room for his son-in-law at his feet. The two rocks towards the silted part of the lake are the petrified son and daughter-in-law while the lakelet at the bottom is his son-in-law.

Here one meets shepherds with their flocks. On the first day of their arrival, they kill a sheep and cook their food in well-washed utensils. Before they eat, they place a dish full of cooked rice and meat on the shore of the lake as an offering to the spring deity.

There is a nice camping ground here. The spot selected for the tent should however be such that rain water naturally flows away from it. The first and foremost duty of the camp manager is to dig a trench round the tent and prepare tea.

The north of a place can be found by observing the position of Druv Ji (Pole Star) in the firmament. It occupies the middle position between the constellation of safta Reshi (the Great Bear) and Cassopiea. A line joining the two stars of the Great Bear called pointers passes through the Pole Star, or if the angle in cassopia (lady's chair) in the form of W is trisected will also pass through it. It will add pleasure if other consellation be also located.

The valley is full of marmots' burrows. These animals are as large as a big cat and brown in colour. They have been found living above 9,000 ft. in dreary regions. When they hoot at intruders they stand on their hind legs and join their fore legs in the manner of a Kangaroo or a penguin. They are sometimes killed for their furs. The burrows are formed of Zigzag passages. A copper-coloured lizard is also found at a similar height. The naked-peaks are the haunts of the ibex and the stag, which descend to lower levels in winter and early spring. Brown bears are also sometimes found here.

The valley is inhabited by shepherds, Gujars and Bakörbans. On Fridays the Gujars make milk cakes from buffaloes' milk. The milk is boiled and some churned milk or whey is put into it till it turns sour. It is then strained and cakes are made from the residue. Cakes are also made from churned milk, but they are thicker and not so good. The cakes are fried in oil or ghee and eaten.

It is worth-while surveying the valley. The Western end of the Kolahoi glacier gives rise to a torrent which drains the whole of the Har Bhagwan valley and enters the Amar Nath stream (Pantsatarni) at Baltal. It is worth-while to climb up the edge of the glacier made through the torrent and have a glimpse of the frowning crevasses of the glacier. The ice has turned pink and blue and it seems that the water too is of pink colour. It may be that the rocks contain some pink stuff which colours the water. No attempt should be made to negotiate the glacier itself, because its fissures are deep and slippery. It is possible to go over his pass to the Kolahaoi valley but it is not a pony track.

There must have been a time when this glacier extended right into the valley and joined the other glacier from the adjoining mountains in the valley and scooped out the Lake. But now it has receded and skirt the Kolahoi mountain which is popularly called Gawashi Brör (the goddess of light) because it catches the rays of the sun first in the morning. There are no trees here except a few juniper bushes.

This valley is the meeting place of several routes. One, which is not a pony track, goes along the Har Bhagwan Galli (14,086 ft.). At Rabi Marg there is a lake on the way where, according to the story of a shepherd, one may meet fairies and hear them singing and if a person gets enamoured of them he loses his life. At the foot of the pass lies Astan Marg. The other route with goes along Razdön Pass (13,200 ft.) is longer but easier for ponies. The pass leads to Astan Marg which is twelve miles from the Cave of Amar Nath.

Baltal is fifteen miles from here and Sona Marg which is at a distance of ten miles from Baltal is connected by a motorable road with Srinagar.

A Visit to the Cave of Amar Nath

The Cave of Amar Nath is about twenty-nine miles from Pahalgam. The famous pilgrimage to the cave takes place on Sawan purnamasi (July-August full moon). The congregation of pilgrims starts from Pahalgam on Duwadashi shkula pak (twelfth day of the bright fortnight). The route is marked by three stages.

Pahalgam to Tsandanwari eight and half miles.

Tsandanwari to Vaovajen eight miles.

Ascent to Pisu Hill (11,081 ft.) pony track.

No fuel except juniper is available during this part of the journey which is marked by a superb view of Shishiram Nag. There are some sheds for Sadhus en route.

Vaovajen to Pantasatarni eight and quarter miles.

Pantasatarni to Cave four miles.

On the return journey too some sheds of Sadhus are met with. On other days weather permitting, this journey can be performed in two days. A person starting early on horse-back will spend the night at Vaovajen. Early next morning he will visit the Cave and return to Pahalgam in the evening. There may possibly be a seasonal hotel at Vaovajen.

CHAPTER 17

SMILES FROM KASHMIR

By

Krishan Lal Shridharani

I

PALE HANDS OF SHALIMAR

The second time I visited Kashmir it was all smiles. The snow-capped peaks were smiling in the sun. The myriad brooks were tumbling with laughter. The Dal Lake got pink because the rays of the rising sun were tickling the Chinar trees and those white-waisted, slender, tall maidens of the Poplar tribe. The Shikara-men had the twinkle in their eyes, so characteristic of those good-hearted super-salesmen.

The first time I visited Kashmir it was all tears. It was more than a decade back, in 1947. The raiders were being pushed back and Baramulla was liberated only the day before our arrival. I had flown in from Delhi in Pandit Nehru's party. There was no electricity in Srinagar because the power house was destroyed by the raiders. Even to go to Shalimar Gardens across the Dal Lake was a risk because a ferocious, bearded Afridi face might come out of the shrubs in place of the pale hands.

THEN AND NOW

And then we neared Baramulla. We saw corpses of slain tribesmen still lying by the roadside. There were tears in Pandit

Nehru's eyes as he saw the demolition and desolation of a Catholic monastery. Pale girls, trembling, approached Indira Gandhi and showed their torn ear lobes as the raiders had no patience to unhook their gold ear-rings during the orgy of loot and rape. Empty houses and shops haunted, oppressed one as a deserted village would. I wrote a despatch in which I said that "some day the people of India will raise a monument to the lost virginity of Baramulla!" Had the raiders not stopped there overnight to plunder and to rape, they would have taken the dusty airstrip of Srinagar before the Indian troops could land the morning after. Kashmir would have been lost.

That was more than a decade back. Now, during my second trip, it was all serene and peaceful. Here was Kashmir without tears. Compared to Srinagar even Delhi appeared an agitated capital. Kashmir was having its biggest tourist season since independence. Yet there was not a single report of theft. Ornaments forgotten by foreigners were being returned by boatsmen. There were gaiety and song in the air. There were smiles on ivory faces. Indeed "There Are Smiles From Indiana," but here were Smiles from Kashmir, the best of the blossoms of the Valley of Gods. Only an outsider like me was aware of the "normalcy" because to the Kashmiris "normalcy" was a normal thing. I was given a clinching proof of normalcy. I was told that the wives of most of the United Nations Observers were in the family way; the men seemed to have very little to do at the front.

Thus I have seen Kashmir only twice, once when it was in tears and then again when it was full of smiles. It is a pity that I have been there only twice; I should have been there two hundred times. There is nothing in the world I would exchange Kashmir for; it is beauty and elegance incarnate. Kashmir is the most precious part of the Indian landscape. And the Kashmiri Muslim is the most precious aspect of the Indian polity; he is the sustenance of India's secularism as he is its source. And he is such a smiling man. He is an aspect of Kashmir's lures. Where every prospect pleases the man is smile, too.

VALLEY OF EYES

The poet has sung about the "The Pale Hands of Shalimar". To the West, therefore, Kashmir has meant pale hands — women of extraordinary clear complexion and dainty, carved-ivory beauty. And yet there is not a single houseboat, or a shikara, or a cocktail lounge named "Pale Hands". Would it not be thrilling for one European tourist to say to another : "See you at the Pale Hands this evening"? And this is the valley of tourists. Tourists, tourists everywhere. In the season, no houseboat, no hotel room is available for the love of money. V.I.P.s are dime a dozen. White European and American faces do not stand out, as they do in Madras, amidst the fair faces of the Kashmiris. Thus they are generally more numerous than would appear at first sight. Should not they be provided with a rendezvous place called "Pale Hands"? Every pilgrim has a rendezvous with destiny and every tourist a tryst with adventure.

Holding hands, however, is not a Kashmiri custom, nor an Indian one. One has to, therefore, believe the poet without a personal check-up. But faces are there, smiling and friendly, intelligent too, all around you. And what faces ! Chiselled out of pale marble ! The purest Aryan specimen ! Some sharp, curved Jewish noses too.

Srinagar is a city of faces, all kinds, and it takes all kinds. You see them on the Bund bordering the Jhelum. You see them in the bazaars. You see them in the windows. You see them peeping out of the small square windows of the boats that heave elbow to elbow in the river. You see them as the women bend down from the boat windows to wash utensils in the water that flows only a foot below. You see them in clusters of women surrounded by bigger clusters of children, as they wash clothes on the paved and straircased banks. Yes, Srinagar is a city of faces.

It is something even more precise. Srinagar is the Valley of Eyes! The most striking feature of the ivory face of a Kashmiri is his eyes. And here is a valley full of Eyes! Eyes as green as jade or the water of Anantnag (Nag means a brook in Kashmiri). Eyes as gray as the snow over the surrounding mountain peaks at noon. Eyes as blue as the ones that the princess had in the fairy tale you read when you were a dreamy boy. Eyes as black as the hair of a Kathakali dancer from Madras. Here are eyes that speak. They speak out the sophisticated language of the Kashmiri Pandit. But more often, far more often, far far more often, they twinkle with the practical wisdom of the unlettered. Sometimes these eyes of the mountains can be suspicious of the plainsmen, but they show self-confidence too. They have seen things. They are heavy with memories. Srinagar is the Valley of Eyes.

II

A BOUQUET OF ZAFFRAN

Everything auspicious is marked with Kumkum in India. Kumkum comes from saffron or zaffran, and saffron comes from Kashmir and Kashmir alone, from the vast plateaux of Pampur (ancient Padampur). One of the names of Kumkum, therefore, is Kashmiraja. Kashmiraja (like Kashmiriana) would thus be a fragrant title for any grab-bag which contains things exclusively Kashmiri and the essentials that annoint Indo-Kashmir relations. Here is my bouquet of zaffran, or Kashmiraja.

SO MUCH BEAUTY!

The late Gopalaswami Ayyangar, once the Diwan of Jammu and Kashmir and then the Indian Representative on the Kashmir Question, is credited with a classic remark. Emerging out the Chashma-Shahi Rest House he looked at the Dal Lake and the majesty of the mountains reflected in it. "We can't trust our neighbour with so much beauty!" he observed. A pro-Pakistan foreign correspondent told me with a twinkle in his eye : "I think Kashmir should go to Pakistan, but not so long as I am here to enjoy its beauty". Other more valid arguments are indeed there, but how can an Indian think of entrusting any neighbour or a stranger with so much beauty!

The enchanting vale of Kashmir resembles the snow-white foot- print of Parvati, daughter of the Himalayas, set in an expanse of murky mountains. This heavenly saucer with 52 petals is held by the Himalayas in its lap at an average height of about 6,000 feet above the sea. Around eighty-four miles in length, Kashmir is only twenty to twenty-five miles in breadth. On three sides it is ringed by snow-peaked mountains that cut it off from the world, while on the fourth side rocky barriers sixty miles in width separate it from the Punjab in the south. It is at Baramulla that the fortress is broken a bit to let Jhelum pour the heart of the mountains on the plains. Few people realize it. but Kashmir is further north than Tibet. The mountains in the north rise to a height of 18,000 feet, while on the south they obligingly dip down to 9,000 feet to enable India to hold Kashmir's pale hands over the Banihal Pass.

Larger and far more varied in its offerings than Switzerland, the Vale of Kashmir is an oval palm with fifty-two tapering fingers. One valley is different from another and even the looming mountains look sculptured into the shapes of pyramids and temples. Lakes, myriad murmuring springs, emerald turf, the lattice-work of tall, slender poplars and the haunting grooves of chinars, tall snow-capped mountains led by the Nanga Parbat — make it the playground of the gods. It can't be called a rock-bound prison as the mountains stand there not to keep the Kashmiris in but to keep undesirable outsiders out. It is a fortress which opens its gates to friends.

At one moment the mountains look like foamcrested waves. But the scenes shift quickly here and at another moment the drooping snow lines look like strips of white confetti being thrown by gods hiding on the other side. Each snow-white mountain peak looks like the face of Radha with a pitcher of milk on her head. The invisible Krishna must be mischievously throwing pebbles and puncturing the pitcher; for, there are many jets of milk in the form of brooks tumbling down the mountain sides. The sand at the bottom glows like the pulverized resistance of the rocks.

KASHMIRI VILLAGE

We Indians are apt to poetize our village. Personally I do not see in them much besides dust and fleas and dung. But the Kashmiri hamlet is a different thing. My mental picture of a Vedic Rishi's hermitage would not be much different. Out of the foliage of plane-trees or walnut, apple or apricot trees, peeps the cultivator's cottage. It has a kitchen garden at the back, and a sentry-box like wooden granary in the front. More often than not a clear sparkling stream flows under its upraised porch. On its grass banks do idle in the morning children and ducks and dogs — the dogs of the valley are real "Satyagrahis" because they do not budge an inch from the path of ten-ton lorries. There are streaks of coral red flowers before battalions of terraces of rootless, tender rice plants. The house-roofs are made of birch bark with earth spread on them, so in time grass grows on them dotted with iris. The cottages are far apart, not like the shoulder-to-shoulder hovels of villages in Uttar Pradesh. In such surroundings the Kashmiri villager lives, never separated from three things — Kangri (a portable stove), tobacco and tea.

CITY'S SEVEN BRIDGES

New York, stretching long along the Hudson, is measured by "up-town" and "down-town". "Meet me down-town for dinner tonight," a New Yorker would say to a friend. Srinagar, snaking long along the Jhelum, is measured by its bridges. "You will get aspirin near the Third Bridge", they would say. Or, "I live at the Sixth Bridge". The best "gustaba" (Kashmiri meatballs), for instance, might be had near the Fifth Bridge. It is a city of seven bridges and it is determined to remain so. For instance, there are two more bridges, recently built, which would give the present first bridge the number three, and the present seventh bridge the number nine. But these two upstarts have failed to enter Srinagar's folklore. Like a Hindu wife who is ashamed to call her husband by his name, Srinagaris are ashamed to call them by their numbers. They just don't talk about them, although they walk on them.

NOT A SNOWMAN

Eternal snow is all around the valley. The oval bowl is itself full of snow in winter. And yet Yuvraj Karan Singh, Sadar-i-Riyasat, saw the falling snow for the first time in New York, just as the present pen-pusher did. The Administration in the Maharajah's time moved from Srinagar to Jammu, as it does now, before the winter set. Last year the Yuvaraj saw the falling snow-flakes for the first time in his life in the valley, because it came early and surprised the Administration.

THE MOST CERTIFIED MAN

No people on earth are such collectors of certificates and testimonials and chits. Your might see hanging from the wall of a shoemaker a recommendation from Pandit Jawaharlal Nehru, all in his handwriting. The massage man has a treasure trove of certificates, and he would tell you one story invariably : "Such and such English or American Sahib had massages in Sweden and Turkey and Russia and everywhere, but he said mine was the best, and he wanted to take me along with him." The Kashmiri salesman is as deft a names-dropper as a society columnist in America. By the time he has sold you more goods than you came to buy, you have the satisfaction of knowing that many and much more important people are going around the world in clothes and shoes that you are just now purchasing. The collection of certificates of a houseboat owner would fill a shelf. And you are enticed into adding your own before you are through. Every Kashmiri seems to be certified. He is the most certified man in the world.

THE QUESTION OF ISA

The characters from Ramayana and Mahabharata have been in the habit of having been every-where in India. So you see places in Kashmir where they had slept or played or slayed. But the hero of the New Testament also seems to have visited the vale. The tradition is that Jesus Christ was for years in the vale and in Ladakh and that he even went down to Dwarka. Otherwise, the missing seven years of his life (or are they six ?) cannot be explained. The legend tries to be logical. Anyway, there is an alleged tomb of Christ right in Srinagar. Yuvraj Karan Singh explained, however, that it is the tomb of Kazi Isa; hence the confusion; some people have come to believe that it belongs to Isa (Jesus) Masih.

Brimming with legends, the vale has a tradition of recorded history also. Spangler asserts that we Indians have no historical sense. Kashmir seems to have it, anyway, and it might not be surprising if Pandit Nehru's yen for history is due to the fact that he is a Kashmiri Pandit. Kalhana's Rajtarangini records Kashmir's history from the earliest time.

WHITE SHAHTUSH

I had read and written poems about Chukor without having ever seen one, just as Avanindranath Tagore had painted the Taj Mahal without setting eyes on it. The bird to me was a poetic concept rather than a reality, so faithful to his mate and intoxicated only on the wine of moon-light. This bird, known to Europeans as the Greek Partridge, I saw for the first time on the Banihal mountain and near Verinag. An illusion was thus broken by Kashmir, because Chukor looks like a glorified partridge.

But another illusion was built by Kashmir. It is about shahtush, the ring shawl, the thing Kashmiri that the Kashmiri Pandit Nehru likes most. It does pass through a ring, is softer than an infant's brow, and warmer, according to Kashmiri salesman, than the sun. It is indeed the warmest wool, and they talk about so many degrees. White shahtush, I am told, is the rarest of things. It comes from the small white star on the forehead of the shahtush sheep. It takes 15 years to collect enough white shahtush for a shawl. I can't wait, but my purse can.

NISHAT VERSUS SHALIMAR

Srinagaris as well as all visitors from outside are divided in two camps : those who believe that Shalimar is more beautiful versus those who believe that Nishat is prettier. Shalimar was built by Jahangir for "The Light of Harem", Nurjahan. It is like a Japanese scroll whose beauty cannot be taken in at one glance, from one spot. It is also a bit gloomy in order to spread the traditional melancholia of the Mughal love lore. Nishat, on the other hand, although larger, can be comprehended, taken in, at one glance, from one spot. The ten terraces and the water falling down them from fountains focus easily.

But, for the glory and magnificent use of natural water streams, there is nothing to beat Achhabal, full of full-blown chinar grooves and water cascades. It is there that your see the remnants of a Mughal hamam (Turkish Bath). Those boys knew how to live ! And the girls caught on quickly.

A CALL TO COLOURS

The flowers of Kashmir are a rainbow of colours. The mountain tops become a symphony of hues at dawn and dusk.

But the clothes of men and women are drab, jet black and a dirty white. (How is it that desert people, in Rajputana, Saurashtra, Kutch, have more colourful costumes! Perhaps man there tries to make up for nature's monotony!)

It seems to me that cottages and houses can also improve by a dash of colour. Swiss chalets, with their painted windows and walls, add to the natural beauty of the Alps. The costumes of Kashmiris can take something more than colour. The big blown-up gown debars lines and folds that set woman apart from man. Laurence, the great authority on the vale, calls the Kashmiri gown effeminate and quotes folklore to the effect that it is this portable tent which has made the Kashmiri "goat-hearted". Of course, the Kashmiri regards the gown as a house for his Kangar ("What Laila was on Majnu's bosom, so is the Kangar to a Kashmiri"). And this voluminous gown hides not only the Kangar but many a burn-marks. I was heartened to find in Laurence an observation I had made on my own. The famed Kashmiri beauty and complexion is more to be found in Srinagar than in the countryside.

GILLMARG

Dr. P.S. Gill, whom I knew in America during his and mine student days, a cosmic-rays expert from Aligarh University, has perched himself on the highest point in Gulmarg to look after the Gulmarg Research Observatory. Among other things, he measures the increase in radio-activity due, perhaps, to the Russian nuclear tests in southern Siberia. Perhaps Dr. Homi Bhabha does not pay him enough attention, (scientists being more jealous then women), but he is becoming so well-known in his summer nest that Gulmarg may be renamed Gillmarg.

MAHA-GUJARAT

Of all the provincials of India, it is the Gujaratis, it seems, who frequent Kashmir most. You see them everywhere, especially in Srinagar and Pahalgam—they do not like Gulmarg so much. Their vegetarian restaurants and hotels are to be found everywhere. There are some houseboats which specialize in vegetarian food simply to attract Gujaratis. There is a hotel named "Girnar" after a famous mountain in Saurashtra which is not known outside Saurashtra. The Nedou's Hotel has become the hotbed of Parsis, a special variety of Gujaratis. If the Kashmir Government is not alerted by the advocates of the Samyukta Maharashtra, Kashmir might become a part of Maha-Gujarat !

CHAPTER 18

LAKES AND FLOATING GARDENS

By

C. G. Bruce

Life in a Kashmir house-boat is very like a summer holiday spent in one on the Thames. But how infinitely more enchanting are our surroundings ! We find no notice boards nailed up to bar our progress, and we are told that we may go and camp in one of the famous gardens, baghs as they are called.

Some of these gardens are famous on account of the royal heads which planned their planting. Nur Mahal, the beloved wife of the Mogul Emperor Jehangir, had evidently the gift of imagination when she superintended the laying out of marble terraces, plashing fountains, long canals, and stately walks. And we breathe in old romance as we wander through the summer-houses with their black marble columns so richly carved. Great must have been the love of her royal husband in the indulgence of these plans of his beloved wife, for the marble hailed from Delhi, and the workmen too. That his love remained constant we are convinced by seeing merely a picture of the white marble tomb he erected to her memory—the Taj Mahal at Agra.

True gardeners and foresters must be possessed of imagination or else of deep unselfishness, for they can seldom hope to see the matured beauty of their cherished plans and planting. This is partly why such doings are ennobling, for they give of their best to future generations. The kind fairy, called Compensation, sees to it that they have a very fair share of the pleasure all the same. There is such intense delight in watching the growth in the concrete of one's abstract hopes. And so here we bow ourselves, under the shade of the plane trees in these lovely gardens, to the memory of her who planned them. The Shalimar and Nasim Baghs, and the Nishat or Garden of Gladness, have provided themes for many songs of sentiment and romance.

The Kashmiris love flowers, and, like the Japanese, have their spring expedition to view the blossom. They will go out en masse to the foot of the hill on which is the fort to admire the peach blossom, and again, later, on to the Nishat Bagh to visit the lilacs when in full bloom, just as Londoners go to Bushey Park on "Chestnut Sunday."

The Dal lake is one of the great attractions to Kashmir's visitors. the water is so clear that the reflections of the surrounding mountains are perfect. Some of the photographs of the Dal lake are equally clear, whichever side you turn them. Chenars and willows, picturesque chalets, dark cypresses, blue distance, and snow mountains, make a picture hard to equal anywhere. Graceful little fishing-boats, called "Shikharas," skim about with sails like white wings.

This lake is not one sheet of water, but it is all the prettier for that reason. Little canals intersect the floating gardens and small islands, while villages and orchards are dotted about its banks, which cover about five miles in length and two in breadth.

Of the outlying lakes, Manasbal is quite lovely. It lies between the Sind river and the mountains, locked in and reached by a narrow channel through which only narrow boats can be piloted. It also has the remains of another Mogul garden.

The Wular lake has at its head the village of Bandipura, which is the point from which the road to Gilgit starts. This lake, in which the rivers Sind and Jhelum and other waters all mingle, is charming in spring and early summer, and again in late autumn, but it is very dangerous by reason of the swarms of mosquitoes during July, August, and September—indeed, we are wise to avoid all the waterways of Kashmir during these months.

Another lake of some interest is Gangarbal, which is cradled in the rocky centre of Haramouk, above the Wular lake. It lies at a height of 12,000 feet, and is held sacred by the natives, some of whom declare it to be the source of their holy river Ganges.

A unique and fascinating feature of the Dal lake consists in a series of floating gardens. Masses of weeds are woven into a kind of basket in which rich earth is placed, and melons, cucumbers, tomatoes, and purple egg plants flourish in them, needing no other water than that which their roots touch. And so they float in a tangled mass rich with colour. We constantly meet boat-loads of fruit and vegetables being piloted along the canals which interlace these gardens and the lake itself.

Modern gardening is not neglected in Srinagar, though there is nothing on the scale of the Empress Nur Mahal's stately pleasances. The pretty villas have delightful gardens, and that of the British Residency is charming, especially in spring and early summer; bright with many familiar flowers and shrubs, gay with birds, and, for a background, views of the everlasting hills and their purity.

As we have said, the Emperor Jehangir loved Kashmir, and took his queen there with him. We can picture the great cortege slowly wending its way through the burning Panjab plains, stopping at the rest-houses on the way. We can follow Jehangir in imagination as he reined in his horse with its gay saddlecloth and trappings beside the curtained palanquin of Nur Mahal as they neared the top of the Pir Pangal Pass, and then commanding the bearers to pause, as he held back the curtain and bade her gaze on the grand view of snow mountains : those wonderful ranges of dazzling peaks and snow-fields, of which they were never to lose sight during the summer months spent in that happy retreat.

Imagine Nur Mahal and the ladies of her court drawing their soft Indian shawls (woven in Kashmir and trophies of Jehangir's first visit) closer round their slender forms as the first mountain breezes met them. Think of the gorgeous state barge moored in waiting for the Imperial party beneath stately chenar trees and drooping willows; and of how Nur Mahal appreciated the beauties of her new country we have ample proof, for we see how she planted even the approach to Srinagar with royal avenues. And then what joy they must have had planning the lovely gardens, laying out terraces and stately walks, planting little cypress trees which were to become the sentinels of her fountains and marble summer-houses !

We can with reason imagine river trips and long summer evenings on the lakes, and moonlight nights under the clear skies, the snows silhouetted in soft "moonstone" blues, while the water's silver tinkle alone broke the stillness as the little waterfalls plashed over marble and fern grottos. Rich subject-matter for the writers of poetry and romance !

To breathe the air of Kashmir is to breathe poetry, and endless cantos could be sung by one capable of voicing her charm, her colour, her majesty, in verse. In the description of the colours of her scenery and flowers, even of her art, we must not forget the skies, for they are part of the pictures which artists have striven to paint.

The sunrises and sunsets are the occasion for such colouring, both rich and delicate, as few parts of the world, if any, can eclipse. Though alike in many effects, the opening and close of day have many contrasts too.

When the sun rides over a mountain ridge in the East and floods the whole horizon with his glorious beams, he flings a dazzling veil over the grey garments of the dawn and instantly transforms the valley. The neutral sky becomes shot with rose and yellow; the sullen blue of the mountains and valleys turns to royal sapphire. The snows light up and sparkle and glisten. The rice-fields burst into vivid emerald, and the trees become alive with lights and mysterious shadows. The lakes gleam like cloth of silver, and in their still depths mirror forth in duplicate mountain and countryside. The rising sun goes forth to conquer by his light and warmth, eager for what the new day, untried and untarnished, will yield.

And the sunset paints for us the going to rest of the conqueror. In skies of saffron, banked with purple clouds, or soft with amethyst vapour, he seeks retirement. In a trail of crimson and gold he withdraws the magic of his presence. There is a veil of haze again, but this time it is mellowed with experience, and is golden rather than silver. Many things have been witnessed. Sorrow, sin, and suffering, as well as joy, and work, and beauty, have been found to exist even under those genial rays, and there is a suspicion of tears in the triumphant majesty and brilliance. The reflections are still faithfully rendered by peaceful lakes, but even in their peace there is pathos. A smile lingers, but there is pity in it.

And then Nature's tender voice calls all to rest, and she lays aside her coloured robes of day for night's soft trailing garments, and the moon sails out, and Kashmir sleeps.

(1915)

CHAPTER 19

THE VALLEYS OF KASHMIR

By

C. G. Bruce

The word valley has always a ring of charm about it. One instantly pictures a river winding through pretty country, and a walk running along that river. The valley of the Thames, for instance, though criticised by many people from a health point of view, is one of the most attractive of valleys.

But in our present trip we have to realise the difference in scale of the country. The whole of Kashmir proper is much larger than the extent of country called the valley of the Jhelum. Even this valley is split up again by other rivers into many other valleys, which take their names from the rivers which flow through them.

The ancient history of most valleys is that they were once lakes, and the old legend about Kashmir is that its vast lake was first of all drained of water by a grandson of the god Brahma, and that he then placed Brahmans there to cultivate and populate it, and that the rocky gorge at Baramulla was the lip of the vessel out of which he poured the waters. Such quaint ideas and superstitions are common to all unlettered people.

For instance, when the late Maharajah of Kashmir died no one was allowed to fish, because, it was declared, the spirit of the Maharajah had gone into a fish. Unfortunately he was caught by some disobedient subject, and there was a fearful commotion.

The principal valleys in Kashmir are the Sind, the Lidar, the Wardwan, and the Lolab, though there are many more.

The Sind river flows through sixty miles of charming scenery, sometimes foaming along, or pressing through narrow channels, again widening out into placid reaches and winding through flowery meads with wooden huts dotted here and there.

This river rises in the Ladakh mountains, and, working its way down through the defile of the Zoji La at Baltal, flows through Sonamarg, and later on casts in its lot, as do the other Kashmir rivers, with the Jhelum.

Along the path which follows the course of the river we find the wild home of the raspberry and black-currant and gooseberry; but though to a wayfarer even such crude fruit is welcome, we cannot compare them with their cultivated step-brethren in our kitchen gardens.

As we ride or walk along the Sind valley through miles of grassy orchard-land, and rest beneath spreading walnuts, there seems to be a sense of homeliness and quiet country life, quite untouched by the roar and whirl of modern life, and feeling of peace and content comes over us.

When travelling once, years ago, through this very valley, we put up for a night at a large wooden shelter which had been erected for native troops, but was still in the carpenters' hands. A wet day and the absence of the workmen induced us to camp in it, and our camp-beds were put into a large room in which the kind person left in charge quickly spread a carpet of birch-bark. To weary feet the pearly satin of these sheets of paper-like substance was a cooling and healing touch, and so was the fragrant ozonous scent of the freshly sawn pine wood.

The Lidar valley is the next rival in our affection. The river has gradually slipped down from large glaciers, wanders through grassy uplands, through birch and pine forests, till it widens out at Eishmakam into a wide stretch. A rocky hill crowned with an old monastery is seen through the trees from the spreading walnut giant under whose branches we are encamped, and an old fakir has come trotting down with a basket of peaches and pears to offer us. We shall send him away happy with some tea and sugar in exchange.

To-morrow's march will take us fourteen miles to Pahalgam, a sanatorium of pine trees much liked for standing camps. The scenery grows wilder beyond that point, and one delightful diversion is to turn up a little side valley to Aru and on into the big forests at the foot of the Kolahoi peaks.

But the main branch of the valley leads on and up to Shisha Nag, and yet higher to Amarnath, famous for its sacred cave, to which thousands of pilgrims come every year. This is 13,500 feet above sea-level. The great pilgrimage takes place in August, and from every part of India all sorts of people bravely plod their way. It lies among steep rocks and bare greyish red limestone country, without trees, surrounded by towering peaks. There are splendid views of the Koh-i-nur mountains as neighbouring peaks. A very poor stone statue of the sacred bull of Shiva, one of the Hindu gods, and some fluttering pigeons supposed to be the expression by the god that the pilgrimage is accepted, is the poor end to the weary marches of the pilgrims.

There is a passage (only passable at certain times of the year) not far from here between the two important valleys, the Lidar and the Sind.

The Wardwan river drains the Suru mountains and flows down the east side of Kashmir. Little farmsteads and peasants' huts stand in their fields on the banks of the river. In the autumn the harvesters shade curious eyes as we pass, and woollen-frocked children scream to each other and rush out, a band of merry faces. The valley is a high one, about 2,000 feet, and is so beautiful that artists can find much to paint : chalet-like villages backed with dark forest slopes of pine, and brightened with the wonderful crimson millet and amarnath and bright pasture-land on each side of the river. Wooded knolls rise here and there, from which one gets a glimpse of the Kolahoi peaks.

The Lolab valley is chiefly attractive from its rural character. We might almost fancy here and there that we were camping on a Surrey common or among the hills of Berkshire. Regular villages and large barns add to the picturesque effect, and splendid groves of walnut trees are to be found at every stage. The river takes us through most beautiful country, now flat, now undulating, but shut in with fir forests, beyond which on one side we come close up to the grand barrier of the Kaj-i-Nag.

The whole of the valley is cultivated richly, for it is a very easy matter to farm here. There is good soil and plenty of water; the sun never scorches, though it warms up in July and August. But we see the lazy character of the Kashmiris on every hand. Fences are made by supporting branches on forks of wood just as they are cut up; the villagers do not even trouble to drive the stakes into the ground.

Why should they trouble ? they answer, when we ask why they don't make good fences and keep their houses and barns in better repair. There is plenty of food and firing and water, and they weave woollen garments from the long wool of their flocks of fat sheep.

One march nearing the end of the valley which leads us back towards Baramulla gives us a splendid view of Haramouk's rough old head. His coiffure is less snowy in the autumn, for hot sunshine during several months has clipped his white locks close; still, at whatever time and from whatever place he is seen, he is a fine old mountain, and any valley is the richer for a sight of him.

(1915)

CHAPTER 20

THE DAL LAKE AND MOGHUL GARDENS

By

Dermont Norris

This lovely sheet of water, which lies close on the outskirts of Srinagar, has been held to be the most beautiful in the world, and, even if this is admittedly an exaggeration, it would be a difficult task to name any other so beautiful a lake situated almost at the door of a large city. The lake itself is five miles long and nearly half as broad, but it is divided by causeways into two distinct portions, each of which has a number of minor off-shoots, and a large proportion of its surface is covered with floating gardens and beds of rushes, which grow in size as the summer advances, so that the general effect is then somewhat spoilt. But the ring of high mountains, which extend almost to the edge of the water on the northern and eastern sides, and which are still capped with snow when spring in the valley is far advanced, the delicate colouring of the poplar and willow trees, and those beautiful islets, Sona and Rupa Lank, all combine to render a very perfect picture of natural beauty; a picture that is duplicated in every detail in the clear snow-fed waters of the lake.

Beautiful though the Dal lake is at every season of the year, it is, however, incomparably at its best in mid-summer, when the lotus is in flower. The masses of these great pink water-flowers, which cover large areas of the surface of the lake, are a wonderful sight, and though they may, perhaps, be seen to even better advantage at Manasbal, they bring thousands of admirers from the city to view them, and even attract some of the less ardent golfers from their cool links at Gulmarg.

The floating gardens, which are mostly situated on the western side of the lake, are well worth a short visit. They are prepared in early spring when the level of the water is at its lowest. Rushes are cut and tied together in large masses, which are then towed to a suitable site, where they are bound in strips a few feet wide and perhaps forty or fifty yards in length. These strips are staked to the muddy floor of the lake, and water-weeds and a certain amount of earth are piled on the foundation so formed. A large variety of excellent vegetables are grown in these floating gardens and are sent daily into Srinagar, where they find a ready market.

Leaving the Dal Gate, which is the narrow entrance to the lake from the Tsunt-i-Kol, the canal which connects it with the Jhelum, and through which the water rushes with such force that it is frequently a matter of considerable difficulty to get the heavy and awkward house-boats through in safety, the visitor will proceed in his shikara down a long lane of clear water, bordered on either side by rows of moored house-boats and masses of tall rushes and water-weeds, until, after a mile or so, the lake opens out. To the right there are more hose-boats, but in the opposite direction there is an extensive view and the full beauty of the lake can be first appreciated.

At Gagribal, lying almost in the shadow of the Takht, there is a large expanse of clear water, where, according to tradition, in the days when the shawl-making industry was at its height, the rarest and the best shawls were taken to be washed in the cold spring water, which was supposed to have the effect of imparting a peculiar softness to the fabric. To-day it is used chiefly as a bathing place and a raft is moored some way out for the bathers to rest on.

A word of warning regarding bathing in the Dal lake, or elsewhere, except in recognised bathing places, is desirable, as the water-weeds, which grow to a great length, are sometimes dangerous. Divers get entangled among them and cannot escape, and numerous drowning tragedies have occurred in this way.

Many people do not like bathing at Gagribal owing to the number of house-boats and doongas that are moored near by, and prefer, instead, to go to Nagim, which is undeniably cleaner and more pleasant, but has the disadvantage of being a good deal further away. A popular form of amusement, when the moon is full, is to arrange a bathing picnic at Nagim with supper afterwards, either on the lake, or at one of the dozens of attractive spots along its shores, and it would be difficult to imagine a pleasanter setting for such an affair.

Round the shores of the lake there are numbers of places of interest, the chief of which are, of course, the far-famed Moghul gardens. Most of these places can easily be reached by motor car along the road that runs past the foot of the Takht and through the village of Gupkar, but it is usually more convenient and less tiring to visit them by boat.

Starting on the circuit of the lake in an anti-clockwise direction, Chasma Shahi is the first place that should be visited. It is situated at some distance back from the lake and consists of a beautifully situated spring of clear water gushing from the mountain side, round which the Emperor Shahjehan laid out a garden and built a pavilion. A considerable area of land in this neighbourhood is covered with vines, and years ago, under the direction of an enterprising Frenchman, a very fair wine was prepared from these Kashmir grapes, but phylloxera appeared, the quality of the wine deteriorated and the industry is now moribund.

Two miles further and we come to the Nishat Bagh, which, owing to its beautiful situation and easy accessibility, is the most visited of the gardens and is a popular resort of the townsfolk, crowds of whom, dressed in their best clothes, resort there on Sundays and holidays.

The garden, which is enclosed by a high wall, covers a considerable area and extends far up the hill-side in a series of twelve terraces carpeted with turf. Behind tall bare mountains rise precipitously. A stream runs through the middle of the garden in a series of cascades and fountains, and, when the fountains are playing, the effect is, of course, vastly improved. The presence of this stream must have gladdened the eyes of the Moghul gardeners, whose chief difficulty in the plains was the provision of the copious supply of water, on which they relied so greatly to produce the effects that they admired.

The garden has suffered from years of neglect. Many of the pavilions are in ruins and, delightful though it still is, Nishat would no doubt bring tears to the eyes of its Moghul builders, who, as their sole crumb of comfort, would be forced to admire the incomparable chenars that adorn the upper terraces, which now are the chief glory of the garden, and which could have been no more than newly planted saplings in their day. These upper terraces rise to a considerable height above the lake and delightful views can be obtained from them framed in the foliage of the chenars.

A full understanding of these Moghul gardens, the ideas of their originators, and the difficulties that they had to contend with, will lead to a greater appreciation of their beauties, in the same way that a piece of fine music can only be fully understood by the educated listener. Mrs. C. M. Villiers Stuart's book, "The Gardens of the Great Moghuls," supplies this information, and makes one realise how it was that a formal garden, with conventional watercourses, fountains and cool pavilions, though entirely different from the natural effects that are generally sought after to-day, was the obvious form suited to the severe limits and the heat and dust of such places as Delhi and Lahore, in which they were perfected.

At Harwan, some way beyond the Nishat Bagh, and close to the Shalimar garden, the reservoir, which supplies Srinagar with drinking water, is situated at a distance of two miles or more back from the lake. Modern visitors, perhaps, may not realise what a boon this supply of pure water is to a city, which is for ever threatened by an outbreak of cholera in epidemic form, and how rarely such a supply is to be found in any but the largest eastern cities. The water is stored in an artificial reservoir, which was built in 1901. All human inhabitations have been removed from the catchment area of the valley in which it is situated, and no person is allowed to enter this area on any account, so that the chance of the supply being contaminated at its source is thus reduced to a minimum.

At Harwan, also, a successful trout hatchery has been established with ovae sent from Europe. A number of streams in the valley have been stocked with trout in recent years, and some of the fish attain to a considerable size, rise freely to an artificial fly, and now afford very fair fishing. Near by there is the Maharajah's Model Farm, stocked with animals and pouluy imported from England.

Shalimar Bagh, two miles further on, is not so well situated as the Nishat Bagh, as it is on almost level ground and is separated from the lake by a considerable expanse of low-lying land. It is approached along a narrow canal shaded by chenar trees. The garden is laid out in a series of low terraces and is surrounded by a wall. At the further end, which was reserved for the ladies of the Imperial harem, there is a very handsome pavilion of black marble with beautifully carved pillars standing in the middle of an artificial reservoir lined with marble. There is a tradition that this garden was once much larger than it is to-day, and the remains of ancient masonry outside the wall which surrounds it, and between the garden and the lake, lend weight to this assumption.

After leaving the Shalimar Bagh and passing the mouth of the Arrah, or Telbal river, which is navigable for some distance from its mouth, Nasim Bagh, on the western side of the lake, is reached. Nasim is now hardly more than a park, as the wall that surrounded it has almost disappeared and the ruins of its buildings are hidden by low mounds of grass-covered earth. But its fine chenar trees, now, alas, far past their prime, and its air of ancient neglect are so completely in accord with the indefinable melancholy of a still summer evening, that it is, perhaps, at times the most charming spot on the shores of this delightful lake.

Some little distance from the Nasim Bagh there is the large mosque, or ziarat, of Hazratbal, which is celebrated as containing a supposed hair of the Prophet, purchased, so tradition has it, by a wealthy merchant for a lakh of rupees a thousand years ago. Festivals are held here from time to time, and twice a year, in May and August, the hair is produced before vast numbers of devout Mahommedans assembled together from all parts of the valley.

Hazratbal virtually completes the circuit of the lake, for, although it is still almost an hour's journey back to the Dal Gate, the remainder of the distance lies through a canal and a series of small open spaces of water, and here, except for the ever-changing display of the domestic life of the inhabitants of the city, there is not much of interest to detain the sight-seer.

CHAPTER 21

NINE LAKES OF KASHMIR

By
S. N. Dhar

Kashmir is a land of lakes like Italy or Switzerland. No smoky European steamboats disfigure their smooth expanse. Picturesque shikaras—canoe-like gondolas of the East—comfortable doongas and well furnished and tastefully decorated houseboats, carry the visit or from the Jhelum to the Dal Lake and thence to the Anchar, the Manasbal and the Wular lakes. The shores of the Kashmir lakes are not steep and rocky but soft and marshy, so that they are reclaimed for cultivation purposes or for planting lines or willows and poplars.

1. The Dal Lake. Conveniently situated at the door of Srinagar, the lake is enclosed within the Dal Gate. Its length is about 5 miles with an area of 10 sq. miles. A net-work of canals, bearing hamlets and the unique floating gardens on their sides, as also, a Moghul causeway across it, intersect it. Its smooth waters reflect a ring of mountains which rise three to four thousand feet above its level.

Aquatic plants and picturesque birds abound. Two islets, Sona Lank (Golden isle), Rupa Lank (Silver isle) dot it beautifully.

2. The Anchar Lake. This shallow lake starts from the northern boundary of Srinagar and is reached from Dal Lake through the Mar Canal—the gift of Zain-ul-Abdin. It provides a

delightful alternative water route to Ganderbal. In summer it measures three miles in length. In winter it is a place for duck shooting. Lilies abound in mid-summer, July-August.

3. The Wular Lake. At the west end of the valley, it is the largest fresh-water lake in India. Indeed it is one of the most beautiful sheets of water in India being 14 miles broad in summer. Full of weeds, it is also full of fish, especially mahasheer, which travels up from the sea through the Indus and the Jhelum. Surrounded by high mountains of the Pir Panchal range, it is prone to changeful moods. Sudden storms occur in the afternoon. Though it can be crossed in a house-boat or doonga, generally, however, shikaras are used and the crossing is done in the morning.

4. The Manasbal Lake. Situated at a distance of 18 miles by road, via Sumbal from Srinagar, this small circular lake lies near Ganderbal. About 2 miles long its deep bed shelves steep from the bare ridges surrounding it. Interesting remains of a Moghul Garden exist on its northern side. It is reputed for the transparency of its water and its lotus blossoms which cover miles together in August.

5. The Gangabal Lake. Situated at a height of 11,714 ft., this mountain lake impressively nestles close to the rocky foot of Mt. Haramoukh. It is about 5 miles in circumference and a quarter of a mile in diameter. The water is of torquoise blue colour in which the reddish-blue steep crags of Haramoukh, below the snow line, are beautifully reflected.

6. The Shishanag. 15 miles from Pahalgam, through upland, flowery valleys of Pisa. One of the most beautiful lakes of Kashmir. 11,730 feet above sea level, it is enclosed within a mountain amphitheatre of steep and snow-capped high mountains, whose glaciers feed it from the eastern side and whose jagged peaks produce fantastic reflections in the water of the lake.

7. The Tar Sar and Mar Sar Lakes. The Tar Sar is a beautiful mountain lake in the Kolohai Valley at a height of 12,500 ft., 10 miles from Lidderwat and 24 miles from Pahalgam. At some distance, on its eastern side, lies the Mar Sar Lake. Sona Sar, Chanda Sar, Hoka Sar, Dudh Sar and other mountain tarns are also found in the Liddar Valley, when trekking to Mt. Kolohai (18,000 ft.).

8. Konsarnag. At a height of about 12,000 ft., this fig-shaped, mountain lake is surrounded by a ring of Pir Panchal range summits. It is three-quarters of a mile broad and its greatest length is about 3 miles. The depth is as much as 150 feet. Icebergs may be seen floating in it in June. During autumn its water is clear and sapphire blue.

The lake is reached from Shopian—a town at a distance of 34 miles from srinagar. On the bridle path from Shopian to Konsarnag, the tourist comes across Ahrabal waterfalls, which reach a height of about 200 feet. Forest Rest Houses are provided at Kungawattan and at Ahrabal.

9. The Pangong Lake. This is a salt lake in the frontier district of Ladakh, about 8 miles long. But it is bottle-necked, varying in breadth from half a mile to two miles. The greater part of the lake stretches towards the plateaux of Tibet.

NOTE FOR VISITORS TO THE LAKES

The Valley lakes are best visited during spring months of April and May or during late autumn in October. To see the lotus in blossom, visit them in August.

During mid-summer it is delightful to trek up to the mountain lakes.

The Dal lake is crowded with bathers in summer. They should use only the recognised bathing places where the bathing house-boats are moored. At other places the lake is weedy and there is the danger that a diver may get seriously entangled among the weeds.

To safeguard against cholera and other tropical diseased, the water of the valley lakes should not be used for drinking or cooking purposes.

(1945)

CHAPTER 22

THE MOGHAL GARDENS IN KASHMIR

By
Sachchidananda Sinha

When some face
Whilst butterfly and bee
O'er happy flowers, hovering, say
"We love thee! Only thee!"
Sweet, drowsy flowers closing up
Their dewy cups; the sun
Is sinking low, still late bees sup
'Til lingering day is done.
From "A Garden in Gulmarg" in Mrs. Percy
Brown's Chenar Leaves.

A GENERAL SKETCH

Like the Taj Mahal, at Agra, the two principal Moghal gardens, in Kashmir—situated on the Dal lake, close to Srinagar—are such, in their own line, as to beggar all description, and frustrate the effort of the pen or the brush to depict, delineate, or capture their charm, since their loveliness, being a perfect harmonious blend between man's handicraft and natural beauty, is indescribable. To see the far-famed Shalamar gardens, laid out by the Emperor Jehangir, or the no less famous Nishat Bagh, the garden beloved of his Empress Noor Jehan, of a summer afternoon, with their enchanting marble pavilions, the limpid water jutting out of the beautifully-fretted marble-slides, and the slender, sparkling fountains beneath the towering chenar trees, is to feel with the poet, that the scene is truly reminiscent of

> when some face
> Divinely fair unveils before our eyes,
> Some woman beautiful unspeakably,
> And the blood quickens, and the spirit leaps.

All the Moghal gardens, in Kashmir, are beauty-spots worth staying at, for some time, to enjoy their loveliness to the full. No visitor to Srinagar should omit to visit the Shalamar and the Nishat Baghs, and also the Chasma Shahi, the three renowned Moghal gardens, built near Srinagar, by Jehangir and Shah Jehan, for their wives. Fascinating marble pavilions, silvery cascades, gushing fountains, and tier upon tier of terraces laden with lovely banks of flowers, lend supreme attractiveness to those haunts of pleasure and delight—the Shalamar and the Nishat—especially when the fountains play on Sundays and fete days. Groups of pleasure parties, in shikaras and doonga boats, visit these glorious gardens in spring and summer, to spend the day out, under the delightful shades of the chenar trees, to inhale the fragrance of the spring flowers, and to drink the cool waters of the fountains—than which there could be no better holiday-making.

The most famous of the Moghal gardens—the Shalamar, and the Nishat—the former the Emperor Jehangir's garden, and the latter that of his Empress, Noor Jehan—are each, in its own way, supremely beautiful. They both comprise fretted-marble water-slides, handsome fountains spouting limpid water, masses of loveliest flowers, with chenar trees of immense size casting their shade over velvet lawns. Every Sunday, throughout the summer, the fountains play and the gardens are then thronged with people in gorgeous raiment. The Dal lake, with its floating gardens, the late-summer lotuses that abound in it, and the peaks of the rugged mountains all round, reflected in its clear and calm waters, with these glorious gardens on its edge, is not surpassed, on the authority of even experienced travellers, by even the world-famous Italian lakes—and though this view is not shared by a qualified visitor, Mr. Aldous Huxley, yet even he (in his Jesting Pilate) writes as follows :—

"The little Chashma Shahi is architecturally the most charming of the gardens near Srinagar. And the loveliest for trees and waters is Achhbal, at the upper end of the valley; while far-off Verinag, where Jehangir enclosed the blue deep source of the Jhelum in an octagonal tank, surrounded by arcades, has a strange and desolate beauty all its own. If the Kashmiri gardens are beautiful, that is the work not much of man as of Nature. The formal beds are fully of zinnias and scarlet cannas. The turf is fresh and green. The huge chenar trees go up into the pale, bright sky; their white trunks shine between the leaves, which the autumn has turned to a rusty vermilion. Behind them are the steep bare hills, crested already with snow. Their colour, where the sun strikes them, is a kind of glamourous gold, and, in the shadows, a deep intense indigo. Below, on the other side stretches the Dal lake, with the isolated fort crowned hill of Hari Parbat on the further shore."

If towards afternoon you leave for any of the Moghal gardens on the Dal, the sun blazing on the lake, you see boats, in its light, glowing like brass, steal away, their colours fading with the sun, into the violent shadows. The sun at last sinks behind the yellow gilt-edged hills, and the whole circle of the lake gleams with prismatic colours. The high crests of the Pir Panjal have that remote and crystal air, as of great jewels, and the benediction of evening settles upon the water, like the peace of God which passeth all understanding :—

As some tall cliff, that lifts its awful form,
Swells from the vale, and midway leaves the storm;
Though round its breast the rolling clouds are spread,
Eternal sunshine settles on its head.

THE NASEEM BAGH

Akbar was the first of the Great Moghals to visit Kashmir. Having built the massive fort at Hari Parbat, which even now overlooks Srinagar, he is said to have laid out the Naseem Bagh, on the slopes of the Dal lake, of which nothing but a few ruins and the avenues of chenar trees now remain to remind one of the first of the Moghal gardens in Kashmir. But it is even to-day the shadiest and the most picturesque of camping grounds in Kashmir, and a sufficiently long stay here in tents is delightful. The Naseem is the antithesis of the Nishat, for while the latter, with its rushing waters and sparkling fountains, is still in the prime of life, the Naseem is long since overtaken by serene, old age. In fact, it is truer to say that the Naseem is now no more a garden but a beautiful old park, with deep glades, through which the sunlight and shadow fall upon its velvet sward. It has in its grand way a touch of a deer-park; but it is no longer a work of Art. For one can measure its proportions, and see right through it now the mauve waters of the lake, and to the snow-spangled mountains beyond. The trees, still beautiful, are old and even dying. Most of them are hollow, and the central trunks of many of them are black and withered, their life prolonging itself for a space in the great lateral branches—like an Empire in its decline.

Its old surrounding walls, that long shut out the vulgar world, have all but disappeared. You can trace them here and there, and their great foundations by the lake, but they and the conduits, and its pavilions and belvederes, its gardens of roses, narcissus and lilac, have long since passed into self-swelling mounds and grassy hollows. Yet the Naseem Bagh as a park lies open, a beautiful and ancient woodland, through which the lake breezes blow, making it the very abode of serene and tranquil peace, while its white iris clusters lend it an ethereal charm. Nightingales now sing in it, and doves coo and murmur; rooks make their homes in its hollow trees, and the little sparrows feed undisturbed upon its lawns. Kites wheel above it in the blue bays of the sky. The cattle of the country-side wander through its glades, and sheep browse upon its herbage; while upon days of festival, long files of the village people drift across it to the neighbouring Ziarat of Hazrat Bal. It is now an ideal place to idle in, camp out, and to ruminate on the passing show and vanity of life, since it is now a place of benedictions, chanting softly in undertones its nunc dimitties; a place for those who have turned the sunny side of the hill, and see before them the long shadowy vale of evening with its quiet joys and subdued enjoyments; a beautiful mellow old place such as one might come upon in only a very pleasant dream.

THE SHALAMAR BAGH

O Shalamar! O Shalamar!
A rythmic sound in thy name rings
A dreamy cadence from afar
Within those syllables which sings
To use of love and joyous days;
To cast their spell on all who gaze
Upon this handiwork of love—
Reared in Jehangir's proudest days
Homage for Nur Mahal to prove.

From "The Shalamar Bagh" (A Mughal Garden on the Dal Lake) in Mrs. Percy Brown's Chenar Leaves

Many of the Moghal gardens in Kashmir—besides the Naseem Bagh—have disappeared, but fortunately the State maintains carefully two of the most interesting ones—namely, the Shalamar and the Nishat. The first of these was laid out by

Jehangir in 1619. Beautifully situated on the shores of the Dal lake, about nine miles from Srinagar, the Shalamar ("The Abode of Love") is probably the finest known example of a Moghal summer residence, and is a typical example of Moghal gardening. It is approached, from Srinagar, both by a motor road, and also from the water along a tree-lined canal which connects the main entrance of the garden with the Dal lake. Six hundred yards long, and two hundred and sixty yards broad, it is divided into three parts, the whole being surrounded by a lofty wall. The entrance from the canal is the public garden, in which is a large pavilion known as the Diwan-i-Am. The central stream, which runs through the garden, emerges from beneath a black marble throne on which the Moghal Emperor used to sit when holding public audience.

The second, or the middle, part of the garden was reserved for the use of the Emperor, and consists of two shallow terraces. In the centre is another pavilion known as The Hall of Private Audience. Unfortunately, only the carved stone base of the original building still remains. The entrance to the third part, or the ladies' garden, is flanked by two small guardrooms. Inside the ladies' garden stands the main building—a beautiful pavilion of black marble surrounded by a tank in which play numerous fountains. The vista from this pavilion down the terraces, and over the Dal, is entrancingly beautiful, while behind, and overshadowing the whole, tower the snow-capped hills. As it is carefully looked after by the State, its original lay- out has not completely disappeared as yet.

The water for the fountains is obtained from a stream, which rises in the hills behind the garden, and now on Sundays and fete days, during spring and summer, they are made to play. Bernier, the French traveller, who visited Kashmir during Aurangzeb's time, wrote of this garden :—"The whole of the interior is painted and gilt, and on the walls of the chambers are inscribed certain sentences, written in dark and beautiful Persian characters. The four doors are extremely valuable being composed of large stones and supported by two beautiful pillars. The doors and pillars were found in some of the idol temples, demolished by Shah Jehan, and it is impossible to esteem their value. I cannot describe the nature of the stone, but it is far superior to porphyry or any species of marble."

If you do not choose to drive in a car to the Shalamar, but prefer to do so on the return journey, you will in that case have to ply your shikara of an afternoon across the silver, silver-grey water of the Dal, to the sound of plashing oars, and of the songs of party out for a holiday. The bright colours of the shikaras, with their pink, red and orange, awnings, are reflected in the water, and scene is one of the brightest animation. The approach lies through shallow marshy waters, lined with willows and covered with green scum. It is not till you reach the Diwan-i-Khas of Shah Jehan, that the dignity of the garden falls upon you. Here the black and green marbles are superb; and even in the dusk you can trace the amphitheatre of crags and mountains, and the snow-capped peak of Mahadeo, which rises majestically over the scene. Yet withal, this garden, suggests a pleasance, rather than an Imperial residence; which at one time it was.

"I ordered a stream to be diverted, so that a garden might be made, such that in beauty and sweetness there should not be in the inhabited world another like it." So wrote Jehangir in his famous Memoirs, and he evidently did achieve his object, as even now when, on a holiday, Shalamar is thronged with holiday-folk and the fountains are playing, its cascades of silver, quivering with light and animation, as they fall in rapturous music into the shining pools, present a spectacle, of a summer afternoon, which once seen cannot be obliterated from the mind.

THE NISHAT BAGH

"Garden of Gladness!" The name doth echo
Adown the centuries, and in us wakes

A chord responsive to the art which makes
The Mughal Court far-famed :
Which was the admiration of all eyes :
Still what a spell those stately gardens hold
And memories romantic oft recall
Of Kings and Queens—the fairest Nur Mahal,
Whose names live on, enshrined in their rich mould.

From "A Legend of the Nishat Bagh." (A Mughal Garden on the Dal Lake) in Mrs. Percy Brown's Chenar Leaves.

Close to the Shalamar, and also situated like it on the edge of the Dal lake, lies the Nishat Bagh ("The Garden of Delight"), which was built by Asaf Khan, father-in-law of the Emperor Shah Jehan, and father of Mumtaz Mahal, the Emperor's favourite wife, and the lady of the Taj. While the Shalamar, being a royal garden, has three main divisions, the Nishat, being a private one, has only two—one for the owner and the other for his women-folk. Though built on much the same plan as its neighbour, the Nishat differs in some important respects. It is also called the "garden of terraces", as it has as many as twelve of them rising one above the other, flanked by bright rows of season flowers, relieved at intervals by magnificent chenar trees affording shade to the lawns, and also by slender cypresses standing like sentinels to guard, as it were, the purity of the water in the central water channel. It is thus a typical private garden of the Moghal nobles. The enclosure measures six hundred yards long and about four hundred yards wide. Being a private garden, it is divided—as stated above—into two portions, the one for general use, and the other exclusively for ladies, bounded by a high wall. There are octagonal towers at each end of the wall, and many marble thrones are scattered about the garden. The only roofed pavilion stands on the third terrace looking out over the Dal lake towards the snows of the Pir Panjal. Inside the building is a small tank in which at least one of the original stone fountains can still be seen. The garden is, generally speaking, gayer and less formal than the Shalamar, and during spring and summer the flower beds are a wonderful blaze of colour.

With a lavishness of space, and of height beyond height to the overwhelming lines of the mountains, the Nishat rises in a series of twelve imperial terraces from the water's edge and is of a size and stateliness befitting the Moghal court at the height of its splendour. Much of its architectural beauty has suffered from the passing of the centuries, and many of its details have been lost or obscured in the vicissitudes to which so many of the princely palaces and gardens of that period have succumbed. Yet this superb garden still retains its perfection, and time has even added splendour to its trees, now at the very climax of their lives. It is, indeed, these gigantic chenar trees which, first and foremost, appeal to one's unmeasured admiration. There are groves of them, and each is a giant of its princely race. Then there are the great terraces, as superb in their dignity, and in their proportions, as on the day they were made, and one can not fail to admire the art with which they were designed to convey the impression of infinity, as of an endless series, passing into the high mountains which rise above them. The tenth terrace, which marks the approach to the Zenana, is the loftiest and most impressive, and it indicates the transition from the public to the secluded part of the garden.

At the far summit, where of old the beauties of the harem walked, there is a final belvedere, which commands (without itself being seen) the whole reach of the garden to the lake, and the world of loveliness beyond it. This innermost sanctuary (though now in ruins) is most lovely with its roof-garden, whose violet and purple glow like the robe of an Emperor through the sunlight scene of the chenars. At the wings, also, there are octagonal pavilions from which to look out upon the country-side, but these are now in decay. For the rest, there are beds now of brilliant flowers—roses which not only droop under the weight of their own bloom, but sustain the fame of Kashmir by their perfection and luxuriant growth. Time has, indeed, destroyed much, but is has also added such mellow qualities as time alone can give, and you feel this when you see old brick pavements, once so formal, now become a part of the earth itself. Huge and umbrageous chenar trees stand by the terraces in all their pride of loveliness. The grass below is like a thick, high-class carpet, and the roof above a marvellous fabric of painted leaves dappled with light and shadow, of grey boughs, and little spaces of blue sky. There is light, vivid and splendid, all about you, but none that directly penetrates this natural canopy. The hot sunlight, and the gently zephyrs of the garden, as they come, blown in ripples across the lake, combine to provide you with an Elysian climate, while the soaring fountains fill the garden with a mist, upon which there are graven all the colours of the prism. The colour note of this green and purple; its character majestic; its proportions so noble that, notwithstanding the high mountains and precipices that rise so far above it, it conveys the sense of dignity and greatness.

THE NAGINA BAGH AS THE BATHING CENTRE

The Nagina Bagh—which is six miles from Srinagar by road,—lies upon a secret water, a lake within a lake, and you may come upon it by chance, of an afternoon, when the sun blazing over the Dal, suggests an escape to some quieter and more sheltered spot. A canal by the bridge of Kraliyar carries the shikara into this side water, and lands you at the Nagina Bagh. Here you may have tea, and enjoy the reflections of mountain and woodland in the still deep waters; and, in the evening cool walk up the main thoroughfare of the old garden, through its avenue of huge chenars, and its fields of poppied corn. A slumberous stillness, broken only by the murmuring of doves, lies upon this secluded garden, far as it is from the frequented highways of the lake. Its old buildings and towers, its pavilions, water-courses and flagged paths have all departed, its terraces lie hidden under grass, its formal beauties under the waving corn; yet it retains the sentiment of vanished days.

The Nagina Bagh faces the Takht-i-Sulaiman, the image of which dreams at its feet in the tranquil waters. Upon its right as one looks on this beautiful reflection, there is the castled hill of Hari Parbat, and beyond it the majesty and arctic splendour of the Pir Panjal. On its left there is the sun-warmed, peak of Mahadeo, and the whole line of moutains which overhang the Nishat and the Shalamar, and brood in their serrated beauty over the northern and eastern shores of the Dal lake. Late in the evening when the sun is nearly gone, they are seized with a passionate glow of colour, that is of a crystal line, red or crimson, peculiar to them at this transitory moment; and it is here in the cool deeps of this inner water about the Nagina Bagh that one may look to perfection upon their motionless reflections, and entrancing beauty. As the glorious orb of the sun goes down slowly behind the snow-topped mountains, you see the startling colours fade, as though the glow which animated them were too ardent to last for more than a few rapturous moment. The stars now shine out, and Hari Parbat, outlined against the sky, ceases for one instant to be the proud citadel of a kingdom, and becomes in its amethystine loveliness the gossamer fabric of one's dreams. These wonders may be seen even by careless eyes, on a summer night, as one's boat passes slowly over the waters, on its homeward course from the Nagina Bagh to the exit of the waters of the Dal lake.

Long neglected, so popular has Nagina Bagh now become that during the summer months house-boats :—with dressing rooms and diving boards—ring the entire lake and, except at the beginning of the season ghats are very difficult to get; a row of shops has sprung up on the road behind the lake, and a number of garages have been built. There is even a Post Office to save visitors the trouble of sending two miles for their letters and other amenities, including some good shops, are fast springing up. Bathing boats here have spring boards, and platforms of different heights for divine and shutes. On the main deck are dressing rooms for men and women, while the upper deck makes a splendid place for sun-bathing, and the display of multi-coloured and attractive swimming suits. Each boat possesses two or three wide smoothly-planed planks on which one can lie at ease, and by the gentlest paddling motion of the feet, drift slowly round amongst the more energetic swimmers. All this is provided for the sum of four annas per day, or at a slightly lower rate, if weekly or monthly tickets are taken.

Yet, even without these amenities, life at the Nagina Bagh can be very pleasant. A bath about 11 a.m. followed by a long sun-bath till lunch; a quiet reach or sleep; early tea; another bath, followed by a strong brings one to dinner time. As night falls, the lake ringed with the twinkling lights of the house-boats, are shikaras are seen crossing from boat to boat as visits a exchanged. The sound of gramophones and laughter softened by distance, floats across the water—are Nagina Bagh then truly transforms itself into an earth paradise. Though there are several places round about the Dal lake, where one may live delightful days, turning the warmer months—either in a houseboat, or in camp, there are few pleasanter than the Nagina Bagh, which has now become—owing to the craze for moonlight bathing picnics—a charming Lido for those who enjoy refreshing baths and active life, coupled with the amenities of civilisation.

THE CHASHMA SHAHI

To the Chashma Shahi, or the "Royal Spring" you drive along the highway, with its tall poplars like a regiment in line, in the incomparable freshness of the morning. You presently come to an orchard, in which you fain pause and gather a handful of cherries. For "the cherry", wrote the Emperor Jehangir, in his famous Memoirs, "is a fruit of pleasant flavour, and one can eat more of it than of other fruits. I have in a day eaten up a hundred and fifty of them"; an example that you may try to emulate upon a fine summer morning, on your way to the Chashma Shahi. And again; "there was an abundance of cherries on the trees, each of which looked, as it were, a round ruby, hanging like globes upon the branches", which is a very just observation of Jahangir's . At the Chashma-i-Shahi the Emperor, Shah Jehan, built in 1632, a pavilion, and laid out a little garden with fountains and waterfalls, in terraces lifted high above each other; and here one may still pass a day of enjoyment, and drink of the spring which gushes forth with the same purity and unfailing abundance as it did in his day. The Moghal buildings, with their graceful form, have passed away beyond recognition; and newer and less worthy ones (built by the last but one Sikh Governor, in 1842, and later restored by the Maharajas of Kashmir) have taken their place; but the beauty and seclusion of the spot survive. Here was never any pomp or ceremonial, but it was and is place of exquisite repose; and it continues to this day haunted, as of old, by the divinity of the spring, and overlooked by mountains whose plumes are as the irridescent sheen of a peacock. It is now used sometimes as a State guest-house, but it is usually open to visitors.

HABBAK BAGH

The garden at Habbak, to the north of the Naseem Bagh, was laid out by Saif Khan, the Moghal Governor of Kashmir, from 1655 to 1668, and it was called Saifabad after him. As he desired to make it excel the Nishat and the Shalamar in beauty, he brought a stream of water from the Sindh river, to feed the fountains, grottos and cascades in his garden. But before the work of construction was completed, he was summoned back to Delhi by Aurangzeb. As he had suddenly to depart, the garden has remained shadowless for want of the chenar and cypress trees, which he had deferred planting pending the suply of water. Yet the terraces of Habbak catch the eye from afar; and when one arrives at the garden, one realises that this was in plan and purpose the most stately of all the old Moghal gardens on the Dal Lake.

Its ruined walls and outer bastions, its far-flung terraces and steep water-falls, its carved waterways and sunk pools still linger, in all the sadness of a great failure, to remind one of those glorious days. Here more than elsewhere, upon the borders of the Elysian lake, one is struck with the havoc that is so seldom absent from splendour in the East. All the old buildings are shattered beyond recovery, and the channels that glided are choked with weeds. Yet in their midst the roses of a past age still struggle to live; yet are there some beautiful places in this garden of desolation. If you stand at its centre upon its loftiest terrace, where two aged cypresses still mount guard as sentinels, you will see about you fields of scarlet poppies, the lake shining below, and the snow-spangled mass of the Mahadeo hill rising into the mist of the morning sunlight, over its high walls and princely terraces. It is even now well worth a visit of an afternoon.

THE ACHHBAL GARDENS

Thy murmuring waters seem to bless,
As with a tender soft caress,
All who are lulled here by their fall
In garden fair of Achhbal :

From "The Mughal Garden at Achhbal" in Mrs. Percy Brown's Chenar Leaves.

Thirty-two miles by road from Srinagar lies Anantnag, otherwise known as Islamabad, the second city of Kashmir, and important as the starting place foreign cursions to Verinag, Achhbal, Martand, Pahalgam, and many other interesting places. Verinag, the source of the river Jhelum, was the favourite garden of Noor Jehan, and though long since in ruins, it still possesses splendid fruit orchards which produce the best and sweetest apples in the valley, for which there is very great demand in and outside Kashmir. There is another beautiful Moghal garden at Achhbal, about seven miles from Anantnag, along a good motor road. The garden is in three terraces, each terrace having a separate water-fall, and tanks and fountains. There is a small enclosure for trout culture near the garden, which also deserves a visit. Achhbal, laid out as a stately garden by Jehangir, and known as his favourite pleasure resort, is smaller but is, in some respects, lovelier than the more famous Shalamar and Nishat Baghs on the shore of the Dal lake. Like them, it nestles in the gentle sloping lap of a mountain, and derives much of its picturesque beauty from the surrounding fir-clad mountains and valleys.

Whereas Shalamar and Nishat are dependent on distant sources for the water which enhances their charms so greatly, Achhbal glories in the most remarkable spring in Kashmir, which is described in the Ain-i-Akbari as "a fountain which shoots up to the height of a cubit, and is scarce equalled for its coldness, limpidity, and refreshing qualities; the sick that drink of it and persevere in a course of its water recover their health". Bernier wrote about it : "The water is so abundant that it ought rather be called a river than a fountain, and there is a lofty cascade which in its fall takes the form and colour of a large sheet, thirty or forty paces in length, producing the finest effect imaginable—especially at night when innumerable lamps fixed in parts of the wall, adapted for that purpose, are lighted under the sheet of water". A baradari with graceful arches spanned this water-course and, cooled by fountain-spray and rushing icy water, furnished an ideal retreat for the midday siesta.

The original building at Achhbal, having fallen into disrepair, was replaced (during the reign of Maharaja Ranbir Singh) by a building in Kashmiri style, erected on the old foundations. But the hammam of Jehangir still stands, and the earthen pipes used for conveying water to the Royal bath-room from the uppermost terrace of the garden are still intact. Scores of magnificent chenar trees, some probably dating back to the laying-out of the garden, are scattered throughout the grounds, and also line the waterway as it takes its course, along the terraces, before assuming its natural role of a dashing mountain torrent. Spacious lawns and beds of exquisite flowers arranged in characteristic Moghal style, and interspersed with dressed-stone walks, add the final touches to the beauty of one of the great Moghal gardens of Kashmir. With the pomp and regal splendour of the old court days gone, and with all its natural beauty enhanced by the passage of time, Achhbal provides a unique setting for a mela in mid-June, which is thus the best occasion to visit the place. But it is charming and delightful all through the spring and the summer.

VERINAG

The famous spring called Verinag, from which the Jhelum rises, is situated at the foot of the Banihal pass, and there are the relics here of an old Moghal garden. This spring was originally a shapeless pond, and water, oozing out from different places in it, spread about and formed a little marsh. The Emperor Jehangir, whose artistic taste is well known, built, in 1620, round the spring the octagonal tank of sculptured stones so that all the water was collected therein. Jehangir's son, Shah Jehan, who was no less a lover of natural beauty, constructed, in 1627, cascades and aqueducts through and around a fine garden, which he laid out in front of the spring. The water from the spring issues from the north-eastern side of a high and well-wooded hill, and is received into an octagonal stone basin ten feet deep. There are two stone slabs built into the southern and western walls round the spring, on which inscriptions in Persian prose and verse, in praise of the spring, and the dates of the construction of the tank and aqueduct, are inscribed. The gardens are now in ruins, but they still produce some of the finest apples in Kashmir. Verinag, which has some excellent camping grounds, can be easily visited by a slight diversion, near Upper Munda from the road leading up or down from the Banihal pass, which is the main traffic route between Jammu and Srinagar.

(1944)

CHAPTER 23

SPRINGS AND LAKES

Springs

Achhabal : This spring is seven miles from Anantnag. It is situated at the foot of an extensive range of pine-covered hills. The stream runs through the Achhabal garden and supplies water to the fountains and waterfalls.

Kokarnag : This is a beautiful spring about ten miles from Achhabal. Its waters are delicious. The spring is a favourite place for trekkers and anglers.

Verinag : This spring is situated below a range of thickly wooded hills. This spring is the principal source of river Jhelum and is surrounded by a beautiful garden.

Tulmula : This spring is situated in village Lar near Ganderbal. Its water changes colour occasionally. Sometimes it becomes pink and sometimes green. The local Hindu population worships here.

Chashma Shahi : It is a spring famous all over the world for its pure, transparent and cold water nearly a mile from the south- eastern margin of the Dal Lake. This spring is situated at the south end of a beautiful garden of three terraces containing a central canal, tanks, waterfalls and fountains all fed by it. The garden was laid out by Emperor Shah Jehan in 1632 A.D.

Lakes

There are beautiful lakes in the Valley which yield plenty of water-nuts, lotus-roots, and fish. Some of these lakes contain floating gardens producing pumpkins, water melons, musk melons, cucumbers and other vegetables. In them are also found geese, duck, teal and other game birds.

Dal Lake : On the outskirts of Srinagar, the Dal Lake is a vast expanse of water five miles long and nearly half-a-mile broad. It is divided by causeways into several portions, each of which has a number of minor offshoots with floating gardens.

Wular Lake : This lake is the largest fresh-water lake in India, and is situated at a distance of 40 miles from Srinagar. This lake is nearly 12 miles long and 8 miles broad. Its surface is covered with the lotus, Shinghara and other water plants.

Manasbal Lake : It is about 13 miles away from Srinagar. Although quite small, it is the deepest lake in the State. The charm of the lake consists in its deep azure-blue water and the pink lilies.

Sheshnag : It is situated about 16 miles beyond Pahalgam on the way to the scared cave of Amarnathji at a height of 11,730 ft. It lies in between three high peaks, which rise majestically to the right of the lake. The lake is fed by melting snow of the glaciers in the mountains towering about it.

Alpathar Lake : This mountain-lake is situated beyond Khilanmarg at a height of 13,000 ft. above sea-level. This lake is also called the frozen lake, because of its freezing cold water. It remains snow-covered for most of the year.

Nilnag Lake : The lake is situated to the south of Gulmarg at a height of 6,800 ft. This is fed by mountain-springs.

Gangabal Lake : It is situated at the foot of the Harmukh peak and is about three miles long and a mile wide. The water of this lake is juicy sweet.

Mansar : This is 1/2 x 3/4 mile lake in the Samba Tehsil of the Jammu Province. In recent years the Government have spent considerable money for the development of the area around this lake. It is connected with a motorable road with the Jammu-Pathankote national highway. Mansar is also headquarter of the Block Development Officer.

Saruinsar : This is another 1/4 x 1/2 mile lake in the Samba tehsil of the Jammu Province, located in really fascinating surroundings.

In ancient times the area situated between Samba and Saruinsar was called Dogarths which in the course of time has been shortened into Dogar or Duggar and the people inhabiting this area are known as Dogras.

In addition to the above, there are 22 other lakes in Jammu and Kashmir State, mostly situated in mountains at heights over 14,000 ft.

(Kashmir Today)

CHAPTER 24

CAMP LIFE IN KASHMIR

By

C.G. Bruce

The very phrase "going into camp" gives one a pleasing thrill. People who have never slept outside four walls have missed a great deal, and are advised to do their best to sleep in a tent, even if it is only by riverside or moor or park. But wild camping when one is far away from modern civilisation is at the same time more delightful and more difficult. Going into the wilds entails knowledge and forethought, or our expedition may turn out a failure indeed.

Before camping in the Kashmir valley we have to visit one of the general provision shops which are on the riverside. We moor our boat to the bank, and have quite an amusing hour picking out our groceries (which we must cut low unless we are rich globe- trotters), also a small share of precautionary medicines, writing-paper, bootlaces, and little odds and ends, perhaps even some good old homely butter-scotch and bull's-eyes.

We see the things packed into our kiltas, the leather-covered baskets which are made in Kashmir and are shaped like barrels. When the lids are padlocked some responsible person takes the keys and we convey the kiltas back to our boat.

We have already hired tents and camp furniture and engaged servants, having only brought the bearer with us. He is a capital person at making what is called a bundobast, an arrangement; and, like all Panjabi servants, he is very happy at coming to Kashmir, the land of milk and honey, and fruit and firewood.

We have brought books and sketching materials, and cameras too, as we shall need plenty of resources to fall back on for wet days. For the women-folk, sewing and knitting correspond to the soothing influence of smoking for the men; for boys and girls scrap-book diaries, a game or two, as well as books. Undiluted views and joys of the wild, even when well punctuated by meals, marching, and sleep, are apt to pall sometimes, and the mind needs feeding as well as the senses. Besides, days must come in camp when all is not delightful—rain and wind, heat and cold—and so we will guard against any possibility of getting bored or regretting we came.

The pack ponies (for there is no wheeled traffic or real roads on the Kashmir side of Srinagar) are to meet us at Ganderbal, at the head of the Sind river, about fourteen miles from Srinagar. This is also a favourite camping-ground, though we personally mean to camp in the Chinar Bagh on our way back, and must not delay now.

Several white tents gleam amongst the trees, and under a large willow tree Rahim Ali, our bearer, points out proudly the result of his bundobast, for there are the ponies awaiting us. The servants are soon busy carrying off the baggage and sorting it into loads. Sometimes an unwilling pony backs away from the loaders, and they tumble head over heels with the rolls of tents, while the triumphant creature canters away with a whinny and rolls over and over on the grass. He is soon recaptured, and this time there is to be no nonsense. Two men hold his head and one his tail, while two more shift and bind his load. The silly thing doesn't mind a bit really, and begins to crop grass, paying no heed whatever to the bundles on his back.

Mule-and pony-men invariably start by giving trouble, and perhaps, not yet knowing the Kashmiri, we are taken in by the piteous plea that the animals will be killed and we shall have to replace them—yes, each pony is worth fifty to a hundred rupees, and so on. But at this critical moment up comes a kind Samaritan in the person of a veteran traveller. He takes in the situation instantly, and turning to the head-man utters one laconic order, "Lado," which means "Load up."

Without a word, but with tears in his eyes, which soon increase to sobs, he waves his satellites into submission, and in a few minutes, after grateful thanks to our unknown friend, we start, with a rattling of pails and empty kerosene oil tins and kettles to cheer us on.

These empty tins are indispensable to every household in India which indulges in baths, for the hot water is boiled in them, and for cold water carriers they are clean and capacious. The tears of the pony-men were crocodile tears. They knew perfectly well that the loads were moderately sized up, and that even so two spare ponies were engaged in case of a sore back or other casualty. But we shall soon cease worrying over Kashmiri tears. They spring too easily, and these fine big men are sure to cry again before the day is over. It will be too hot, or it will rain, or they will be tired and cannot collect wood. Poor things, one has still to pity them, for their weak, cringing characters come from the many generations, indeed centuries, of tyranny under which they have suffered; and to resist all authority, and weep if they cannot resist it successfully, is part of their nature now.

A modest request when we reach the first village to the lumbadar or head-man that he will provide chickens, eggs, and milk meets, perhaps, with the assurance that there are none. This village is so poor that the people themselves have no food, we are told. And this with fowls scratching and clucking, and a mooing of cows just coming home to be milked! On one such occasion, when camping in Kashmir, we failed to move the lumbadar, a great fine man with a big black beard, snowy turban, and white clothes. He just sat himself down under the spreading walnut tree, and with folded arms watched our discomfiture.

But one of our staff, a Gurkha orderly, crept off round the tree with a pony's food pail in his hand. Filling this at the spring, and before we could speak, he emptied it over the head of the lumbadar. The effect of the pail fitting like an extinguisher was so funny, and the damage so slight, that we laugh still when we recall that scene. Coughing and spluttering, the man threw himself on to the ground, yelling out that he was killed. Other men rushed up and joined their cries that he was killed, without doubt killed. (Kashmiris certainly seem to consider bathing a danger to health!) As they all cried and sobbed together they rubbed the lumbadar vigorously from head to foot. At last, with deep groans, he sat up, and with tears rolling down his cheeks ejaculated that we might have whatever we wanted. The villagers dispersed to procure farm produce such as we stood in need of. Before we parted, the price of these luxuries and a small "tip" in his hand to make up for the shower-bath, we conversed cheerfully with the lumbadar. He inquired our route, told us plenty of provisions could be obtained (from his neighbours), and even escorted us a hundred yards or so on our way, with a retinue of villagers and children. Thus the Kashmiri.

There are such endless tours through the happy valley that it is better for an intending traveller to consult a guide-book. We can here only give specimens of the charm of camp life.

The two favourite valleys to visit are the Sind and the Lidar, and we have already seen these in the description of the valleys. So we will now talk only about the actual life in camp.

The first day, perhaps, we feel stiff and tired, for we have not braced up our muscles by life on board ship or in the train and tonga. Every day, however, that we go to bed almost with the sun and get up perhaps before he does, leaves us better and brighter. The perfect scenery ad scents, the picturesque sights and country sounds of this simple life, act as a charm to body and soul. The first night in camp stands by itself, perhaps. We do not fall asleep quickly. To ears accustomed to noises, such as passing wheels and shutting doors, common to a house at nightfall, there seem to be hosts of strange and mysterious sounds. For there is no silence in Nature except in a desert. We hear her breathing, gentle as it is. The sound of the pine trees is like distant lapping of waves on a silver shore. Every now and then there is the sleepy twitter of a bird or gentle hoot of an owl, and a cool breath of fragrance wafts from jasmine and musk roses and newly trodden grass where our camp has invaded the grassy glade.

Now and then a moth flutters to our camp lanterns, but harmlessly, for they are turned low. In the distance camp-fires still burn bright, and dark figures are silhouetted against them as the natives cook their evening meal. Let us hope the wind is the right way for us, for we can spare them the odour of their ghi, or butter, as it cooks. The bark of a dog guarding a peasant's hut makes our dogs mutter a sleepy challenge, but they are too tired to bark.

Gradually the fires die out. The forms lately gathered round them are satisfied, and are now rolled inside their blankets something like Bologna sausages, for neither head nor feet are visible. And then comes with deeper silence that strange sense of aloofness One is alone, and yet feels nearer, perhaps, than one has ever felt tot he Universal Heart of Love which broods over all, wise and unwise, just and unjust, full of pity and protection and yearning; able to bear the sorrowful and sinful stumblings of these children through the knowledge that it has bestowed eternal life, and that they are learning by slow degrees to tread the path of life.

The stars twinkle a welcome to another child of earth who has come to sleep under their lofty skies, and the well-known "Ursa Major" and his attendant stars twinkle the friendly message, "We are watching over the friends in the West too"; and as we sigh, "How I wish they were here too !" the first night in camp ushers one by a new door into the well-known Land of Nod.

The next thing we know is less enchanting—the stern bearer's voice rousing us for the early march as he pushes a tray with our morning tea and toast under the flap of the tent. It was not easy to rouse from the deep sleep we were wrapped in. We are stiff and achy, and the morning is chilly. Washing and dressing are performed in a very limited space, the former rather in the "lick an' a promise style" for which we were chastised by old nursery goddesses in the old days. We lace our dusty boots—no time to clean them till we reach our standing camp—and a little crossly emerge on grass drenched with dew. In a twinkling the good camp servants have our tents down, and we are told breakfast has been taken on to half-way.

So we start our march before the first sunbeam has found its way over the tops of the hills. The dogs race ahead. They have long chafed to be off. The river flows along in swift current, here and there churned up into a creamy lather by rocks lying in silent brown pools under bending willows, while silvery bays of sand are dotted about with flowering rushes under banks of wild roses and honeysuckle.

A bend in the river brings us round a cliff, and there, spread out before us, is a valley already flooded on one side with golden sunshine. Cheerful sounds reach us of cattle being driven out to pasture, and a shepherd's reed flute shows that some of them are already up the hillside. Another bend of the path and we come upon a sight at which we draw breath. There is a great snow mountain. A veil of golden haze cast over its crest, garments of sparkling white, a soft blue in the folds, with deeper sapphire blue velvet wrappings shading into cool grey—for the sun has not yet reached the deep valleys—is a sight to repay us for our early start.

Sometimes we make a standing camp in a lovely centre, such as Sonamarg or Pahalgam, and dismiss our pack ponies. There are endless excursions in all directions to occupy at least a month. Days in the deep shady forests, or fishing in the river. Days in the jungle for sprotsmen after bear. Days with camera and sketch-book for those who wish to carry away mementoes of these who wish to carry away mementoes of these happy hours. Rambling walks for the botanist and butterfly collector. And health and spirits improving with each of these happy hours.

Of course there is a shady side to every street, and camp life is not always perfect. Hot, long marches over stony paths or hills; rainy days, when everything is soaked, and the servants seem to lose their wits and we our tempers, must come occasionally. But the memory of them does not linger as the golden days do even after years have passed. In such a country of mountains, forests, rivers, lakes, valleys and gardens, woodland glades, and flowers and fruits, is it any wonder that they should so linger, served up with such a climate ? Is it any wonder that we should again look forward with joy to visiting a country which, to us fortunate visitors, is a thing of beauty and a joy for ever ?

(1915)

CHAPTER 25

PLACES OF PILGRIMAGE

Amarnathji Cave : Situated at an altitude of 13,900 ft. in a long glacial gorge high among the eastern mountains it contains a self-formed lingam of ice which increases and decreases with the waxing and waning of the moon. It is visited by thousands of Hindu pilgrims every year from various parts of India on the full moon day of Sawan (July-August).

Hazrat Bal : Situated at a distance of four miles from the city of Srinagar, this great Muslim shrine commands an excellent view of the Dal Lake. This shrine attracts large numbers of Muslims on every Friday, and a common prayer is held in the mosque in which thousands of votaries participate. The shrine contains a hair of Prophet Mohammad.

Shah Hamdan Mosque : This is a famous shrine situated on the bank of the River Jhelum in Srinagar. It draws thousands of votaries of various castes and creeds. A big fair is held here in which Hindus and Muslims participate and pay homage to the patron saint popularly known as Shah Hamdan.

Chrar-i-Sharief : This shrine is situated in the village of Chrar, about 18 miles from Srinagar. It is dedicated to a great patron saint, named Sheikh Noor-ud-Din, popularly known as Nund Reshi who preached communal amity and brotherhood through the vehicle of verse. He was the contemporary of the famous poet-saint Lal Ded who hailed from Pampore.

The Shrine of Khirbhawani : The shrine of Tulamula, sacred to the Khirbhawani or Ragini Devi, is one of the most popular places of pilgrimage among the Hindus in Kashmir. The shrine is situated in the vicinity of a spring, 14 miles to the north of Srinagar. The water of the spring changes colour frequently, sometimes becoming purple, sometimes green and so on. It is a very ancient shrine and even Rajtarangini contains its mention. There is a legend that his goddess was originally in Ceylon in the house of Demon King Ravana and after his death Hanumanji brought it here. Every year in the month of June a fair is held here when thousands of Kashmiri Hindus assemble to offer prayers at the shrine.

Vaishnow Devi Cave : This cave is situated in a mountain, 6,000 ft. high in Reasi Tehsil, about thirty-nine miles to the north of Jammu City. During the months of September and October, people from all parts of India visit this cave to have darshan of the goddess who is enshrined at the extreme end of the long cave. There are also many self-formed images of gods. The nine-mile ascent to the cave begins from Katra, the main starting point. There are two routes leading to the cave; one of these is pony road and the other a foot-path, which is more commonly used. This place is snow-bound during winter months.

(Kashmir Today)